Lecture Notes in Computer Science

Edited by G. Goos and J. Hartmanis

20

Joost Engelfriet

Simple Program Schemes and Formal Languages

Springer-Verlag
Berlin · Heidelberg · New York 1974

Jost Engelfriet
Technical University Twente
Department of Applied Mathematics
Enschede/Nederland

AMS Subject Classifications (1970): 68A05, 68A30
CR Subject Classifications (1974): 5.24, 5.23

ISBN 3-540-06953-4 Springer-Verlag Berlin · Heidelberg · New York
ISBN 0-387-06953-4 Springer-Verlag New York · Heidelberg · Berlin

Offsetdruck: Julius Beltz, Hemsbach/Bergstr.

Preface

This work grew out of my research in the field of program schemes during the years 1971 and 1972, and it is a direct descendant of the notes that I had to prepare while lecturing on the subject of program schemes.

I have lectured on this topic in Utrecht in the "Seminar on some syntactical and semantical problems in theoretical computer science "(organized by G. Rozenberg), in Oberwolfach during a "Tagung über Formale Sprachen und Programmiersprachen" (organized by W. Händler, G. Hotz and H. Langmaack), in Rocquencourt in a seminar "Théorie des algorithmes, des langages et de la programmation" (organized by M. Nivat), and in Oberwolfach during a "Tagung über Automatentheorie und Formale Sprachen" (organized by G. Hotz and H. Langmaack).[†]

I have not indicated in which degree the results in this work are original, which is always a difficult problem when a uniform approach to a subject is presented. However, most of the results of section 19 (published in Engelfriet [1973]) and of sections 20 and 21 (not published before) seem to be new.

---

† See Engelfriet [1971 b, 1971 a, 1972 a, 1972 c] respectively.

Acknowledgments

I would like to express my gratitude to Grzegorz Rozenberg for his constant stimulation of my research in theoretical computer science, and for his energetic guidance and encouragement during the preparation of this work.

I am grateful to those people who made this investigation possible by their helpful discussions and valuable comments. I am also indebted to the Department of Applied Mathematics, and in particular to the Computer Science Group, of the Technical University Twente, Netherlands, for providing pleasant working conditions.

I would like to express my thanks to Posy Rietman for her excellent typing of the manuscript.

Finally I want to thank Louco Engelfriet for trying to understand the difference between a program scheme and a formal language.

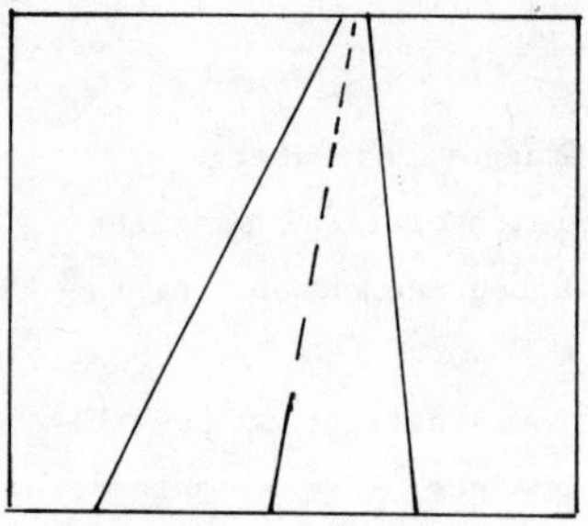

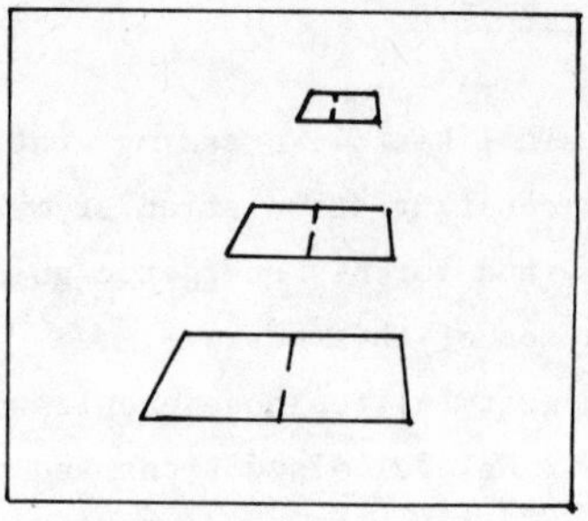

Note to the reader.

We have tried to make the reading structure of this book to be something in between a regular highway and a highway for grasshoppers. If the reader wishes to read this book in a "continuous" fashion, then we hope that he can easily do so. However, if the reader wishes to "grasshop" through the book, then he will find a number of facilities which should make it easy also for him.

These facilities include diagrams of the interrelations between sections within each Part and two indexes (of terms and of symbols used). To make the use of crossreferences easier, all theorems, lemmas, remarks, etc., are numbered consecutively. Thus "Lemma 10.8" refers to the 8th numbered item in section 10 (which happens to be a lemma). We are using the sign /// to indicate the end of proofs, examples, remarks, etc. To take full advantage of these facilities the reader is advised to read carefully the introductions to the various Parts and in particular the text below the headings "Diagram of Sections" and "More Terminology".

Finally we want to indicate that

(1) occasionally the symbols $\Rightarrow$ and $\Leftrightarrow$ are used for the phrases "implies" and "if and only if" respectively, and

(2) references to the literature are given in the following style: Name(s) of author(s) [year(s) of publication, eventual details].

Table of Contents

INTRODUCTION

AND

TERMINOLOGY

0. Introduction

0.1. Program schemes - a way of looking at the control structure of programs

One of the most important and frequently investigated aspects of a computer program is its control structure. As this notion is an informal one, there are various ways of capturing it in a precise definition. One way of doing this is to abstract from the meaning of the basic operational instructions of the program. In that case the resulting object is called a program scheme.† Thus a program scheme is obtained from a program by replacing its instructions by instruction symbols††, and consequently it represents a family of programs. To obtain a specific program from this family it suffices to provide the given program scheme with a suitable interpretation of its instruction symbols. In this context an interpretation is understood to be a construct I consisting of a set D, called the domain of I, (representing the set of data on which the program under consideration operates) and a set $\{I(\sigma) | \sigma$ is an instruction symbol$\}$ each element of which is a relation on D (representing the effect of executing the given instruction on an arbitrary element of D)†††. Consequently one may view a program as a pair (program scheme, interpretation), where the program scheme represents its control structure, whereas the interpretation represents the meaning of its instructions.

---

† One should observe the analogy with propositional logic, where the logical structure of a proposition is investigated by abstracting from the meaning of the elementary propositions from which the proposition is build up with the help of logical connectives. Thus, in this analogy, the control structure of a program corresponds to the logical structure of a proposition, whereas a program scheme corresponds to a formula of propositional logic.

†† These instruction symbols play the same role in a program scheme as the propositional variables do in a formula of propositional logic.

††† Observe that a pair $(\sigma, I(\sigma))$ might be called an instruction (σ being its name and $I(\sigma)$ its meaning). We would like to point out that we allow for nondeterministic instructions.

A program may be investigated from a syntactic and a semantic point of view. From a syntactic point of view one can consider a program to be a sequence of symbols with an underlying grammatical structure, or a flowchart of a particular form, or any other object expressing the "form" of the program. From a semantic point of view a program represents a relation on its data set. To be more precise, if P = (U,I) is a program and D is the domain of I, then this relation (often referred to as the relation "computed by P", and denoted by I(U)), is the set of all pairs (x,y) from D × D such that an "execution" of P on ("input") x may yield (an "output") y.† I(U) is also called the relation computed by the program scheme U under the interpretation I.

Consequently, a program scheme may also be investigated from a syntactic and a semantic point of view. From a syntactic point of view, a program scheme and a program, the control structure of which the program scheme represents, coincide, except perhaps for the form of the instructions. From a semantic point of view, a program scheme represents the family of all relations that are computed by programs, the control structure of which is specified by the program scheme. Following this division line we distinguish two kinds of properties of program schemes. A syntactic property of a program scheme is a property which is concerned with the form of the program scheme (with its underlying "grammatical description"). A semantic property of a program scheme is a property which can be defined in terms of the family of relations represented by the program scheme.

The above considerations constitute the basic point of view of the theory of program schemes - a (now fashionable) area of theoretical computer science.

---

† Note that we explicity allow for nondeterministic programs. Obviously a deterministic program computes a partial function (if its instructions are deterministic), but a nondeterministic program may compute a relation which is not a partial function. For the relevance of nondeterminism to programming, see Floyd [1967].

0.2. Some of the goals of the theory of program schemes

Thus the theory of program schemes investigates programs through their control structures. This is accomplished by studying those properties of a program which are invariant under a change of meaning of the instructions used by the program. In other words the theory of program schemes is mainly concerned with those properties of a program scheme which result from the requirement that a property holds for all programs that can be obtained from the program scheme by any interpretation of its instruction symbols.†

For example, if two programs compute the same relation, then this fact may be due to particular properties of the data and instructions involved, but it may also be entirely due to the control structures of the programs. The latter case holds if these programs are indistinguishable, as far as the relations computed by them are concerned, no matter how the meaning of the instructions involved is changed. In other words, the corresponding program schemes should compute the same relation under all interpretations of the instruction symbols. If this is the case, then the program schemes are called equivalent. The equivalence of program schemes (which clearly is a semantic property) is one of the main research topics in the theory of program schemes.

One of the goals of the theory of program schemes is to construct formal systems in which various properties of program schemes (from a certain class) can be proved or even decided. This naturally leads to an investigation into the recursive enumerability or decidability of such properties.

Another important goal of the theory of program schemes is the investigation and comparison of different programming features.

----

† Clearly, it is often the case that one does not want to admit arbitrary interpretations of the instruction symbols, but one fixes part of their meaning a priori. For example, one may require a particular instruction symbol to represent an assignment involving a certain number of variables, or one may require one instruction to be the "inverse" of another, etc. In such cases one should appropriately restrict the class of admissible interpretations and only consider those programs that can be obtained from the program scheme by an interpretation from the restricted class.

Usually the control structure of a program is build up with the help of a number of programming features (such as recursion, variables, conditional instructions, markers, nondeterminism). In order to compare the power of these features one defines different classes of program schemes in each of which one (or more) of these features is modeled. Then one asks whether the class of program schemes modeling one feature is "translatable" into the class of program schemes modeling another feature, were the translatability means that for each program scheme in the first class there is an equivalent one in the second class. (If that is the case, then one concludes that the programming feature embodied in the second class is at least as powerful as the one of the first class).

0.3. Aim and outline of this work

Many results in program scheme theory have been proved by using techniques and results from formal language and automata theory (see Igarashi [1963], Rutledge [1964], Paterson [1967, §4], Ito [1968], Kaplan [1969], Rosen [1972], Ashcroft, Manna and Pnueli [1973], Indermark [1973], Chandra [1973, §2.2 and §3.3]). Clearly, still much more has to be done in this direction. Quoting Book [1973], "it is hoped that more applications of results from formal languages theory will be made in this area since in many cases it is only a matter of rephrasing such results in new terms".

It is the aim of this work to fit a part of program scheme theory into a formal language theoretic framework in such a way that

(1) semantic properties of program schemes can be translated into syntactic properties of formal languages, and

(2) results from formal language theory need only to be "rephrased" in order to be applicable to program schemes.

In pursuing this aim we have restricted ourselves to rather simple program schemes, which are known in the literature under the technical term of "single variable monadic program schemes".

This work is organized as follows.

We start Part I by demonstrating how formal languages can be used to compute relations, provided an interpretation of the symbols of the underlying alphabet is given.

Thus formal languages can be viewed as program schemes, and for this reason we call them "L-schemes". Then we introduce several specific classes of program schemes. This is done because

(1) several of these classes will be investigated in Part III,

(2) in this way the uninitiated reader is introduced into the theory of program schemes, and

(3) it gives us a chance to demonstrate the usefulness of the concept of L-scheme. In fact we show that with each of the program schemes from the classes considered one can associate an equivalent L-scheme.

In this way these classes of program schemes can be "semantically embedded" in the class of all L-schemes.

In Part II we start developing a general theory of L-schemes. Several semantic properties of L-schemes (and thus of program schemes in general) are investigated. We prove that every L-scheme can be brought into "standard form", the usefulness of which stems from the fact that semantic properties of L-schemes can be translated into syntactic properties of their standard forms. We also consider the effect which various restrictions on the class of admissible interpretations have on some semantic properties of program schemes.

It is worth mentioning that we have used as a descriptional tool (in Parts I and II) an algebraic structure which is a combination of a complete lattice and a monoid.

In Part III the general theory of L-schemes, developed in Part II, is used to show that several specific problems for specific classes of program schemes can be solved by rephrasing them as formal language theoretic problems the solutions of which are already available. Among the topics considered in Part III are decidability of several program scheme properties, translatability between specific classes of program schemes, and augmenting program schemes with variables over a finite domain.

A more detailed outline of Parts I, II and III can be found in their introductions.

0.4. Some bibliographical comments

After (or before, or instead of) reading this book the reader may wish to consult one of the following survey papers of program scheme theory: de Bakker [1969, section 2], Ershov [1971], Paterson [1972], Manna [1973] and Chandra and Manna [1973].

As far as specific research topics is concerned one can roughly divide existing papers into four areas.

(1) Formal systems for the expression of properties of program schemes (see, for instance, Ianov [1960], Engeler [1967], de Bakker and Scott [1969], Manna [1969], Cooper [1971], Cherniavsky and Constable [1972], de Bakker and de Roever [1973]).

(2) Decision problems concerning various properties of program schemes (see, for instance, Ianov [1960], Kaplan [1969], Luckham, Park and Paterson [1970], Ashcroft, Manna and Pnueli [1973], Chandra [1973, Chapter 3]).

(3) Investigation and comparison of various programming features (see, for instance Knuth and Floyd [1971], Constable and Gries [1972], Brown, Gries and Szymanski [1972], Garland and Luckham [1973], Chandra [1973, §2.3], Chandra [1974]).

(4) Algebraic considerations concerning program schemes (see, for instance, Scott [1971], Elgot [1971], Goguen [1972, §7], Nivat [1973], Burstall and Thatcher [1974]).

It is our hope that the present work clearly demonstrates that a merge of the theory of program schemes and the theory of formal languages is fruitful for both disciplines.

1. Terminology and preliminary definitions

The reader is assumed to be familiar with

(1) the basic concepts from elementary set theory and elementary algebra,

(2) formal language theory, e.g. most chapters of the book of Hopcroft and Ullman [1969].

Although this text is self-contained with respect to the theory of program schemes, the reader will find some knowledge of this field useful to help him understand the meaning of concepts and results.

In this section we review a number of concepts which will be used in the sequel. The reader is advised to take notice of the terminology with respect to relations, functions and predicates in 1.1, and of the notion of a "cslm" in 1.3.

The section is divided into the following subsections:

1.1. Sets, relations, functions and predicates.

1.2. Words and languages.

1.3. Algebra.

1.4. Grammars and machines.

1.5. Decidability and enumerability.

1.1. Sets, relations, functions and predicates

1.1.1. Sets

Let D,E and D_j, for each j in some index set J, be sets.

If x is an element of D, then we write $x \in D$. Otherwise we write $x \notin D$.

The set of those elements x such that the statement P(x) is true, is written as $\{x \mid P(x)\}$. We write $\{x \in D \mid P(x)\}$ to denote the set $\{x \mid x \in D \text{ and } P(x)\}$, and we write $\{t(x_1,\ldots,x_n) \mid P(x_1,\ldots,x_n)\}$ to denote the set $\{y \mid$ there exist $x_1,\ldots,x_n$ such that $y = t(x_1,\ldots,x_n)$ and $P(x_1,\ldots,x_n)\}$, where $t(x_1,\ldots,x_n)$ is an expression and $P(x_1,\ldots,x_n)$ is a statement about $x_1,\ldots,x_n$. Furthermore we write $\{t(x_1,\ldots,x_n) \in D \mid P(x_1,\ldots,x_n)\}$ with obvious meaning.

If D is a finite set with elements $x_1,\ldots,x_n$, then D is written as $\{x_1,\ldots,x_n\}$. The number of elements in a finite set D is denoted by $\#(D)$.

The <u>empty</u> set is denoted by $\emptyset$.

If D is a <u>subset</u> of E, then we write $D \subset E$. We also say that D is <u>included</u> in E. Note that $E \subset E$.

The union of D and E is denoted by $D \cup E$. The union of the sets D_j is denoted by $\bigcup_{j \in J} D_j$. If J is the set of nonnegative integers, then we also write

$$\bigcup_{j=0}^{\infty} D_j.$$

The intersection of D and E is denoted by $D \cap E$. If $D \cap E = \emptyset$, then D and E are said to be disjoint.

The difference of D and E is denoted by $D - E$. The operation of taking the difference is called subtraction.

The cartesian product of D and E is denoted by $D \times E$.

The set of all subsets of D is denoted by $P(D)$.

An ordered pair with first element x and second element y is denoted by (x,y). Thus, $D \times E = \{(x,y) | x \in D \text{ and } y \in E\}$.

1.1.2. Relations and functions

1.1.2.1. Let D and E be sets. A relation from D into E is any subset of $D \times E$. If $D = E$, we also say that the relation is on D.

Note that $P(D \times E)$ denotes the set of all relations from D into E.

Let f be a relation from D into E. Since we shall often think of f intuitively as a multi-valued function, the following terminology will be used. For any x in D and y in E, if (x,y) is in f, then we say that y is a value of f for the argument x; we also say that y is obtained by applying f to x. For any x in D, if there exists y in E such that (x,y) is in f, we say that f is defined for x.

Example. Let D be the set of integers. Consider the set $f = \{(x,y) \in D \times D | x = y^2\}$. Clearly, f is a relation on D. For the argument 9, f is defined and has the values 3 and -3. ///

1.1.2.2. A partial function from D into E is a relation f from D into E, which has at most one value for any argument in D. As usual, we write $f: D \to E$. Also, if f is defined for x in D, the unique value of f for x is denoted by f(x). Occasionally, a partial function will be called a deterministic relation.

For partial functions, the terms onto, one-to-one and inverse will be given their usual meaning.

A partial function f from D into E, defined for all x in D, is said to be a total function, or mapping from D into E.

Example. Let D and f be as in the previous example. Obviously, f is not a partial function.

Let $g = \{(x,y) \in D \times D \mid x=y^2 \text{ and } y \geq 0\}$. Then g is a partial function from D into D. Clearly, g is not total.

Finally, consider $h = \{(x,y) \in D \times D \mid y=x^2\}$. Obviously, h is a total function from D into D. ///

1.1.2.3. Let D, E and F be sets.

For relations f, from D into E, and g, from E into F, the composition of f and g, denoted by $f \circ g$, is the relation from D into F defined by

$$f \circ g = \{(x,y) \mid (x,z) \in f \text{ and } (z,y) \in g \text{ for some } z \text{ in } E\}.$$

The identity function on D, denoted by id_D, is the function $\{(x,x) \mid x \in D\}$.

For a relation f on D, we define $f^0 = id_D$ and, for $n \geq 0$, $f^{n+1} = f^n \circ f$.

For a relation f on D, the transitive-reflexive closure of f, denoted by f^*, is the relation on D defined by

$$f^* = \bigcup_{n=0}^{\infty} f^n.$$

Alternatively, f^* is the set of those pairs (x,y) in $D \times D$, for which there exists a sequence $x_1, x_2, \ldots, x_n$ of elements of D, such that $n \geq 1$, $x_1 = x$, $x_n = y$, and $(x_i, x_{i+1}) \in f$ for all i, $1 \leq i \leq n-1$.

Example. Let D be the set of integers, and consider the total function $f = \{(x,y) \in D \times D \mid y=x+1\}$ on D. Then it is easy to see, that, for $n \geq 0$, $f^n = \{(x,y) \in D \times D \mid y=x+n\}$, and $f^* = \{(x,y) \in D \times D \mid x \leq y\}$. Note that f^* is not a partial function. ///

1.1.2.4. If f is a relation on the set D, then we often write "xfy" for "$(x,y) \in f$".

For relations on a set D, the terms reflexive, transitive, symmetric, and antisymmetric will be given their usual meaning.

Note that the transitive-reflexive closure of a relation f on D is the smallest transitive and reflexive relation on D, including f.

As usual, a reflexive, transitive and antisymmetric relation on D is called a partial ordering on D. Also, a reflexive, transitive and symmetric relation on D is called an equivalence relation on D.

Example. For any set D, the relation $\subset$ is a partial ordering on $P(D)$.

Let us call partial functions $f,g : D \to D$ similar, if, for any x in D, f is defined for x if and only if g is defined for x. It is easy to see that similarity is an equivalence relation on the set of all partial functions from D into D. ///

1.1.3. Predicates

1.1.3.1. Let D be a set. A partial predicate on D is an ordered pair (p,q) of partial functions from D into D such that

$$p \cup q \subset id_D \quad \text{and} \quad p \cap q = \emptyset.$$

Remark. Usually, a partial predicate is defined to be a partial function from D into {true, false}. It can be shown as follows that these two concepts are equivalent. Firstly, let (p,q) be a partial predicate on D. Define the partial function f from D into {true, false} by

$f(x) = \text{true}$ if $(x,x) \in p$,
$f(x) = \text{false}$ if $(x,x) \in q$, and
f is undefined for x otherwise.

Secondly, let f be a partial function from D into {true, false}. Define the partial predicate (p,q) on D by

$$p = \{(x,x) \in D \times D \mid f(x)=\text{true}\}, \text{ and}$$
$$q = \{(x,x) \in D \times D \mid f(x)=\text{false}\}.$$

It should be evident that these definitions establish a one-to-one correspondence between partial predicates on D and partial functions from D into {true, false}. ///

Therefore, for any x in D, we say that the partial predicate (p,q) has the value true (or false) for x, if (x,x) is in p (or q respectively).

Example. Let D be the set of integers. Consider the pair of partial functions (p,q) where $p = \{(x,x) \in D \times D \mid x \text{ is even}\}$ and $q = \{(x,x) \in D \times D \mid x \text{ is odd}\}$. Clearly, (p,q) is a partial predicate on D. The corresponding partial function f from D into {true, false} is total, and f(x) = true if and only if x is even. Thus, for instance, (p,q) is true for 6, and false for 7. ///

1.1.3.2. A total predicate on D is an ordered pair (p,q) of partial functions from D into D such that

$$p \cup q = id_D \quad \text{and} \quad p \cap q = \emptyset.$$

Thus, trivially, any total predicate is a partial predicate.
Similar to the case of partial predicates, it can easily be shown that

total predicates on D correspond to total functions from D into {true, false}.

Since, in what follows, we shall be mainly concerned with total predicates, the term predicate will be used rather than total predicate. Note therefore that predicates and mappings are always total.

Example. The partial predicate in the previous example is clearly also a total predicate. ///

1.1.3.3. Let $\tilde{p} = (p,q)$ be a partial predicate on D, and let f and g be relations from D into D. Then we write $(\tilde{p} \to f,g)$ to denote the relation $(p \circ f) \cup (q \circ g)$ from D into D. In other words, for any x and y in D, $(x,y) \in (\tilde{p} \to f,g)$ if either $\tilde{p}$ is true for x and $(x,y) \in f$, or $\tilde{p}$ is false for x and $(x,y) \in g$.

Example. Let D be the set of integers. Consider the total predicate (p,q) from the previous example. Define the total function f from D into D by $f(x) = x - 1$ for x in D. Let g be the relation $(\tilde{p} \to f, id_D)$ where $\tilde{p} = (p,q)$. Clearly, g is a total function from D into D, and, for any x in D, g(x) is the largest odd integer $\leq x$. ///

1.2. Words and languages

1.2.1. Words

An alphabet is any set. The elements of an alphabet are called symbols. Unless indicated otherwise, all alphabets under consideration are assumed to be finite.

Let Σ be an alphabet.

A word over Σ is any finite sequence $\sigma_1\sigma_2\cdots\sigma_n$ $(n \geq 0)$ with σ_i in Σ for all i, $1 \leq i \leq n$. The word over Σ with $n = 0$, called the empty word, is denoted by ε.

The set of all words over Σ is denoted by Σ^*.

If $\phi = \sigma_1\sigma_2\cdots\sigma_n$ and $\psi = \sigma'_1\sigma'_2\cdots\sigma'_k$ are words over Σ with $\sigma_1, \sigma_2, \ldots, \sigma_n, \sigma'_1, \sigma'_2, \ldots, \sigma'_k$ in Σ, the product of ϕ and ψ, denoted by $\phi\cdot\psi$ (or simply by $\phi\psi$), is defined to be the word $\sigma_1\sigma_2\cdots\sigma_n\sigma'_1\sigma'_2\cdots\sigma'_k$.

For words ϕ and ψ over Σ, we say that ϕ is a prefix of ψ if $\psi = \phi\omega$ for some ω in Σ^*.

For σ in Σ and ϕ in Σ^*, we say that σ occurs in ϕ, denoted by σ in ϕ, if $\phi = \phi_1\sigma\phi_2$ for certain ϕ_1, ϕ_2 in Σ^*. Furthermore we write ϕ in ψ, for ψ in Σ^*, if $\{\sigma\in\Sigma \mid \sigma \text{ in } \phi\} \subset \{\sigma\in\Sigma \mid \sigma \text{ in } \psi\}$, that is, each symbol occurring in ϕ also occurs in ψ.

Example. Let Σ be the alphabet $\{a,b\}$. The product of the words aab and b is the word aabb. The words ε, a and ab constitute all prefixes of the word ab. Finally, the following are true: a in ba, abb in ba, aaa in ba, aaa in a, ε in a. ///

1.2.2. Languages

1.2.2.1. Let Σ be an alphabet.

A language over Σ is any subset of Σ^*. Thus, $P(\Sigma^*)$ denotes the set of all languages over Σ.

If A and B are languages over Σ, the product of A and B, denoted by $A \cdot B$ (or simply by AB), is defined to be the language $\{\phi\psi \mid \phi\in A \text{ and } \psi\in B\}$.

For a language A over Σ, we define $A^0 = \{\varepsilon\}$, and, for $n \geq 0$, $A^{n+1} = A^n \cdot A$. The closure of A, denoted by A^*, is defined to be the language

$$A^* = \bigcup_{n=0}^{\infty} A^n.$$

Furthermore, the set $A^* - \{\varepsilon\}$ is denoted by A^+.

Remark. To simplify notation, we shall in the sequel identify the word ϕ in Σ^* with the language $\{\phi\} \in P(\Sigma^*)$. Thus $\Sigma^* \subset P(\Sigma^*)$.

As an example, let $\Sigma = \{a,b,c\}$, and A a language over Σ. Then, $a^2bA \cup c = \{a\}^2 \cdot \{b\} \cdot A \cup \{c\} = \{aab\} \cdot A \cup \{c\}$. ///

Example. Let Σ be the alphabet $\{a,b\}$. Then the following are languages over Σ: $\{ab,baa\}$, a, ε, Σ, the set of all words over Σ of even length.

The product of the languages $\{ab,b\}$ and $\{a,b\}$ is the language $\{aba,abb,ba,bb\}$. Finally, the following equalities are true: $a^0 = \varepsilon$, $a^2 = aa$, $(aa)^n = a^{2n}$ for $n \geq 0$, $(aa)^* = \{a^{2n} \mid n\geq 0\}$, $a \cup b = \{a,b\}$. ///

1.2.2.2. Let Σ and Δ be alphabets.

A substitution from Σ into Δ is a mapping from Σ into $P(\Delta^*)$. If Σ = Δ, the substitution is said to be on Σ.

If s is a substitution from Σ into Δ, then

(1) it is extended to words over Σ as follows:

$s(\phi\sigma) = s(\phi)\cdot s(\sigma)$ for any $\phi \in \Sigma^*$ and $\sigma \in \Sigma$, and

$s(\varepsilon) = \varepsilon$;

(2) it is extended to languages over Σ as follows:

$s(A) = \bigcup_{\phi\in A} s(\phi)$ for any $A \subset \Sigma^*$.

The so extended substitution s is a mapping from $P(\Sigma^*)$ into $P(\Delta^*)$ (according to usual conventions, we use the same symbol to denote both the mapping from Σ into $P(\Delta^*)$, and its extension to languages).

Example. Let Σ = Δ = {a,b}, and define the substitution s on Σ by $s(a) = (ab)^* \cup b^*$ and $s(b) = a^*$. For the language $A = a^*b$, we have $s(A) = ((ab)^* \cup b^*)^*\cdot a^*$. ///

1.3. Algebra

1.3.1. A monoid is a triple (M,*,e) where

(1) M is a set,

(2) * is a mapping from M × M into M, called the product operation, and

(3) e is an element of M,

and, for any x, y and z in M,

(i) $x * (y*z) = (x*y) * z$,

(ii) $x * e = e * x = x$.

Note that, for any x and y in M, we write $x * y$ to denote $*((x,y))$.

Example. Let Σ be an alphabet. Both $(\Sigma^*,\cdot,\varepsilon)$ and $(P(\Sigma^*),\cdot,\varepsilon)$ are monoids. Also, if D is a set, $(P(D\times D),\circ,id_D)$ is a monoid. ///

1.3.2. A complete semilattice † is a triple $(S,\leq,\bigvee)$ where

---

† More precisely, a complete join-semilattice, see Birkhoff [1967, Chapter II, §2].

(1) S is a set,

(2) $\leq$ is a partial ordering on S, and

(3) $\bigvee$ is a mapping from $P(S)$ into S, called

the <u>join operation</u>

and, for any D in $P(S)$,

(i) if x is in D, then $x \leq \bigvee D$, and

(ii) if y is in S, and, for all x in D, $x \leq y$,

then $\bigvee D \leq y$.

Note that, for any $D \subset S$, we write $\bigvee D$ instead of $\bigvee(D)$.

<u>Notation</u>. If $(S,\leq,\bigvee)$ is a complete semilattice, then we denote $\bigvee\emptyset$ and $\bigvee S$ by $\underline{0}$ and $\underline{1}$ respectively. Clearly, for any x in S, $\underline{0} \leq x$ and $x \leq \underline{1}$.

Furthermore, if x and y are in S, then we write $x \vee y$ for $\bigvee\{x,y\}$.

Finally, if for each j in some index set J, x_j is in S, then we write $\bigvee_{j\in J} x_j$ for $\bigvee\{x_j | j\in J\}$. Note that, in particular, if $J = \emptyset$, then $\bigvee_{j\in J} x_j = \underline{0}$.

///

<u>Remark</u>. Note that $\leq$ and $\bigvee$ depend on each other in the following sense:

(1) If $(S,\leq,\bigvee)$ is a complete semilattice, and x,y are in S, then $x \leq y$ if and only if $x \vee y = y$. This fact enables us to regard a complete semilattice as a pair $(S,\bigvee)$ where S is a set, and $\bigvee$ a mapping from $P(S)$ into S with certain properties.

(2) Given a set S and a partial ordering $\leq$ on S, there is at most one mapping $\bigvee$ from $P(S)$ into S, such that $(S,\leq,\bigvee)$ is a complete semilattice. Thus, when defining a specific complete semilattice, it suffices to specify S and $\leq$, and to show that $\bigvee$ exists. ///

<u>Example</u>. Let E be a set. Let $S = P(E)$, and, for any A,B in S, let $A \leq B$ if $A \subset B$. This defines a complete semilattice $(S,\leq,\bigvee)$, where for any $D \subset S$, $\bigvee D = \bigcup_{A\in D} A$. Thus, $(S,\leq,\bigvee) = (P(E),\subset,\bigcup)$. Note that $\underline{0} = \emptyset$, and $\underline{1} = E$. ///

1.3.3. A <u>complete lattice</u> is a 4-tuple $(S,\leq,\bigvee,\bigwedge)$ such that

$(S,\leq,\bigvee)$ is a complete semilattice, and

$(S,\geq,\bigwedge)$ is a complete semilattice, where, for any x,y in S, $x \geq y$ if $y \leq x$.

For any x,y in S, we shall denote $\bigwedge\{x,y\}$ by $x \wedge y$.

It is easy to see that any complete semilattice $(S,\le,\bigvee)$ can be made into a complete lattice $(S,\le,\bigvee,\bigwedge)$ by defining, for every $D \subset S$, $\bigwedge D = \bigvee\{y\in S \mid y\le x \text{ for all } x \text{ in } D\}$. Thus, from the point of view of the partial ordering, the two concepts coincide. Nevertheless, as algebras they are different.

In what follows we shall be mainly concerned with complete semilattices.

A complete Boolean algebra is a complete lattice $(S,\le,\bigvee,\bigwedge)$ such that the following holds: for each x in S there exists y in S such that $x \vee y = \underline{1}$ and $x \wedge y = \underline{0}$.

Example. The complete semilattice of the previous example, together with set-intersection, is a complete Boolean algebra. ///

1.3.4. We now define a concept which will be of importance in the study of program schemes and languages from an algebraic point of view.

A cslm † is a 5-tuple $(S,*,e,\le,\bigvee)$ such that

(1) $(S,*,e)$ is a monoid,

(2) $(S,\le,\bigvee)$ is a complete semilattice, and

(3) if x is in S, and, for each j in some index set J, y_j is in S, then

$$x * (\bigvee_{j\in J} y_j) = \bigvee_{j\in J} (x*y_j) \text{ , and}$$

$$(\bigvee_{j\in J} y_j) * x = \bigvee_{j\in J} (y_j*x).$$

Thus, a cslm is an algebraic structure which is both a monoid and a complete semilattice, and has the distributivity property of the product

---

† "Cslm" abbreviates "complete semilattice monoid".

The notion of cslm appears in Birkhoff [1967, Chapter XIV, §5] under the name of "cl-monoid" (abbreviation of complete lattice-ordered monoid).

A similar notion, called "net", is defined by Blikle [1971,1973] who, independently, realized the importance of this concept in programming and formal language theory.

See also Goguen [1973, § 6.4].

operation with respect to the join operation. Note that condition (3) is equivalent to the following condition (3')

(3') for x in S and D in $P(S)$,

$$x * (\bigvee D) = \bigvee\{x*y \mid y \in D\}, \text{ and}$$
$$(\bigvee D) * x = \bigvee\{y*x \mid y \in D\}.$$

<u>Remark</u>. Whenever $*$, e, $\le$ and $\bigvee$ are understood we use S to denote $(S,*,e,\le,\bigvee)$. Similarly for other algebraic structures. ///

We now prove some elementary, but useful, properties of a cslm $(S,*,e,\le,\bigvee)$:

(i) For any x in S, $x * \underline{0} = \underline{0} * x = \underline{0}$.

Proof. Recall from 1.3.2 that $\underline{0} = \bigvee\emptyset$. Now take $J = \emptyset$ in condition (3) of a cslm.

(ii) For any x,y and z in S, if $x \le y$, then

$$x * z \le y * z \quad\text{and}\quad z * x \le z * y.$$

Proof. Suppose that $x \le y$. Then, obviously, $x \vee y = y$. Thus $(x \vee y) * z = y * z$. Hence, by condition (3), $(x*z) \vee (y*z) = y * z$. Consequently, $x * z \le y * z$.

The proof of the second inequality is similar.

(iii) $\underline{1} * \underline{1} = \underline{1}$.

Proof. Recall from 1.3.2 that, for any x in S, $x \le \underline{1}$. Thus, $\underline{1} * \underline{1} \le \underline{1}$. Also $e \le \underline{1}$, and so, by (ii) above, $e * \underline{1} \le \underline{1} * \underline{1}$. Hence, $\underline{1} \le \underline{1} * \underline{1}$. Consequently, $\underline{1} * \underline{1} = \underline{1}$.

<u>Example 1.3.4.1</u>. Let Σ be an alphabet. Then it is easy to see that $(P(\Sigma^*),\cdot,\varepsilon,\subset,\cup)$ is a cslm (cf. the examples in 1.3.1 and 1.3.2). ///

<u>Example 1.3.4.2</u>. Let D be a set. Then it is easy to see that $(P(D\times D),\circ,id_D,\subset,\cup)$ is a cslm (cf. the examples in 1.3.1 and 1.3.2). ///

<u>Example 1.3.4.3</u>. Let k be a positive integer. Let N^k denote the set of all sequences of k non-negative integers. Clearly, if + is coördinate-wise addition, and $\overline{0}$ is the sequence of k zeros, then $(N^k,+,\overline{0})$ is a monoid. Also, if, for any A and B in $P(N^k)$, $A + B = \{\overline{a}+\overline{b} \mid \overline{a}\in A \text{ and } \overline{b}\in B\}$, then $(P(N^k),+,\{\overline{0}\},\subset,\cup)$ is a cslm. ///

Example 1.3.4.4. (For readers familiar with the notion of category). Consider a category with a set K of objects and a set M of morphisms. Composition of morphisms is denoted by $\star$, and the identity morphism on the object A is denoted by e_A. For arbitrary subsets P and Q of M, we define $P \star Q = \{f \in M \mid f = p \star q \text{ for certain } p \in P \text{ and } q \in Q\}$.

It is easy to see that $(P(M), \star, \{e_A \mid A \in K\}, \subset, \cup)$ is a cslm.

Note that the cslm's in the previous examples are specific cases of this cslm.

In the case of Examples 1.3.4.1 and 1.3.4.3 this is obvious (a monoid may be regarded as the set of morphisms of a category with one object).

In the case of Example 1.3.4.2, consider the category with D as set of objects, and $D \times D$ as set of morphisms. For x,y and z in D, let (x,y) be the unique morphism from x into y, and let $(x,y) \star (y,z) = (x,z)$. It is left to the reader to show that by applying the above construction to this category, the cslm of Example 1.3.4.2 is obtained. ///

1.3.5. Let $\underline{S} = (S, \star, e, \leq, \vee)$ and $\underline{T} = (T, \star, e, \leq, \vee)$ be cslm's. A cslm-morphism from $\underline{S}$ into $\underline{T}$ is a mapping $f: S \to T$, such that

(1) $f(e) = e$;

(2) if x and y are in S, then $f(x \star y) = f(x) \star f(y)$;

(3) if x_j is in S for each j in some index set J,

then $f(\bigvee_{j \in J} x_j) = \bigvee_{j \in J} f(x_j)$.

Note that condition (3) is equivalent to the following condition (3'):

(3') if D is in $P(S)$, then $f(\bigvee D) = \bigvee \{f(x) \mid x \in D\}$.

$\underline{S}$ and $\underline{T}$ are said to be isomorphic cslm's if there exists a one-to-one cslm-morphism from $\underline{S}$ onto $\underline{T}$.

We now prove some elementary, but useful, properties of a cslm-morphism f from $\underline{S}$ into $\underline{T}$:

(i) $f(\underline{0}) = \underline{0}$.

Proof. Take $J = \emptyset$ in condition (3), or equivalently, take $D = \emptyset$ in condition (3').

(ii) If f is onto T, then $f(\underline{1}) = \underline{1}$.

Proof. Take D = S in condition (3').

(iii) For any x and y in S, if $x \leq y$, then $f(x) \leq f(y)$.

Proof. Suppose that $x \leq y$. Hence $x \vee y = y$. So $f(x \vee y) = f(y)$. Thus by condition (3), $f(x) \vee f(y) = f(y)$. Hence $f(x) \leq f(y)$.

Remark 1.3.5.1. Consider the cslm $P(\Sigma^*)$ of all languages over Σ, see Example 1.3.4.1. $P(\Sigma^*)$ is the "free cslm generated by Σ" (that is, for each mapping $f: \Sigma \to S$, where $\underline{S} = (S,*,e,\leq,\bigvee)$ is any cslm, there exists a unique cslm-morphism $\tilde{f}$ from $P(\Sigma^*)$ into $\underline{S}$, such that for any σ in Σ $\tilde{f}(\sigma) = f(\sigma)$). The easy proof of this fact is left to the reader. ///

Example. Consider the cslm $P(N^k)$ from Example 1.3.4.3. Let $\Sigma = \{\sigma_1,\sigma_2,\ldots,\sigma_k\}$ be an alphabet with k symbols. For σ in Σ and ϕ in Σ^*, let $n(\phi,\sigma)$ denote the number of occurrences of σ in ϕ. We define the mapping f from $P(\Sigma^*)$ into $P(N^k)$ as follows:

(i) for ϕ in Σ^* , $f(\phi) = (n(\phi,\sigma_1), n(\phi,\sigma_2),\ldots,n(\phi,\sigma_k))$,

(ii) for A in $P(\Sigma^*)$, $f(A) = \{f(\phi) \mid \phi\in A\}$.

It is easy to see that f is a cslm-morphism from $P(\Sigma^*)$ onto $P(N^k)$. ///

1.3.6. Let $\underline{S} = (S,*,e,\leq,\bigvee)$ be a cslm. A cslm-congruence on $\underline{S}$ is an equivalence relation $\equiv$ on S, such that

(1) if x_1, x_2, y_1 and y_2 are in S, $x_1 \equiv x_2$ and $y_1 \equiv y_2$, then $x_1 * y_1 \equiv x_2 * y_2$;

(2) if, for each j in some index set J, x_j and y_j are in S and $x_j \equiv y_j$, then $\bigvee_{j\in J} x_j \equiv \bigvee_{j\in J} y_j$.

Let $\equiv$ be a cslm-congruence on $\underline{S}$, and let $S/\equiv$ denote the set of all equivalence classes $[x] = \{y\in S \mid y\equiv x\}$ with x in S. Then it is easy to show that $S/\equiv$ can be made into a cslm by defining, for any x and y in S,

$[x] * [y] = [x*y]$, and

$[x] \leq [y]$ if $x \vee y \equiv y$.

Furthermore, if f is a cslm-morphism from $\underline{S}$ onto $\underline{T}$, then it can be shown by standard algebraic techniques, that the cslm's $S/\equiv$ and $\underline{T}$ are isomorphic, where $\equiv$ is the "kernel congruence" of f (that is, for any x and y in S, $x \equiv y$ if $f(x) = f(y)$).

Example. Let Σ be an alphabet. For any ϕ in Σ^*, let $\ell(\phi)$ denote the length of ϕ. For A in $P(\Sigma^*)$, let $\ell(A)$ denote the set $\{\ell(\phi) \mid \phi\in A\}$. For A,B in $P(\Sigma^*)$, we define $A \equiv B$ if $\ell(A) = \ell(B)$. It is easy to see that $\equiv$ is a cslm-congruence on $P(\Sigma^*)$. ///

1.3.7. Note that in any cslm $\underline{S} = (S,*,e,\leq,\bigvee)$ a "closure operation" can be defined as follows:

for x in S, we define $x^o = e$, for $n \geq 0$, $x^{n+1} = x^n * x$, and the closure of x (denoted by x^*) by $x^* = \bigvee_{n=0}^{\infty} x^n$.

In the cslm's $P(\Sigma^*)$ and $P(D\times D)$ (see Examples 1.3.4.1 and 1.3.4.2) this closure is equal to the closure of a language and the transitive-reflexive closure respectively.

1.4. Grammars and machines

1.4.1. Grammars

1.4.1.1. A type 0 grammar is a 4-tuple $G = (N,\Sigma,R,Z)$, where

(1) N is an alphabet (of nonterminals),

(2) Σ is an alphabet (of terminals) disjoint with N,

(3) R is a finite subset of $(\Sigma \cup N)^* \times (\Sigma \cup N)^*$;
an element (α,β) of R is called a rule, and is usually denoted by $\alpha \to \beta$,

(4) Z is a distinguished element of N (the start symbol).

For α and β in $(\Sigma \cup N)^*$ we write $\alpha \underset{G}{\Rightarrow} \beta$ (or $\alpha \Rightarrow \beta$ when G is understood) if there exist α_1, β_1, γ and δ in $(\Sigma \cup N)^*$ such that $\alpha = \gamma\alpha_1\delta$, $\beta = \gamma\beta_1\delta$ and $\alpha_1 \to \beta_1$ is in R.

Thus $\underset{G}{\Rightarrow}$ is a relation on $(\Sigma \cup N)^*$. As usual, $\overset{*}{\underset{G}{\Rightarrow}}$ (or $\overset{*}{\Rightarrow}$ when G is understood) denotes the transitive-reflexive closure of $\underset{G}{\Rightarrow}$.

We define the language generated by G, denoted by L(G), to be $\{\phi \in \Sigma^* | Z \overset{*}{\Rightarrow} \phi\}$. A language is called a type 0 language if it is generated by some type 0 grammar.

Example. Let $N = \{S,D,L\}$, $\Sigma = \{a\}$, $Z = S$ and $R = \{S \to SD, S \to L, aD \to Daa, LD \to La, L \to a\}$. Then $G = (N,\Sigma,R,Z)$ is a type 0 grammar. We have, for instance, $LDD \Rightarrow LaD$, $LDD \overset{*}{\Rightarrow} Laaa$, and $S \overset{*}{\Rightarrow} aaaa$. One can show that $L(G) = \{a^m | m=2^n \text{ for some } n\geq 0\}$. ///

1.4.1.2. A context-free grammar is a type 0 grammar $G = (N,\Sigma,R,Z)$ in which each rule is of the form $S \to \alpha$, where S is in N and α in $(\Sigma \cup N)^*$.

A language is called a context-free language if it is generated by some context-free grammar.

Let $G = (N,\Sigma,R,Z)$ be a context-free grammar.

For S in N, we denote by $R(S)$ the set of all rules of G with left hand side S. Formally, $R(S) = R \cap (\{S\}\times(\Sigma\cup N)^*)$.

A rule of the form $S \to \varepsilon$ is called an <u>ε-rule</u>.

G is said to be <u>reduced</u> if for each nonterminal S there exist words ϕ,ψ and ω in Σ^* such that $Z \overset{*}{\Rightarrow} \phi S\psi$ and $S \overset{*}{\Rightarrow} \omega$. It is well known, that for any context-free grammar, generating a nonempty language, a reduced context-free grammar can be found, generating the same language (Hopcroft and Ullman [1969, Theorem 4.3]).

<u>Example</u>. Consider the context-free grammar $G = (N,\Sigma,R,Z)$ with $N = \{S,T\}$, $\Sigma = \{1,+,=\}$, $Z = S$ and $R = \{S \to 1S1,\ S \to +T,\ T \to 1T1,\ T \to =\}$. Then, $L(G) = \{1^n+1^m=1^{n+m} \mid n,m\geq 0\}$. Note that G is reduced. ///

1.4.1.3. A <u>regular grammar</u> is a context-free grammar G in which each rule is of one of the forms $S \to \phi T$ or $S \to \phi$, where S and T are non-terminals and ϕ is in Σ^*.

A language is called a <u>regular language</u> if it is generated by some regular grammar.

<u>Example</u>. $G = (\{A\},\{a,b\},R,A)$ with $R = \{A \to aaA, A \to b, A \to \varepsilon\}$ is a regular grammar, generating the regular language $(aa)^*b \cup (aa)^*$. ///

1.4.1.4. An <u>s-grammar</u> (or "simple deterministic" grammar) † is a context-free grammar $G = (N,\Sigma,R,Z)$ such that

(1) each rule is of the form $S \to \sigma\alpha$, where S is in N, σ is in Σ, and α is in N^*,

(2) If $S \to \sigma\alpha$ and $S \to \sigma\beta$ are rules with $\alpha, \beta \in N^*$, then $\alpha = \beta$.

Also, by definition, each grammar of the form $(\{Z\},\Sigma,\{Z \to \varepsilon\},Z)$ is an s-grammar.

---

† The notions of s-grammar and s-language were introduced by Korenjak and Hopcroft [1966]. Our definition differs slightly from theirs in that we consider $\{\varepsilon\}$ as an s-language, while they do not.

A language is called an <u>s-language</u> if it is generated by some s-grammar.

<u>Example</u>. Let $G = (\{T,S,B\},\{a,b\},R,T)$ with $R = \{T \rightarrow aS, S \rightarrow aSB, S \rightarrow b, B \rightarrow b\}$. It is easy to see that G is an s-grammar, generating the language $\{a^n b^n | n \geq 1\}$. ///

1.4.1.5. Let $X = \{x_1, x_2, x_3, \ldots\}$ be a denumerably infinite set of symbols. Define $X_o = \emptyset$ and, for $k > 0$, $X_k = \{x_1, x_2, \ldots, x_k\}$.

A <u>macro grammar</u> † is a 5-tuple $G = (N, r, \Sigma, R, Z)$ where

(1) N is an alphabet (of <u>nonterminals</u>),

(2) r is a mapping from N into the set of nonnegative integers (for S in N, r(S) is called the <u>rank</u> of S),

(3) Σ is an alphabet (of <u>terminals</u>) disjoint with N,

(4) R is a finite set of <u>rules</u> of the form

$$S(x_1, x_2, \cdots, x_k) \rightarrow t$$

where $k = r(S)$ and t is in $T[X_k]$ (the set $T[X_k]$ is defined below),

(5) Z is a distinguished element of N (the <u>start symbol</u>) with $r(Z) = 0$.

For each $k \geq 0$ we define the set of <u>terms over</u> X_k, denoted by $T[X_k]$, as follows.

(1) ε is a term, and each element of $\Sigma \cup X_k$ is a term.

(2) If t_1 and t_2 are terms, then $t_1 t_2$ is a term.

(3) If S is in N and $t_1, t_2, \ldots, t_{r(S)}$ are terms, then $S(t_1, t_2, \cdots, t_{r(S)})$ is a term. If $r(S) = 0$, then we write S instead of S( ).

Note that $T[X_k]$ is a subset of $(\Sigma \cup N \cup X_k \cup \{(,),\mathbf{,}\})^*$.

We now define how a macro grammar should be used to generate a language.

- - - - - - - - - - - -

† The notion of macro grammar was introduced by Fischer [1968]. Actually, what we define above is called an "outside-in (OI) macro grammar" in his paper. The corresponding class of macro languages is then called the class of outside-in (OI) macro languages.

For u and v in $T[\emptyset]$, we write $u \underset{G}{\Rightarrow} v$ (or $u \Rightarrow v$ when G is understood) if there exist $\alpha, \beta \in T[\emptyset]$, $S \in N$ with $r(S) = k$, $t_1, t_2, \cdots, t_k, t' \in T[\emptyset]$ and $t \in T[X_k]$, such that

(1) $u = \alpha S(t_1, t_2, \cdots, t_k)\beta$

(2) $v = \alpha t'\beta$

(3) $S(x_1, x_2, \cdots, x_k) \to t$ is in R

(4) t' is the result of substituting t_i for x_i in t for all i, $1 \le i \le k$.

Thus, $\underset{G}{\Rightarrow}$ is a relation on $T[\emptyset]$. As usual, $\overset{*}{\underset{G}{\Rightarrow}}$ denotes the transitive-reflexive closure of $\underset{G}{\Rightarrow}$.

We define the <u>language generated by G</u>, denoted by L(G), to be $\{\phi \in \Sigma^* | Z \overset{*}{\underset{G}{\Rightarrow}} \phi\}$. A language is called a <u>macro language</u> if it is generated by some macro grammar.

<u>Example</u>. Consider the macro grammar $G = (\{S,T\}, r, \{a,b,c\}, R, S)$ where $r(S) = 0$, $r(T) = 2$, and R consists of the rules $S \to aT(b,c)$, $S \to \varepsilon$, $T(x_1,x_2) \to aT(x_1b, x_2c)$ and $T(x_1,x_2) \to x_1x_2$. Then, for instance, $T(b,c) \Rightarrow aT(bb,cc)$, $T(b,c) \Rightarrow bc$ and $S \overset{*}{\Rightarrow} aabbcc$. One can show that $L(G) = \{a^nb^nc^n | n \ge 0\}$. A grammar generating the same language is $(\{S,T\}, r, \{a,b,c\}, R, S)$ where $r(S) = 0$, $r(T) = 1$ and $R = \{S \to T(\varepsilon), T(x_1) \to aT(bx_1c), T(x_1) \to x_1\}$.

1.4.2. <u>Machines</u>

1.4.2.1. A <u>sequential transducer with accepting states</u> † is a 6-tuple $M = (K, \Sigma, \Delta, R, k_0, E)$ where

(1) K is a finite set (of <u>states</u>),

(2) Σ is an alphabet (of <u>input symbols</u>),

(3) Δ is an alphabet (of <u>output symbols</u>),

(4) R is a finite subset of $K \times \Sigma^* \times K \times \Delta^*$;
an element (k_1, ϕ, k_2, ψ) of R is called a <u>rule</u>, and is denoted by $(k_1, \phi) \to (k_2, \psi)$,

(5) k_0 is in K (the <u>initial state</u>),

(6) E is a subset of K (the set of <u>final states</u>).

---

† See Ginsburg, Greibach and Hopcroft [1969].

M realizes a mapping $\overline{M}$ from $P(\Sigma^*)$ into $P(\Delta^*)$, called a <u>sequential transduction</u>, as follows.

(1) For ϕ in Σ^*, $\overline{M}(\phi)$ is the set of all words ψ in Δ^* with the property that there exist $\phi_1,\phi_2,\ldots,\phi_n$ in Σ^*, $\psi_1,\psi_2,\ldots,\psi_n$ in Δ^*, and $k_1,k_2,\ldots,k_n$ in K, such that $n \geq 1$, $\phi = \phi_1\phi_2\ldots\phi_n$, $k_n \in E$ and $(k_i,\phi_{i+1}) \to (k_{i+1},\psi_{i+1})$ is a rule for all i, $0 \leq i \leq n-1$.

(2) For A in $P(\Sigma^*)$, $\overline{M}(A) = \bigcup_{\phi\in A} \overline{M}(\phi)$

<u>Example</u>. Let $K = \{k_o,k_1,k_2\}$, $E = \{k_2\}$, $\Sigma = \Delta = \{a,b,c\}$, and let R consist of the rules

$(k_o,ab) \to (k_o,c)$,
$(k_o,c\ ) \to (k_1,\varepsilon)$,
$(k_1,c\ ) \to (k_1,ab)$,
$(k_1,\varepsilon\ ) \to (k_2,ab)$,
$(k_1,\varepsilon\ ) \to (k_2,c)$.

Then $M = (K,\Sigma,\Delta,R,k_o,E)$ is a sequential transducer with accepting states. We have, for instance, $\overline{M}(ab) = \emptyset$, $\overline{M}(c) = \{ab,c\}$, $\overline{M}(ba) = \emptyset$, $\overline{M}(\{ba,abc\}) = \{cab,cc\}$ and $\overline{M}(\Sigma^*) = c^*(ab)^*(ab\cup c)$. ///

1.4.2.2. A <u>generalized sequential machine</u> (abbreviated gsm) is a sequential transducer with accepting states $M = (K,\Sigma,\Delta,R,k_o,E)$ such that $R \subset (K \times \Sigma \times K \times \Delta^*) \cup \{(k_o,\varepsilon) \to (k,\varepsilon) | k\in E\}$. $\overline{M}$ is called a <u>gsm mapping</u>.

We say that M is <u>deterministic</u> if, for each k in K and σ in Σ, at most one rule of M has left hand side (k,σ). If M is deterministic, then $\overline{M}$, restricted to Σ^*, is a partial function.

For A in $P(\Delta^*)$, define $\overline{M}^{-1}(A) = \{\phi\in\Sigma^* | \overline{M}(\phi)\cap A\neq\emptyset\}$. The mapping $\overline{M}^{-1}$ from $P(\Delta^*)$ into $P(\Sigma^*)$ is called an <u>inverse gsm mapping</u>. Note that, in general, $\overline{M}^{-1}$ is not really the inverse of $\overline{M}$.

<u>Example</u>. Let $K = \{k_o,k_1\}$, $E = \{k_o\}$, $\Sigma = \Delta = \{a,b,c\}$, and consider the gsm $M = (K,\Sigma,\Delta,R,k_o,E)$ where R consists of the rules

$(k_o,a) \to (k_1,\varepsilon)$,
$(k_1,b) \to (k_o,c)$,
$(k_o,c) \to (k_o,ab)$,
$(k_o,\varepsilon) \to (k_o,\varepsilon)$.

Then $\overline{M}$ is a deterministic gsm mapping which, in each word from $(ab \cup c)^*$, changes ab into c and c into ab. Note that $\overline{M}^{-1} = \overline{M}$. ///

1.4.2.3. A pushdown automaton (abbreviated pda) is a 7-tuple $M = (K,\Sigma,\Gamma,R,k_o,Z,E)$ where

(1) K is a finite set (of states),

(2) Σ is an alphabet (of input symbols),

(3) Γ is an alphabet (of pushdown symbols),

(4) R is a finite subset of $K \times \Sigma^* \times \Gamma \times K \times \Gamma^*$; † an element (k_1,ϕ,S,k_2,α) of R is called a rule, and will be denoted by $(k_1,\phi,S) \to (k_2,\alpha)$,

(5) k_o is in K (the initial state),

(6) Z is in Γ (the start symbol),

(7) E is a subset of K (the set of final states).

If k_1 and k_2 are in K, ϕ and ψ are in Σ^*, α and β are in Γ^*, S is in Γ, and $(k_1,\phi,S) \to (k_2,\alpha)$ is in R, then we write

$$(k_1,\phi\psi,S\beta) \vdash_M (k_2,\psi,\alpha\beta).$$

Thus, $\vdash_M$ is a binary relation on $K \times \Sigma^* \times \Gamma^*$. As usual, $\vdash_M^*$ (or $\vdash^*$ when M is understood) denotes the transitive-reflexive closure of $\vdash_M$.

For a pda M we define $L_f(M)$, the language accepted by final state, to be $\{\phi \mid (k_o,\phi,Z) \vdash^* (k,\varepsilon,\alpha)$ for some k in E and α in $\Gamma^*\}$. Furthermore we define $L(M)$, the language accepted by empty store, to be $\{\phi \mid (k_o,\phi,Z) \vdash^* (k,\varepsilon,\varepsilon)$ for some k in $K\}$.

Whenever only $L(M)$ is involved, we describe M as a 6-tuple $(K,\Sigma,\Gamma,R,k_o,Z)$.

It is well known, that the class of languages accepted by pushdown automata by final state (or by empty store) equals the class of context-free languages (Ginsburg [1966, Exercise 2.4.7, Theorem 2.5.1 and Theorem 2.5.2]).

Example. Consider the pda $M = (\{k_o,k_1\},\{a,b\},\{Z,a\},R,k_o,Z,\{k_1\})$ where R consists of the following

---

† Usually, the notion of pda is defined in such a way, that R is a finite subset of $K \times (\Sigma \cup \varepsilon) \times \Gamma \times K \times \Gamma^*$. However, it is well known that this is no restriction on the accepting ability of the pda (Ginsburg [1966, Exercise 2.4.7]).

rules:

$(k_o,ab,Z) \to (k_o,aZ)$,

$(k_o,ab,a) \to (k_o,aa)$,

$(k_o,b,a) \to (k_1,\varepsilon)$,

$(k_1,b,a) \to (k_1,\varepsilon)$,

$(k_1,\varepsilon,Z) \to (k_1,\varepsilon)$,

Then, for instance, $(k_o,b,aZ) \vdash (k_1,\varepsilon,Z)$ and $(k_o,abb,Z) \vdash^* (k_1,\varepsilon,\varepsilon)$. It is easy to show that $L(M) = \{(ab)^n b^n \mid n \geq 1\}$ and $L_f(M) = \{(ab)^n b^m \mid n \geq 1, 1 \leq m \leq n\}$. ///

1.4.2.4. A pda $M = (K,\Sigma,\Gamma,R,k_o,Z,E)$ is said to be deterministic, and is called a dpda, if

(1) R is a subset of $K \times (\Sigma \cup \varepsilon) \times \Gamma \times K \times \Gamma^*$,

(2) for each k in K, S in Γ and σ in $\Sigma \cup \varepsilon$, there is at most one rule with left hand side (k,σ,S),

(3) for each k in K and S in Γ, if there is a rule with left hand side (k,ε,S), then for no σ in Σ there is a rule with left hand side (k,σ,S).

For a dpda M, $L_f(M)$ will be called a dpda language, and $L(M)$ will be called a dpda-ε language.†

It is well known that the class of dpda-ε languages is a proper subclass of the class of dpda languages (Harrison and Havel [1973, Theorem 3.1]), which, on its turn, is a proper subclass of the class of context-free languages (Ginsburg and Greibach [1966, Corollary 1 of Theorem 3.5]).

Example. Consider the pda M of the previous example. Add a state k_2.

---

† In the literature, the dpda and dpda-ε languages are called deterministic context-free and strict deterministic context-free languages, respectively (see Ginsburg and Greibach [1966], Harrison and Havel [1973]). We did not adopt this terminology, since it would interfere with certain terms in the theory of program schemes.

Replace the first two rules of M by the following four rules:

$(k_0,a,Z) \to (k_2,Z)$,

$(k_2,b,Z) \to (k_0,aZ)$,

$(k_0,a,a) \to (k_2,a)$,

$(k_2,b,a) \to (k_0,aa)$.

The resulting pda M' is deterministic. It is easy to see that $L(M') = L(M)$ and $L_f(M') = L_f(M)$. ///

1.5. Decidability and enumerability

The reader is assumed to be familiar with some elementary terminology used in the theory of computability. We shall give short intuitive descriptions of some of the terms which will be used in the sequel. For precise definitions and ample discussion of these concepts, the reader is referred to Hopcroft and Ullman [1969, Chapters 1, 6 and 7], and to Chapters 1, 2 and 3 of Rogers [1967].

Moreover, the reader is assumed to be familiar with the elementary decidability and undecidability results in formal language theory (see, for instance, Hopcroft and Ullman [1969, Chapter 14]).

Let C be a set of "constructive" objects, and D a subset of C.

D is said to be decidable (in C) if there exists an algorithm to determine for an arbitrary element of C whether it belongs to D or not. Such an algorithm is also called a decision method for D (in C). A set which is not decidable is called undecidable.

D is said to be recursively enumerable (in C) if there exists an algorithm which, given an element of C, halts if this element belongs to D, and does not halt if the element does not belong to D.

Note that a relation is a set. Thus, the above terminology also applies to relations.

A question Q(x), depending on x in C, is said to be decidable (or recursively enumerable) if the set $\{x \in C \mid$ the answer to Q(x) is "yes"$\}$ is decidable (or recursively enumerable, respectively).

Let C_1 and C_2 be sets of "constructive" objects, and let P(x,y) be a statement, involving x in C_1 and y in C_2. Suppose that there is an algorithm which, given an element x of C_1, computes an element y of C_2 such that P(x,y) is true. Then we say that, for each element x of C_1, an element y of C_2 can effectively be found such that P(x,y) holds.

Example. Let C be the set of all pairs of context-free grammars, and let D be the subset of C defined by $D = \{(G_1,G_2) \mid L(G_1)=L(G_2)\}$. Then D is undecidable (Hopcroft and Ullman [1969, Corollary 14.1]). Since each context-free language is decidable (in the set of all words over its terminal alphabet), see Hopcroft and Ullman [1969, Theorem 2.2], it is easy to see that the set C - D is recursively enumerable. Thus, it is recursively enumerable to determine for two arbitrary context-free grammars whether they generate different languages. ///

PART I

AN L-SCHEME APPROACH

TO PROGRAM SCHEMES

Survey of Contents

In this Part we introduce the notion of an L-scheme and we motivate its usefulness within program scheme theory.

Section 2 introduces the basic notions of interpretation and L-scheme. The central idea is that a formal language over a given alphabet can compute a relation if each symbol of the alphabet is interpreted as a relation. Thus a formal language may be viewed as a program scheme, and whenever it is viewed in this way it will be called an L-scheme.

In sections 3,4,5 and 6 we consider several classes of program schemes (Ianov schemes, recursive schemes, recursive schemes with parameters and μ-terms respectively). For each of these classes we show that each program scheme from the class may be regarded as a language generating device (yielding, respectively, a regular, context-free, macro and, again, context-free language over its alphabet of instruction symbols). For each of these cases we prove a theorem which says that the program scheme and the language generated by it (viewed as an L-scheme) are equivalent. These theorems alone justify the choice of the notion of an L-scheme as the central one in our investigations.

The above specific examples of classes of program schemes lead to the notion of a program scheme system introduced in section 8. A program scheme system is a class of program schemes satisfying the requirement that for each of its program schemes there exists an equivalent L-scheme. The classes of L-schemes generated by several of the program scheme systems from sections 3 - 6 are compared.

In section 7 it is shown that L-schemes are in a one-to-one correspondence with Ianov schemes that have the form of a finite or infinite tree. Together with the results of sections 3 - 6 this implies the well known fact that to each of the program schemes considered in these sections there corresponds an equivalent finite or infinite tree.

Diagram of Sections

Below we give a rough diagram of the interrelations between the sections of Part I. In this diagram, "x→y" means that some knowledge of section x is required to be able to understand (a part of) section y.

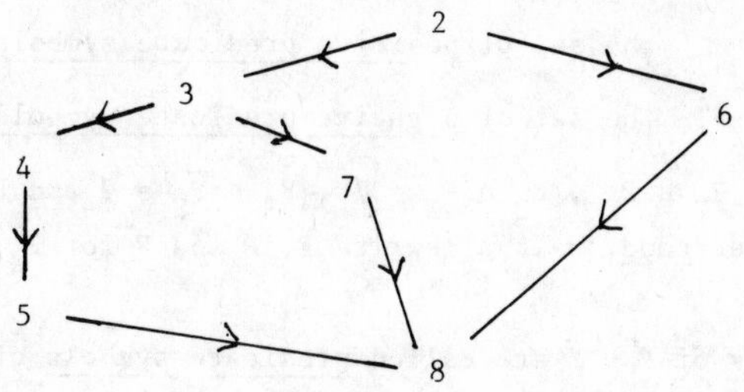

2. L-schemes and interpretations.
3. Ianov schemes and regular schemes.
4. Recursive systems of Ianov schemes and context-free schemes.
5. Procedure parameter schemes and macro schemes.
6. The μ-calculus.
7. L-schemes viewed as infinite trees.
8. Program scheme systems.

Section 2 is basic to Parts I, II and III.

Section 3 includes many details so as to provide an extensive example of a class of program schemes and their corresponding L-schemes.

Section 8 can be read "selectively". To read the definitions only, knowledge of section 2 is sufficient, but for reading more than this the reader may find some knowledge of the other sections needed.

More Terminology

Convention. Whenever an alphabet is denoted by Σ (or by variants like Σ_1, Σ_2, Σ', etc.), we assume that it is divided into three disjoint parts:

F_Σ, the set of function symbols of Σ,

P_Σ, the set of positive predicate symbols of Σ, and

$\overline{P}_\Sigma = \{\bar{p} \mid p \in P_\Sigma\}$, the set of negative predicate symbols of Σ.

Thus, $\Sigma = F_\Sigma \cup P_\Sigma \cup \overline{P}_\Sigma$, $F_\Sigma \cap P_\Sigma = \emptyset$, $F_\Sigma \cap \overline{P}_\Sigma = \emptyset$ and $P_\Sigma \cap \overline{P}_\Sigma = \emptyset$. (When Σ is understood, we shall write F, P and $\overline{P}$ for F_Σ , P_Σ and $\overline{P}_\Sigma$ respectively.)

The elements of $P \cup \overline{P}$ are called predicate symbols of Σ, and the elements of Σ are called instruction symbols. ///

Note that F, P and $\overline{P}$ may be empty. However, it is clear that P is empty if and only if $\overline{P}$ is empty.

Example. Consider the alphabet $\Sigma = \{f,g,p,\bar{p},q,\bar{q}\}$. We divide Σ into $F_\Sigma = \{f,g\}$, $P_\Sigma = \{p,q\}$ and $\overline{P}_\Sigma = \{\bar{p},\bar{q}\}$. ///

We now introduce another operation on languages.

Definition. Let Σ be an alphabet, let A and B be languages over Σ, and let p be an element of P_Σ. Then the conditional composition of A and B with respect to p, denoted by $(p \to A,B)$, is defined by

$$(p \to A,B) = pA \cup \bar{p}B.$$

Example. Let Σ be the alphabet of the previous example. Then, $(q \to f,gf) = \{qf,\bar{q}gf\}$. Also, if $A = (q \to f,gf)$ and $B = \varepsilon$, then $(p \to A,B) = \{pqf,p\bar{q}gf,\bar{p}\}$. ///

2. L-schemes and interpretations

In this section we introduce some basic concepts and facts, to be used throughout the rest of this work.

Firstly, we define the general notion of interpretation of an alphabet of instruction symbols, and its restrictions.

Secondly, we turn languages into program schemes, called L-schemes, by defining the relation computed by a language under an interpretation. Then we discuss the "homomorphic behaviour" of an interpretation with respect to several language-theoretic and set-theoretic operations (Lemmas 2.9 and 2.12). The notion of a cslm turns out to be useful here.

Finally, we point out the obvious intuitive connections between various L-scheme and programming concepts.

Let Σ be an alphabet, fixed throughout this section.

† Definition 2.1. A general interpretation of Σ is a pair $I = (D,h)$, where D is a set, called the domain of I, and h is a mapping from Σ into $P(D\times D)$. (We also write D_I and h_I for D and h respectively).††

Thus, a general interpretation interpretes each instruction symbol σ in Σ as a relation $h(\sigma)$ on D.

---

† In all definitions of this kind (in which something is "of Σ" or "over Σ") we drop the words "of Σ" or "over Σ", whenever Σ is understood.

†† The reader may wonder why we do not define a general interpretation as a triple (Σ,D,h) showing also the arguments of the mapping h. We could of course have done so, however it is conceptually nicer, and also usual in program scheme theory, to separate the objects to be interpreted (in this case, the instruction symbols) from the interpretation itself. In fact, the triple (Σ,D,h) is more like a "set of instructions" (see section 0), since, for each instruction, its name (the instruction symbol σ) and its meaning (the relation $h(\sigma)$) are given.

<u>Example 2.2</u>. Let $\Sigma = \{f,p,\bar{p}\}$ with $F_\Sigma = \{f\}$, $P_\Sigma = \{p\}$ and $\bar{P}_\Sigma = \{\bar{p}\}$. For each j , $1 \le j \le 7$, we define a general interpretation $I_j = (D,h_j)$, where D is the set of all integers, and the mappings h_j are defined as follows:

$h_1(f) = h_2(f) = h_3(f) = \{(x,y) | x \le y\}$,
$h_4(f) = h_5(f) = \{(x,x+1) | x \ge 0\}$,
$h_6(f) = h_7(f) = \{(x,x+1) | x \in D\}$,
$h_j(p) = \{(x,x) | x < 0\}$ for all j, $1 \le j \le 7$,
$h_1(\bar{p}) = \{(x,x+1) | x \ge 0\}$,
$h_2(\bar{p}) = h_5(\bar{p}) = h_6(\bar{p}) = \{(x,x) | x \ge 1\}$,
$h_3(\bar{p}) = h_4(\bar{p}) = h_7(\bar{p}) = \{(x,x) | x \ge 0\}$. ///

Obviously, a general interpretation need not take into account the division of the alphabet Σ into function and predicate symbols. We now define some restricted kinds of interpretation for which this division is essential.

<u>Definition 2.3</u>. A <u>π-interpretation of Σ</u> is a general interpretation I = (D,h) such that, for all p in P_Σ , $(h(p),h(\bar{p}))$ is a partial predicate †. A <u>τ-interpretation of Σ</u> is a general interpretation I = (D,h) such that, for all p in P_Σ , $(h(p),h(\bar{p}))$ is a total predicate. A <u>px-interpretation of Σ</u> (where x is π or τ) is an x-interpretation I = (D,h) such that, for all f in F_Σ , h(f) is a partial function. A <u>tx-interpretation of Σ</u> (where x is π or τ) is an x-interpretation I = (D,h) such that, for all f in F_Σ , h(f) is a total function.

Thus we have π- , τ- , pπ- , pτ- , tπ- and tτ-interpretations.

<u>Example 2.4</u>. Consider the general interpretations of Example 2.2. The following statements are easily seen to be true. I_1 is not a π-interpretation. I_2 is a π-interpretation; however, it is neither a τ-, nor a pπ-interpretation. I_3 is a τ-interpretation, which is not a pτ-interpretation. I_4 is a pτ-interpretation, but it is not a tτ-interpretation. I_5 is a pπ-interpretation; it is neither a tπ-, nor a pτ-interpretation. I_6 is a tπ-, but not a tτ-interpretation, and I_7 is a tτ-interpretation. ///

---

† For the notion of predicate, see 1.1.3.

If P_Σ and F_Σ are nonempty, then all classes of interpretations, defined above, are different (see Example 2.4). If not, then some of the classes coincide. Let, for the moment, g denote the class of all general interpretations of Σ, and x the class of all x-interpretations of Σ (where x is $\pi,\tau,p\pi,p\tau,t\pi$ or $t\tau$). If $P_\Sigma = \emptyset$, then obviously, $g = \pi = \tau$, $p\pi = p\tau$ and $t\pi = t\tau$, and no other equations hold. Thus, if Σ has no predicate symbols, then we have three different classes of interpretations. If $F_\Sigma = \emptyset$, then, obviously, $\pi = p\pi = t\pi$ and $\tau = p\tau = t\tau$, and no other equations hold. Thus, if Σ has no function symbols, then we have three different classes of interpretations, of which two consist of π-interpretations.

Remark 2.5. All the results of this Part are stated for general interpretations. And so, they are also valid for alphabets which are not divided into function and predicate symbols. However, sometimes, in our examples, use will be made of restricted interpretations. ///

We now define the central notion of this work: that of an L-scheme (the term L-scheme abbreviates "language viewed as a program scheme").

Definition 2.6. An L-scheme over Σ is any subset of Σ^*.

Usually, in formal language theory, a subset of Σ^* is called a language over Σ. We shall use both terms "L-scheme" and "language" synonymously. The term "L-scheme" is used to stress the fact that languages can be considered as program schemes.

The relation computed by an L-scheme under some interpretation is defined as follows.

†Definition 2.7. Let $I = (D,h)$ be a general interpretation of Σ. For an L-scheme A over Σ, the relation computed by A under I, denoted by I(A), is defined recursively as follows:

(1) for σ in Σ, $I(\sigma) = h(\sigma)$,

(2) $I(\varepsilon) = id_D$,

(3) for ϕ in Σ^+ and σ in Σ, $I(\phi\sigma) = I(\phi) \circ I(\sigma)$,

(4) for A in $P(\Sigma^*)$, $I(A) = \bigcup_{\phi \in A} I(\phi)$.

---

† Interpreting languages as in Definitions 2.1 and 2.7 was also done, independently, by Mazurkiewicz [1972b, Definition 1]. The idea is also indicated in Elgot [1972].

Thus, a general interpretation I interpretes an L-scheme A as a relation $I(A)$ on D_I, and we say that A "computes" $I(A)$ under I. Although Definition 2.7 does not remind one of a process of computation, it is easy to see that it is equivalent to the following, more computation-like, definition: for any x,y in D_I, $(x,y) \in I(A)$ if and only if there are $\sigma_1,\ldots,\sigma_n$ in Σ and $x_1,\ldots,x_{n+1}$ in D_I (for some $n \geq 0$) such that
$\sigma_1 \cdots \sigma_n \in A$, $x_1 = x$, $x_{n+1} = y$ and $(x_i,x_{i+1}) \in h_I(\sigma_i)$ for all i, $1 \leq i \leq n$.
For another equivalent definition, see Definition 7.10.

Example 2.8. Let $\Sigma = \{f,p,\bar{p}\}$. Consider the L-scheme $A = (pf)^*\bar{p}$, and the tτ-interpretation I_7 from Example 2.2. It is easy to see, that
$I_7(A) = \{(x,0) \mid x<0\} \cup \{(x,x) \mid x \geq 0\}$. ///

We now consider some simple properties of general interpretations.

Lemma 2.9. Let I be a general interpretation of Σ, let A , B , A_j (for each j in some index set J) be L-schemes over Σ, and let p be in P_Σ. Then,

(1) $I(\emptyset) = \emptyset$,

(2) if $A \subset B$, then $I(A) \subset I(B)$,

(3) $I(\bigcup_{j\in J} A_j) = \bigcup_{j\in J} I(A_j)$, in particular, $I(A \cup B) = I(A) \cup I(B)$,

(4) $I(AB) = I(A) \circ I(B)$,

(5) if I is a π-interpretation, then †
$I(p \rightarrow A,B) = (\tilde{p} \rightarrow I(A), I(B))$,
where $\tilde{p}$ is the partial predicate $(I(p), I(\bar{p}))$,

(6) $I(A^*) = (I(A))^*$.

Proof. Most of the easy proof is left to the reader. As an example, consider (6). From (4), and from the fact that $I(\varepsilon)$ is the identity function on D_I, it follows that, for $n \geq 0$, $I(A^n) = (I(A))^n$. Hence, using (3), we have

$$I(A^*) = I(\bigcup_{n=0}^{\infty} A^n) = \bigcup_{n=0}^{\infty} I(A^n) = \bigcup_{n=0}^{\infty} (I(A))^n = (I(A))^*. \qquad ///$$

Given some general interpretation I = (D,h), let us consider the mapping

---

† For definitions, see the introduction to Part I, and 1.1.3.3.

from $P(\Sigma^*)$ into $P(D\times D)$, associating with each L-scheme A in $P(\Sigma^*)$ the relation I(A) in $P(D\times D)$. Let us denote this mapping also by I. † It follows immediately from Definition 2.7(2) and Lemma 2.9(3) and (4), that the mapping I is a cslm-morphism from the cslm $P(\Sigma^*)$ into the cslm $P(D\times D)$ ††. Furthermore, since $P(\Sigma^*)$ is the free cslm generated by Σ (see Remark 1.3.5.1), each cslm-morphism is fully determined by its restriction to Σ. It thus follows that an alternative definition of "general interpretation" may be given as follows.

Definition 2.10 (alternative to Definitions 2.1 and 2.7).
A general interpretation of Σ consists of a set D together with a cslm-morphism from $P(\Sigma^*)$ into $P(D\times D)$. †††

In the same manner a substitution may be redefined as follows.

Definition 2.11 (alternative to 1.2.2.2).
Let Δ be an alphabet. A substitution from Σ into Δ is any cslm-morphism from $P(\Sigma^*)$ into $P(\Delta^*)$.

---

† Double meaning of one symbol is often used in the literature for simplifying notation. The context in which the symbol occurs should indicate which of the two meanings applies. Since this method is often confusing, even to the initiated reader, it should be used with extreme care.

†† For the notions of cslm and cslm-morphism, see 1.3.4 - 1.3.7.

††† In general, the interpretation of an object is often expressed in terms of the interpretations of its unique constituents. This means that, in general, interpretation (or meaning, or semantics) can be viewed as a homomorphism from a free algebra into another algebra. See e.g. Elgot [1971, section 4] and Nivat [1973]. For a discussion of the importance of such homomorphisms in programming, the reader is referred to Burstall and Landin [1969].

In the next lemma we relate general interpretations and substitutions.

Lemma 2.12. Let I be a general interpretation of Σ, and let s be a substitution on Σ. Let $I_s = (D_s, h_s)$ be the general interpretation such that $D_s = D_I$ and, for each σ in Σ, $h_s(\sigma) = I(s(\sigma))$. Then for any L-scheme A over Σ, $I(s(A)) = I_s(A)$.

Proof. It is easy to show that the composition of any two cslm-morphisms is again a cslm-morphism. Hence, by Definitions 2.10 and 2.11, $s \circ I$ is a cslm-morphism from $P(\Sigma^*)$ into $P(D_s \times D_s)$. But, by the definition of I_s, the cslm-morphisms $s \circ I$ and I_s coincide on Σ. Thus, since $P(\Sigma^*)$ is the free cslm generated by Σ, we have $s \circ I = I_s$. Consequently, for any L-scheme A, $I(s(A)) = (s \circ I)(A) = I_s(A)$. ///

Note that, in general, Lemma 2.12 does not hold for restricted interpretations (Definition 2.3). In such a case we have to show that I_s is of the same type as I.

We conclude this section with an informal discussion of the intuitive "programming" concepts behind some of the notions previously introduced. This should indicate to the reader the natural correspondence between the theory of languages and the theory of program schemes.

An L-scheme A together with a general interpretation I can be considered as a program or statement, computing the relation I(A). For an intuitive notion of "execution" of an L-scheme, see Definition 7.10.
Note that, in general, we allow programs to be nondeterministic (that is, a program may compute a relation which is not a partial function). In section 7 we shall consider L-schemes computing partial functions under all pπ-interpretations.

The L-scheme $\emptyset$ computes "nothing" under all interpretations. It can be thought of as, e.g., the Algol statement ℓ: goto ℓ (cf. de Bakker [1971, section 2]).

The L-scheme ε computes the identity function under all interpretations. It corresponds for example to the dummy statement of Algol.

Under any interpretation, the product AB of the L-schemes A and B computes the composition of the relations computed by A and B respectively. Thus, AB, as a program, may be regarded as the serial composition of the programs or statements A and B (in analogy with Algol, one might denote AB by A;B).

The operation of union on L-schemes has no direct analogue in existing programming languages. However, a programming language might very well be imagined in which nondeterministic statements of the form "A or B", where A and B are statements, were allowed. Under some interpretation, the "execution" of A or B, for some input, would consist either of the execution of A, or of the execution of B for this input. Thus, A or B would compute the union of the relations computed by A and B.

The operations of union and product together may be used to obtain Algol-like conditional statements as follows. Let p be a positive predicate symbol, and let A and B be L-schemes. Then the conditional composition $(p \rightarrow A,B)$, defined in the introduction to Part I as $pA \cup \bar{p}B$, obviously corresponds, under any π-interpretation, to the Algol-like conditional statement
if p then A else B (see Lemma 2.9(5)).

Under any interpretation, the closure A^* of the L-scheme A corresponds to a program executing program A an arbitrary finite number of times, nondeterministically. Again, there is no counterpart for this operation in ordinary programming. Nevertheless, it should be evident, that, for p in P_Σ, the L-scheme $(pA)^*\bar{p}$ corresponds, under any π-interpretation, to the Algol-like statement while p do A. In general, closure of L-schemes corresponds to iteration of programs.

We now turn to inclusion. Let A and B be L-schemes such that $A \subset B$. Under any interpretation, program A computes less than program B, in the sense that the relation computed by A is included in the relation computed by B. We might say that A is an "approximation" of B. †

---

† The notion of approximation of programs was introduced, in a different manner, by Scott [1970,1971]. See also the introduction to section 7.

Finally, substitution has the following interpretation in programming. Let A be an L-scheme over Σ. Let s be a substitution on Σ such that, for each instruction symbol σ in Σ, either $s(\sigma) = \sigma$, or no instruction symbol σ_1 with $s(\sigma_1) \neq \sigma_1$ occurs in any word of $s(\sigma)$. Then for each σ with $s(\sigma) \neq \sigma$, $s(\sigma)$ may be regarded as the "body" of the "procedure" σ. Furthermore, an occurrence of σ in a word of A may be viewed as a "call" of the procedure σ. Thus, under any general interpretation, the L-scheme A together with the substitution s corresponds to a program in which nonrecursive procedure calls occur. The non-recursiveness is ensured by the above condition on s. Of course, the relation computed by the program (A,s) should be equal to the relation computed by the program s(A), which is obtained from A by replacing each call of a procedure by its body. It follows from Lemma 2.12 that this is indeed the case.

3. Ianov schemes and regular schemes

Program schemes were introduced by Ianov [1960] as a formalization of the well known concept of flowchart of a program. These program schemes, in the form in which they are used today, will be called Ianov schemes. A connection between Ianov schemes and regular languages (or finite automata) was discovered by Rutledge [1964] and Igarashi [1963], and investigated by Ito [1968], Kaplan [1969] and Elgot [1970], among others.

In this section we define the notion of Ianov scheme (first its non-deterministic and then, at the end of the section, its deterministic version), and we define the relation computed by a Ianov scheme under an arbitrary interpretation.

Then we show that with each Ianov scheme we may associate, in a natural manner, a regular language (see Definition 3.9), which, as an L-scheme, is equivalent to that Ianov scheme (Theorem 3.11). This illustrates the importance of the concept of L-scheme.

We end the section by pointing out that each regular grammar can be viewed as a program scheme, called regular scheme.

We define a Ianov scheme as a directed labelled graph, as for instance in Kaluzhnin [1961]†.

Definition 3.1. A nondeterministic Ianov scheme is a 7-tuple $U = (\Sigma, N, n^o, E, A, e, \ell)$, where

(1) Σ is an alphabet (of instruction symbols),

(2) N is a finite set (of nodes),

(3) n^o is a distinguished element of N (the start node), ††

(4) E is a subset of N (the set of final nodes),

(5) A is a finite set (of arcs),

(6) e is a mapping from A into $N \times N$, and

(7) ℓ is a mapping from A into Σ (if $e(b) = (n,m)$ and $\ell(b) = \sigma$, we say that b is an arc leading from n to m, labelled by σ).

---

† The relevance of graph theory to flowcharts of programs is discussed in Karp [1960].

†† In the sequel, N will also be used as an alphabet. In such a case, n^o will always denote the start node (and not the zeroth power of the symbol n, that is, ε).

If U is defined as above, then we also say that U is a nondeterministic Ianov scheme <u>over Σ</u>.

In the sequel NIAN(Σ), or NIAN when Σ is understood, will denote the class of all nondeterministic Ianov schemes over Σ.

<u>Example 3.2.</u> Let $\Sigma = \{f,g,p,\bar{p}\}$ with $F_\Sigma = \{f,g\}$ and $P_\Sigma = \{p\}$. Consider the nondeterministic Ianov scheme $(\Sigma,N,n^o,E,A,e,\ell)$, where $N = \{1,2,3,4,5\}$, $n^o = 1$, $E = \{4,5\}$ and $A = \{b_1,b_2,b_3,b_4,b_5\}$. The mappings e and ℓ are defined as follows:

$e(b_1) = (1,2)$, $\ell(b_1) = f$,
$e(b_2) = (1,5)$, $\ell(b_2) = g$,
$e(b_3) = (2,3)$, $\ell(b_3) = p$,
$e(b_4) = (2,4)$, $\ell(b_4) = \bar{p}$,
$e(b_5) = (5,1)$, $\ell(b_5) = \bar{p}$. ///

As usual with graphs, to prevent cumbersome notation, examples of nondeterministic Ianov schemes will often be presented in graphical form, as follows.

<u>Convention 3.3</u> (concerning pictures)

Nondeterministic Ianov schemes will be represented pictorially as directed labelled graphs. Nodes will be represented by points, and arcs by directed lines. Each arc is labelled by an instruction symbol. For the purpose of reference a node may be indicated by its name. Thus, an arc from n to m, labelled by σ, will be drawn as $\underset{n}{\bullet}\overset{\sigma}{\longrightarrow}\underset{m}{\bullet}$, or simply as $\bullet\overset{\sigma}{\longrightarrow}\bullet$. Moreover, the start node will be indicated by an arrow, and circles will be drawn around final nodes. ///

<u>Example 3.4.</u> The nondeterministic Ianov scheme of Example 3.2 is represented as follows:

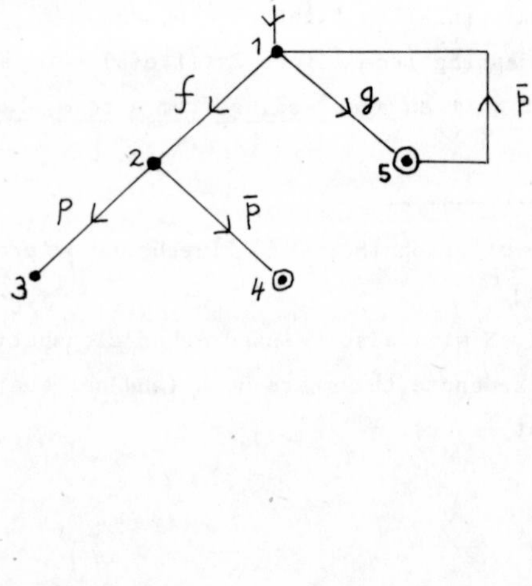

///

Informally, a nondeterministic Ianov scheme $U = (\Sigma, N, n^o, E, A, e, \ell)$ may be "executed" under some general interpretation $I = (D,h)$ of Σ for some "input" x in D, as follows †. At each moment of time execution is "at" some node "with" some element of D. Initially these are n^o and x respectively. Now suppose that execution has arrived at node n with the element y of D. Suppose there is no arc b leading from n such that $h(\sigma)$ is defined for y, where σ is the label of b. Then execution "halts" if n is final, and "sticks" if n is not final. Otherwise execution may either halt (if n is final) or continue with a next step which is selected, in a nondeterministic manner, as follows. First, an arc b leading from n (to m, say) should be chosen such that $h(\sigma)$ is defined for y, where σ is the label of b. That is, an arc should be selected which is labelled by an "instruction applicable to y". Second, an element z in D should be chosen such that (y,z) is in $h(\sigma)$. That is, one of the possible values of $h(\sigma)$ for the argument y should be selected. Execution may now continue at node m with the element z of D. Whenever execution halts (at a final node) with some element of D, then this element is an "output" of U for the input x.

Formally, execution of U under I is defined as follows.

Definition 3.5. Let $U = (\Sigma, N, n^o, E, A, e, \ell)$ be a nondeterministic Ianov scheme, and let I be a general interpretation of Σ. If b is an arc leading from n_1 to n_2, and (x_1, x_2) is in $I(\ell(b))$, then we shall write

$$(n_1, x_1) \vdash_{U,I} (n_2, x_2),$$

thus defining the relation $\vdash_{U,I}$ on $N \times D_I$. Furthermore, as usual, $\vdash^*_{U,I}$ denotes the transitive-reflexive closure of $\vdash_{U,I}$.

Henceforth, whenever it will not lead to confusion, we shall write $\vdash$ and $\vdash^*$ rather than $\vdash_{U,I}$ and $\vdash^*_{U,I}$.

We now define the relation computed by a nondeterministic Ianov scheme under some interpretation.

---

† For some of the terminology used in this section in connection with relations, see 1.1.2.1.

Definition 3.6. For a nondeterministic Ianov scheme $U = (\Sigma,N,n^o,E,A,e,\ell)$ and a general interpretation I of Σ, we define I(U), the relation computed by U under I, to be

$$\{(x,y)\in D_I\times D_I \mid (n^o,x)\overset{*}{\vdash}(n,y) \text{ for some } n \text{ in } E\}.$$

Thus, intuitively, $(x,y) \in I(U)$ if execution of U under I may arrive at some final node with output y, when started at the start node with input x.

Example 3.7. Consider the nondeterministic Ianov scheme U of Example Example 3.2. Let I = (D,h) be the τ-interpretation of Σ, such that D is the set of all integers, and

$h(f) = \{(x,y) \mid x=y^2\}$,

$h(g) = \{(x,y) \mid x\geq 10 \text{ and } y = x+4\}$,

$h(p) = \{(x,x) \mid x \text{ is even}\}$, and

$h(\bar{p}) = \{(x,x) \mid x \text{ is odd}\}$.

Consider the input 9. It has two possible executions, viz. $(1,9) \vdash (2,3) \vdash (4,3)$ and $(1,9) \vdash (2,-3) \vdash (4,-3)$. In both cases execution halts. Thus, for the argument 9, I(U) has the values 3 and -3.

Now consider the input 4. The two possible executions $(1,4) \vdash (2,2) \vdash (3,2)$ and $(1,4) \vdash (2,-2) \vdash (3,-2)$ both stick. Thus, I(U) is undefined for 4.

Finally consider the input 21. It has an infinite number of halting executions. For example,

$(1,21) \vdash (5,25)$,

$(1,21) \vdash (5,25) \vdash (1,25) \vdash (5,29)$, and

$(1,21) \vdash (5,25) \vdash (1,25) \vdash (2,5) \vdash (4,5)$.

In fact, it is easy to see that, for the argument 21, I(U) has an infinite number of values. ///

Example 3.8. Let $\Sigma = \{f,p,\bar{p}\}$ with $F_\Sigma = \{f\}$ and $P_\Sigma = \{p\}$. Consider the nondeterministic Ianov scheme U over Σ, shown below.

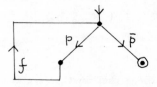

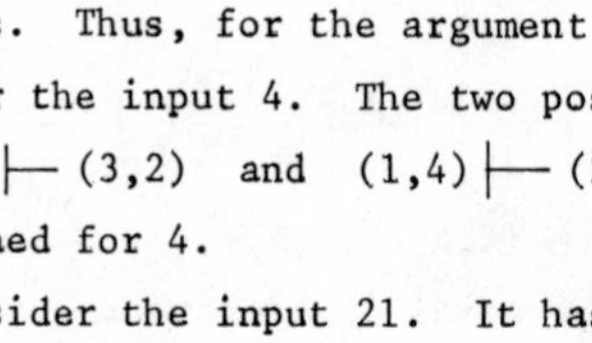

Consider the pτ-interpretation I = (D,h) of Σ, where D is the set of all nonnegative integers, and

$h(f) = \{(x,x-3) | x \geq 3\}$,

$h(p) = \{(x,x) | x \geq 3\}$, and

$h(\bar{p}) = \{(x,x) | 0 \leq x \leq 2\}$.

Intuitively, the Ianov scheme U together with the interpretation I may be regarded as the formal counterpart of the following ALGOL 60 statement:

lab: <u>if</u> x ≥ 3 <u>then</u> <u>begin</u> x := x - 3; <u>goto</u> lab <u>end</u>.

It is easy to show that

$I(U) = \{(x,y) | x \equiv y (\text{mod } 3) \text{ and } 0 \leq y \leq 2\}$. ///

We now show how to associate with each nondeterministic Ianov scheme an equivalent L-scheme. Before defining this formally (Definition 3.9), we give an informal discussion.

Let U be a nondeterministic Ianov scheme. By Definition 3.1, U is a directed labelled graph with a start node and a set of final nodes. Now, it is well known from formal language theory, that such a graph U specifies a (regular) language: the language L(U) of all sequences of labels obtained by following a path in the graph from the start node to some final node, and writing down the labels of the arcs in the order in which they are encountered. In fact, this language is a very natural construct for the Ianov scheme U, because with each particular halting execution of U under some interpretation, one may associate the sequence of instruction symbols encountered during this execution. Since execution of U "follows" a path from the start node to some final node, this sequence belongs to the language L(U), and may be viewed as the "history" or "trace" of the computation performed by U during execution. Therefore, roughly speaking, L(U) consists of all possible histories of computation of U.

Formally, L(U) is defined as follows.

<u>Definition 3.9</u>. Let $U = (\Sigma, N, n^0, E, A, e, \ell)$ be a nondeterministic Ianov scheme. We define L(U), the <u>L-scheme corresponding to U</u>, to be the language generated by the regular grammar † $G_U = (N, \Sigma, R, n^0)$, where R

---

† For the notion of regular grammar, see 1.4.1.3.

consists of the following rules.

(1) For each arc from n_1 to n_2, labelled by σ, the rule $n_1 \to \sigma n_2$ is in R.

(2) For each final node n, the rule $n \to \varepsilon$ is in R.

__Example__ 3.10. Consider the nondeterministic Ianov scheme U of Example 3.2. Then, $G_U = (N,\Sigma,R,Z)$, where $N = \{1,2,3,4,5\}$, $\Sigma = \{f,g,p,\bar{p}\}$, $Z = 1$ and R consists of the rules $1 \to f2$, $1 \to g5$, $2 \to p3$, $2 \to \bar{p}4$, $4 \to \varepsilon$, $5 \to \bar{p}1$ and $5 \to \varepsilon$. It is easy to show that $L(G_U) = (g\bar{p})^*(f\bar{p} \cup g)$. Hence, $L(U) = (g\bar{p})^*(f\bar{p} \cup g)$.

Consider in Example 3.7 the halting execution

$(1,21) \vdash (5,25) \vdash (1,25) \vdash (2,5) \vdash (4,5)$ of U under the interpretation defined in that example. The "history" of this execution is, obviously, $g\bar{p}f\bar{p}$. This word is derivable in G_U as follows:

$1 \Rightarrow g5 \Rightarrow g\bar{p}1 \Rightarrow g\bar{p}f2 \Rightarrow g\bar{p}f\bar{p}4 \Rightarrow g\bar{p}f\bar{p}$. ///

In Theorem 3.11 we shall prove that, for each nondeterministic Ianov scheme U, the corresponding L-scheme is equivalent to U (that is, U and L(U) compute the same relation under any interpretation). Since this result also holds for many other classes of program schemes, as will be shown in the following sections, we first give an informal proof, which is meant to provide an intuitive sense of the truth of the result in general †.

Let U be a nondeterministic Ianov scheme over Σ, and let I be a general interpretation of Σ. We have to show that $I(U) = I(L(U))$. Hence, by Definition 2.7(4), we have to show that, for all x and y in D_I, $(x,y) \in I(U)$ if and only if there exists ϕ in Σ^* such that $\phi \in L(U)$ and $(x,y) \in I(\phi)$.

First suppose that $(x,y) \in I(U)$. Consider the sequence of instruction symbols $\sigma_1,\sigma_2,\ldots,\sigma_n$ encountered during execution of U with input x and output y. Since y was obtained from x by executing the instructions $(\sigma_i,I(\sigma_i))$ for $1 \le i \le n$, it is clear that (x,y) is in $I(\sigma_1\sigma_2\cdots\sigma_n)$. Also, by the definition of L(U), it is obvious that $\sigma_1\sigma_2\cdots\sigma_n$ is in L(U). Now let $\phi = \sigma_1\sigma_2\cdots\sigma_n$.

Conversely, suppose that $(x,y) \in I(\phi)$ for some ϕ in L(U). Let $\phi = \sigma_1\sigma_2\cdots\sigma_n$ for certain $\sigma_1,\sigma_2,\ldots,\sigma_n$ in Σ. Since $\phi \in L(U)$, there is

---

† See also the intuitive discussion of Elgot [1972].

a path through U of which the corresponding labels are $\sigma_1\sigma_2,\ldots,\sigma_n$. Since $(x,y) \in I(\sigma_1\sigma_2\cdots\sigma_n)$, it should be clear that execution of U with input x may follow this path, producing the output y. Thus, $(x,y) \in I(U)$.

We now state the theorem and give its formal proof.

Theorem 3.11. For any nondeterministic Ianov scheme U over Σ and any general interpretation I of Σ, we have $I(L(U)) = I(U)$.

Proof. Let $U = (\Sigma,N,n^o,E,A,e,\ell)$, and let $I = (D,h)$. Let $G_U = (N,\Sigma,R,n^o)$ be the regular grammar with $L(G_U) = L(U)$, see Definition 3.9.

To show that $I(L(G_U)) = I(U)$ we shall prove that, for any n_1 and n_2 in N and any x_1 and x_2 in D,

(*) $(n_1,x_1) \vdash^{*} (n_2,x_2)$ if and only if there is a word ϕ in Σ^* such that $n_1 \overset{*}{\Rightarrow} \phi n_2$ and $(x_1,x_2) \in I(\phi)$.

This is sufficient, since, for any x and y in D,

$(x,y) \in I(U)$

$\Leftrightarrow$ there is a node n in E such that $(n^o,x) \vdash^{*} (n,y)$ (by Definition 3.6)

$\Leftrightarrow$ there are ϕ in Σ^* and n in E such that $n^o \overset{*}{\Rightarrow} \phi n$ and $(x,y) \in I(\phi)$ (by (*))

$\Leftrightarrow$ there is a word ϕ in Σ^* such that $n^o \overset{*}{\Rightarrow} \phi$ and $(x,y) \in I(\phi)$

$\Leftrightarrow$ $(x,y) \in I(L(G_U))$ (by Definition 2.7(4)).

(We have used the obvious fact that, for any ϕ in Σ^*, $n^o \overset{*}{\Rightarrow} \phi$ if and only if there is some n in E such that $n^o \overset{*}{\Rightarrow} \phi n$.)

This proves the theorem. So, let us now prove (*).

The "only if" part is proved by induction on the number of steps in $(n_1,x_1) \vdash^{*} (n_2,x_2)$.

First, if the number of steps is zero, then $n_1 = n_2$ and $x_1 = x_2$. Let $\phi = \varepsilon$. Then obviously $n_1 \overset{*}{\Rightarrow} \phi n_2$ and, by Definition 2.7(2), (x_1,x_2) is in $I(\phi)$.

Now suppose that $(n_1,x_1) \vdash^{*} (n,x) \vdash (n_2,x_2)$ for some n in N and x in D. It follows that there is an arc from n to n_2, labelled by some σ in Σ, such that (x,x_2) is in $I(\sigma)$. Also, by induction, there is a word ψ in Σ^*

such that $n_1 \overset{*}{\Rightarrow} \psi n$ and (x_1,x) is in $I(\psi)$. Let $\phi = \psi\sigma$. Then $n_1 \overset{*}{\Rightarrow} \psi n \Rightarrow \psi\sigma n_2 = \phi n_2$. Moreover, (x_1,x_2) is in $I(\psi) \circ I(\sigma)$, thus, by Definition 2.7(3), it is in $I(\phi)$.

The "if" part is proved by induction on the length of ϕ.

First, let $\phi = \varepsilon$. Thus $n_1 \overset{*}{\Rightarrow} n_2$ and $x_1 = x_2$. Since the rules in R are of the form $n \to \sigma n'$ or $n \to \varepsilon$, it follows that $n_1 = n_2$. Hence $(n_1,x_1) \vdash^{*} (n_2,x_2)$ in zero steps.

Now suppose that $\phi = \psi\sigma$. It follows from the nature of the rules in R that the derivation $n_1 \overset{*}{\Rightarrow} \psi\sigma n_2$ has the form $n_1 \overset{*}{\Rightarrow} \psi n \Rightarrow \psi\sigma n_2$ for some n in N, where $n \to \sigma n_2$ is in R. Since (x_1,x_2) is in $I(\psi\sigma)$, there is some x in D such that (x_1,x) is in $I(\psi)$ and (x,x_2) in $I(\sigma)$. It follows by induction that $(n_1,x_1) \vdash^{*} (n,x)$. Also, since $n \to \sigma n_2$ is in R, there is an arc from n to n_2, labelled by σ. Therefore, since (x,x_2) is in $I(\sigma)$, $(n,x) \vdash (n_2,x_2)$. Thus $(n_1,x_1) \vdash^{*} (n,x) \vdash (n_2,x_2)$, so that $(n_1 x_1) \vdash^{*} (n_2,x_2)$. ///

We illustrate the theorem by the following example.

<u>Example 3.12</u>. Consider the Ianov scheme U and the interpretation I from Example 3.8. It is easy to see, that $L(U) = \{(pf)^k\bar{p} \mid k\geq 0\}$. By induction on k, one can show that, for $k \geq 0$,
$I((pf)^k) = \{(x,y) \mid y=x-3k \text{ and } y\geq 0\}$, and thus
$I((pf)^k\bar{p}) = \{(x,y) \mid y=x-3k \text{ and } 0\leq y\leq 2\}$.
Consequently

$$\begin{aligned} I(L(U)) &= \{(x,y) \mid y=x-3k \text{ and } 0\leq y\leq 2, \text{ for some } k\geq 0\} \\ &= \{(x,y) \mid x\equiv y \pmod 3 \text{ and } 0\leq y\leq 2\} \\ &= I(U). \end{aligned}$$ ///

We conclude this section by defining two other classes of program schemes related to the nondeterministic Ianov schemes: the class of deterministic Ianov schemes (in the next definition), and the class of regular schemes (in Definition 3.16).

<u>Definition 3.13</u>. Let U be a nondeterministic Ianov scheme over Σ. U is called a <u>deterministic Ianov scheme</u> (or simply, <u>Ianov scheme</u>) <u>over Σ</u> if it satisfies the following requirements.

(1) For each node n at most two arcs lead from n.

(2) For each node n, if two arcs lead from n, then there is a p in P_Σ such that one of the arcs is labelled by p and the other by $\bar{p}$. †

(3) No arc leads from a final node.

We shall denote the class of all (deterministic) Ianov schemes over Σ by IAN(Σ), or IAN when Σ is understood.

Intuitively, a deterministic Ianov scheme U gives rise to a "deterministic" execution in the following sense. Let I be a pπ-interpretation (that is, suppose that we have "deterministic instructions"). Then, if execution arrives at some node with some element of D_I, either execution halts, or (at most) one arc is selected for the next step. Moreover, the next element of D_I is uniquely determined. Thus, there is at most one execution for each input from D_I, and I(U) is a partial function (this will be proved formally later on, see Corollary 18.10).

Example 3.14. The nondeterministic Ianov scheme from Example 3.2 is not deterministic, since it does not satisfy requirements (2) and (3) of Definition 3.13 (for nodes 1 and 5 respectively).

The nondeterministic Ianov scheme U from Example 3.8 is obviously deterministic. Note that U computes a partial (even total) function under the pτ-interpretation of that example. ///

Remark 3.15. Note that we did not require, as is usual††, in the definition of a deterministic Ianov scheme, that if an arc is the only one leading from a certain node, it should be labelled by a function symbol. However, for every deterministic Ianov scheme U, we may construct a deterministic Ianov scheme U_1 satisfying this requirement, and computing the same function as U under any pπ-interpretation. We do this simply as follows. Suppose that precisely one arc b is leading from node n, and suppose that $\ell(b) = p$ (or $\bar{p}$), for some p in P_Σ. Then we add to U a new arc b_1 from n to n, labelled by $\bar{p}$ (resp. p). U_1 is obtained by

---

† Such a pair of arcs models a test or predicate. This way of representing a test is due to Karp [1960].

†† See, for instance, Kaluzhnin [1961,§3.1].

repeating this construction until the requirement is satisfied. Then, whenever execution of U sticks at n, execution of U_1 will either stick or enter the "trivial loop" b_1, and vice versa. Thus, obviously, U_1 and U compute the same function under any pπ-interpretation.

Similarly, we could have required that any node from which no arc is leading, is final. ///

We now define regular schemes.

In Theorem 3.11 we showed that, for each nondeterministic Ianov scheme U, U and L(U) compute the same relation under any interpretation. But L(U) is generated, as a language, by the regular grammar G_U. In fact, in the same way as any language is a program scheme (an L-scheme), any regular grammar can be considered as a program scheme. This leads to the following definition.

† Definition 3.16

(1) A regular scheme over Σ is any regular grammar G with terminal alphabet Σ.

(2) The language L(G) generated by the regular grammar G is also said to be the L-scheme corresponding to the regular scheme G.

(3) Given a general interpretation I of Σ, the relation computed by G under I, denoted by I(G), is defined to be I(L(G)).

We shall denote by REG(Σ), or REG when Σ is understood, the class of all regular schemes over Σ.

Note that, for regular schemes, the analogue of Theorem 3.11: "for any regular scheme G over Σ and any general interpretation I of Σ, we have I(L(G)) = I(G)" follows directly from Definition 3.16(3).

---

† Regular schemes were introduced by Ito [1968, section 1] in the form of regular expressions.

4. Recursive systems of Ianov schemes and context-free schemes

Recursive procedures are an essential feature of many programming languages. A theory of recursive procedures was first outlined by McCarthy [1963]. Recursive program schemes were introduced by de Bakker and Scott [1969] as a formalization of the concept of recursive procedure. The connection between recursive program schemes and context-free languages was established in a number of papers, e.g. those of Ito [1968], Garland and Luckham [1973], Ashcroft, Manna and Pnueli [1973] and Rosen [1972].

This section is organized in roughly the same way as the previous one. First we define the notion of recursive program scheme (its nondeterministic version, and at the end of the section we define its deterministic restriction) and the relation computed by a recursive program scheme under an arbitrary interpretation.

Then we show that with each recursive program scheme we may associate, in a natural manner, a context-free language (see Definition 4.8), which, as an L-scheme, is equivalent to the recursive program scheme (Theorem 4.11). This illustrates again the importance of the concept of L-scheme.

We end the section by pointing out that each context-free grammar can be viewed as a program scheme, called context-free scheme.

Recursive program schemes can be defined in a number of equivalent ways. The formalism of de Bakker and Scott [1969] will be discussed in section 6. Here we define recursive program schemes as recursive systems of Ianov schemes, having in mind the following intuitive description of a recursive program.

Roughly speaking, a recursive program consists of a finite set of procedures of which one is the main procedure. Each procedure consists of a a name and a body (for the time being we only consider procedures without parameters). The body of a procedure is an ordinary program of which a flowchart can be drawn. In the body, names of procedures may occur (an occurrence of a procedure name is said to be a call of that procedure).

This is formalized as follows:

Definition 4.1. A nondeterministic recursive system of Ianov schemes (abbreviated by nrsi) is a 4-tuple $U = (\Sigma, \mathcal{F}, Z, b)$, where

(1) Σ is an alphabet (of instruction symbols),

(2) $\mathcal{F}$ is an alphabet (of procedure symbols), disjoint with Σ,

(3) Z is a distinguished element of $\mathcal{F}$ (the main procedure symbol), and

(4) b is a mapping from $\mathcal{F}$ into $NIAN(\Sigma_1)$, where Σ_1 is the alphabet with $F_{\Sigma_1} = F_\Sigma \cup \mathcal{F}$, $P_{\Sigma_1} = P_\Sigma$ and $\overline{P}_{\Sigma_1} = \overline{P}_\Sigma$. (If S is a procedure symbol, then we say that $b(S)$ is the body of S).

If U is defined as above, then we also say that U is an nrsi over Σ. In the sequel, the class of all nrsi's over Σ will be denoted by $NRSI(\Sigma)$, or NRSI when Σ is understood.

Notation 4.2. Let $U = (\Sigma, \mathcal{F}, Z, b)$ be an nrsi. For each procedure symbol S, we denote the nondeterministic Ianov scheme $b(S)$ by $(\Sigma \cup \mathcal{F}, N_S, n_S^o, E_S, A_S, e_S, \ell_S)$. Furthermore, we denote by N_U and E_U the sets $\bigcup_{S\in\mathcal{F}} N_S$ and $\bigcup_{S\in\mathcal{F}} E_S$ respectively.

In the sequel it will be assumed that, for any nrsi $U = (\Sigma, \mathcal{F}, Z, b)$, the sets N_S, with $S \in \mathcal{F}$, are mutually disjoint. ///

Example 4.3. Let $\Sigma = \{f,g,p,\bar{p},q,\bar{q}\}$ with $F_\Sigma = \{f,g\}$ and $P_\Sigma = \{p,q\}$. Then $(\Sigma, \mathcal{F}, Z, b)$, where $\mathcal{F} = \{S,T\}$, $Z = S$ and the bodies of S and T are shown below (see Convention 3.3), is an nrsi.

b(S) =

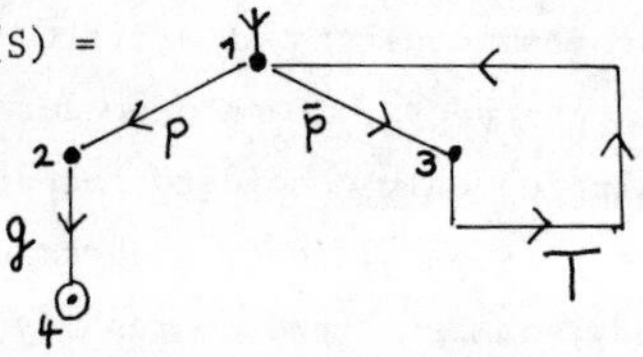

b(T) =

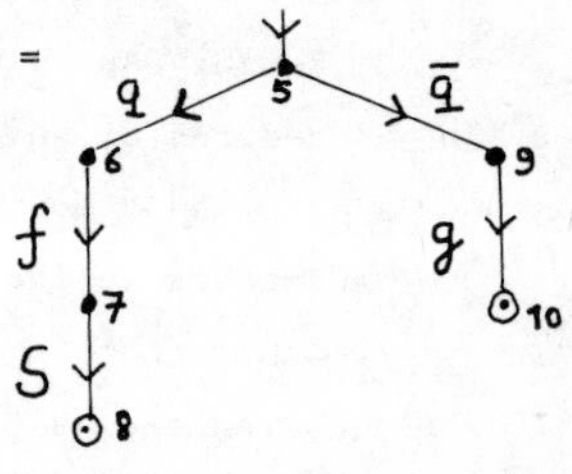

One may regard the above nrsi as formally representing the control structure of the following ALGOL 60 statement:

```
begin procedure S;
      lab:  if p then g else begin T; goto lab end;
   procedure T;
      if q then begin f; S end else g;
   S
end,
```

where it is assumed that procedures f and g and Boolean procedures p and q have been declared outside the block. ///

Example 4.4. Let $\Sigma = \{f,g,k,p,\bar{p}\}$ with $F_\Sigma = \{f,g,k\}$ and $P_\Sigma = \{p\}$. Then $(\Sigma,\{Z\},Z,b)$ with

$b(Z) =$

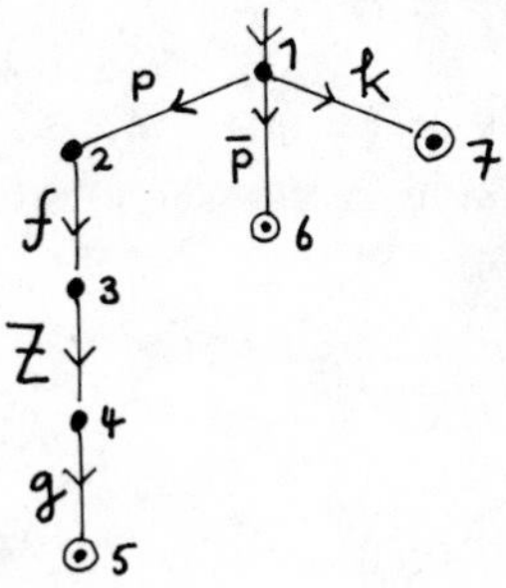

forms an nrsi. ///

We now define "execution" of an nrsi under an arbitrary interpretation.

Definition 4.5. Let $U = (\Sigma,\mathcal{F},Z,b)$ be an nrsi, and let I be a general interpretation of Σ. The relation $\vdash_{U,I}$ (or $\vdash$, when U and I are understood) on $N_U^* \times D_I$ is defined as follows.

(1) If, in the body of some procedure symbol, there is an arc leading from n_1 to n_2, labelled by an instruction symbol σ, and (x_1,x_2) is in $I(\sigma)$, then $(n_1\alpha,x_1) \vdash (n_2\alpha,x_2)$ for all α in N_U^*.

(2) If, in the body of some procedure symbol, there is an arc leading from n_1 to n_2, labelled by a procedure symbol S, then $(n_1\alpha,x) \vdash (n_S^o\, n_2\alpha,x)$ for all x in D_I and α in N_U^*.

(3) If n is in E_U, then $(n\alpha,x) \vdash (\alpha,x)$ for all α in N_U^* and x in D_I.

Furthermore $\vdash^*$ denotes the transitive-reflexive closure of $\vdash$.

Definition 4.6. For an nrsi $U = (\Sigma, \mathcal{F}, Z, b)$ and a general interpretation I of Σ, we define I(U), the relation computed by U under I, to be

$$\{(x,y) \in D_I \times D_I \mid (n_Z^o, x) \vdash^{*} (\varepsilon, y)\}.$$

Intuitively, an nrsi U is executed by the use of a pushdown store which contains at each moment an element α of N_U^*. The top of the pushdown store contains the current node of the current procedure body (that is, the first symbol of α). When, at node n_1, a "call" of a procedure S is encountered (see Definition 4.5(2)), then n_1 is replaced by the "return address" n_2, and the "start address" n_S^o of S is put on top of the pushdown store. When execution of the body of S is completed, then, by Definition 4.5 (3), execution returns to node n_2. Execution of U starts by calling the main procedure, and halts when that call is completed.

Example 4.7. Consider the nrsi U of Example 4.4. Let I = (D,h) be the pτ-interpretation of Σ, such that D is the set of all integers, and

$h(f) = \{(x,y) \mid y=x-1\}$,

$h(g) = \{(x,y) \mid y=x+1\}$,

$h(k) = \emptyset$,

$h(p) = \{(x,x) \mid x>0\}$, and

$h(\bar{p}) = \{(x,x) \mid x\leq 0\}$.

Consider the input 2. It gives rise to the following execution:†

$(n_1,2) \vdash (n_2,2) \vdash (n_3,1) \vdash (n_1n_4,1) \vdash$

$(n_2n_4,1) \vdash (n_3n_4,0) \vdash (n_1n_4n_4,0) \vdash (n_6n_4n_4,0) \vdash$

$(n_4n_4,0) \vdash (n_5n_4,1) \vdash (n_4,1) \vdash (n_5,2) \vdash (\varepsilon,2)$.

Thus, I(U) has the value 2 for the argument 2. In fact it is easy to show that $I(U) = id_D$.

Note, that the sequence of instruction symbols, encountered during the above execution, is $pfpf\bar{p}gg$. ///

One may remark here, that Definition 4.1 augmented by the condition that all procedure bodies are "cycle-free", is obviously equivalent to most of the definitions of recursive program schemes encountered in the literature††. However, one may easily show, that for each nrsi there is an equivalent one satisfying the above condition.

---

† To ensure better readability we denote node i by n_i, for all $i \geq 1$; so, for example, we write $n_6n_4n_4$ rather than 644.

†† See for instance the survey paper of Paterson [1972], where recursive program schemes are called de Bakker-Scott schemes.

We now show how to associate with each nrsi an equivalent L-scheme. As it was the case with Ianov schemes, this L-scheme consists of all sequences of instruction symbols obtained by "following a path through the nrsi".

Definition 4.8. Let $U = (\Sigma, \mathcal{F}, Z, b)$ be an nrsi.
We define L(U), the L-scheme corresponding to U, to be the language generated by the context-free grammar † $G_U = (N_U, \Sigma, R, n_Z^o)$, where R consists of the following rules.

(1) If, in the body of some procedure symbol, there is an arc leading from n_1 to n_2 labelled by an instruction symbol σ, then the rule $n_1 \to \sigma n_2$ is in R.

(2) If, in the body of some procedure symbol, there is an arc leading from n_1 to n_2 labelled by a procedure symbol S, then the rule $n_1 \to n_S^o n_2$ is in R.

(3) For all n in E_U, the rule $n \to \varepsilon$ is in R.

Example 4.9. †† Consider the nrsi U of Example 4.3. Then, $G_U = (N_U, \Sigma, R, n_Z^o)$ where $N_U = \{n_1, n_2, \ldots, n_{10}\}$, $n_Z^o = n_1$ and R contains the rules $n_1 \to pn_2$, $n_2 \to gn_4$, $n_4 \to \varepsilon$, $n_1 \to \bar{p}n_3$, $n_3 \to n_5n_1$, $n_5 \to qn_6$, $n_6 \to fn_7$, $n_7 \to n_1n_8$, $n_8 \to \varepsilon$, $n_5 \to \bar{q}n_9$, $n_9 \to gn_{10}$ and $n_{10} \to \varepsilon$. Obviously, the following smaller set of rules generates the same language: $S \to pg$, $S \to \bar{p}TS$, $T \to qfS$ and $T \to \bar{q}g$ (where we have replaced n_1 by S and n_5 by T). This set of rules can easily be "read off" the bodies of S and T in Example 4.3. ///

Example 4.10. †† Consider the nrsi U of Example 4.4. Then $G_U = (\{n_1, n_2, \ldots, n_7\}, \Sigma, R, n_1)$, where R consists of the rules $n_1 \to pn_2$, $n_1 \to \bar{p}n_6$, $n_1 \to kn_7$, $n_2 \to fn_3$, $n_3 \to n_1n_4$, $n_4 \to gn_5$, $n_5 \to \varepsilon$, $n_6 \to \varepsilon$ and $n_7 \to \varepsilon$. It is easy to see that $L(U) = \{(pf)^m\bar{p}g^m \mid m \geq 0\} \cup \{(pf)^m kg^m \mid m \geq 0\}$.

The word $pfpf\bar{p}gg$ is the history of the execution of U with input 2 (see Example 4.7). It is derivable in G_U as follows:

$$n_1 \Rightarrow pn_2 \Rightarrow pfn_3 \Rightarrow pfn_1n_4 \overset{*}{\Rightarrow} pfpfn_1n_4n_4 \Rightarrow pfpf\bar{p}n_6n_4n_4 \Rightarrow$$

$$pfpf\bar{p}n_4n_4 \Rightarrow pfpf\bar{p}gn_5n_4 \Rightarrow pfpf\bar{p}gn_4 \overset{*}{\Rightarrow} pfpf\bar{p}gg. \quad ///$$

---

† For the notion of context-free grammar, see 1.4.1.2.

†† See the footnote in Example 4.7.

It turns out again (see Theorem 3.11 and the discussion preceding it) that U and L(U) are equivalent program schemes. This is expressed in the following theorem.

Theorem 4.11. For any nrsi U over Σ and any general interpretation I of Σ, we have $I(L(U)) = I(U)$.

Proof. Let $U = (\Sigma, \mathcal{F}, Z, b)$, and let $I = (D,h)$. Let $G_U = (N_U, \Sigma, R, n_Z^o)$ be the context-free grammar with $L(G_U) = L(U)$.†

To show that $I(L(G_U)) = I(U)$, it is sufficient to prove that, for any α_1 and α_2 in N_U^*, and any x_1 and x_2 in D,

(*) $(\alpha_1, x_1) \vdash^* (\alpha_2, x_2)$ if and only if there is a word ϕ in Σ^* such that $\alpha_1 \overset{*}{\underset{\ell}{\Rightarrow}} \phi\alpha_2$ †† and $(x_1, x_2) \in I(\phi)$.

For suppose that x and y are in D. Then,

$(x,y) \in I(U)$

$\Leftrightarrow (n_Z^o, x) \vdash^* (\varepsilon, y)$ (by Definition 4.6)

$\Leftrightarrow$ there is a word ϕ in Σ^* such that $n_Z^o \overset{*}{\underset{\ell}{\Rightarrow}} \phi$ and $(x,y) \in I(\phi)$ (by (*))

$\Leftrightarrow$ there is a word ϕ in $L(G_U)$ such that $(x,y) \in I(\phi)$

$\Leftrightarrow (x,y) \in I(L(G_U))$ (by Definition 2.7(4)),

and this proves the theorem.

Since the proof of (*) is similar to the proof of (*) in Theorem 3.11, it is left to the reader. The only "complication" which arises, is caused by rules of G_U which do not introduce terminals. Therefore, one should first prove that, for any α_1 and α_2 in N_U^*, if $\alpha_1 \overset{*}{\underset{\ell}{\Rightarrow}} \alpha_2$, then $(\alpha_1, x) \vdash^* (\alpha_2, x)$ for all x in D. Intuitively, this follows from the fact that rules without terminals correspond to calls or returns (see points (2) and (3) of Definitions 4.5 and 4.8). ///

We illustrate the theorem by the following example.

---

† For the definition of G_U, see Definition 4.8.

†† Here, $\overset{*}{\underset{\ell}{\Rightarrow}}$ denotes "leftmost derivation", see Hopcroft and Ullman [1969, Lemma 4.1].

Example 4.12. For the nrsi U from Example 4.4 we have that $L(U) = \{(pf)^m \bar{p}g^m | m\geq 0\} \cup \{(pf)^m kg^m | m\geq 0\}$, see Example 4.10. Let us determine $I(L(U))$, where I is defined as in Example 4.7. Firstly, since $I(k) = \emptyset$, $I(\{(pf)^m kg^m | m\geq 0\}) = \emptyset$. Secondly, it is easy to show by induction on m, that for $m > 0$, $I((pf)^m) = \{(x,y) | y=x-m \text{ and } y\geq 0\}$, and thus, $I((pf)^m \bar{p}) = \{(m,0)\}$ and $I((pf)^m \bar{p}g^m) = \{(m,m)\}$. Also, $I(\bar{p}) = \{(x,x) | x\leq 0\}$. Hence, $I(L(U)) = id_D$, and so $I(L(U)) = I(U)$. ///

We conclude this section by defining deterministic recursive systems of Ianov schemes (Definition 4.13) and context-free schemes (Definition 4.15).

Definition 4.13. Let U be an nrsi over Σ. U is called a deterministic recursive system of Ianov schemes over Σ, or shorter, a recursive system of Ianov schemes (abbreviated by rsi) over Σ, if all bodies of procedure symbols of U are deterministic Ianov schemes.

We shall denote the class of all rsi's over Σ by RSI(Σ), or RSI when Σ is understood.

The reader may easily see that, intuitively, an rsi U gives rise to a "deterministic execution" under any pπ-interpretation. In fact, it will be proved later, that I(U) is a partial function for all pπ-interpretations I (see Corollary 18.20).

Example 4.14. The nrsi of Example 4.3 is deterministic. The nrsi of Example 4.4. is not deterministic, since requirement (1) of Definition 3.13 is not satisfied for the start node of the body of the main procedure symbol. ///

We now define context-free schemes. Since, by Theorem 4.11, any nrsi is equivalent to an L-scheme generated by a context-free grammar (Definition 4.8), it is natural to view any context-free grammar as a program scheme.

† Definition 4.15

(1) A context-free scheme over Σ is any context-free grammar G with terminal alphabet Σ.

(2) The language L(G) generated by the context-free grammar G is also said to be the L-scheme corresponding to the context-free scheme G.

(3) Given a general interpretation I of Σ, the relation computed by G under I, denoted by I(G), is defined to be I(L(G)).

We shall denote by CFG(Σ), or CFG when Σ is understood, the class of all context-free schemes over Σ.

Note that each regular scheme G over Σ (see Definition 3.16) is also a context-free scheme over Σ.

Note also that, as in the case of regular schemes, it follows directly from Definition 4.15(3) that each context-free scheme is equivalent to its corresponding L-scheme.

---

† Context-free schemes were introduced in Ito [1968, section 3], where they are called "CF-type program schemes".

5. Procedure parameter schemes and macro schemes

A new kind of program scheme is introduced in this section as a formalization of the concept of a recursive procedure with parameters of type "procedure without parameters". † These schemes will be called "procedure parameter schemes". A similar class of program schemes was investigated, independently, by Langmaack [1973], who also established the connection between these schemes and macro languages.

This section is organized in the same way as the previous one. First we define the notion of nondeterministic procedure parameter scheme (the definition of its deterministic version is left to the reader) and the relation computed by it under an arbitrary interpretation (Definition 5.10).

Then we show that with each procedure parameter scheme we may associate a macro language (see Definition 5.12), which, as an L-scheme, is equivalent to the procedure parameter scheme (Theorem 5.14). This illustrates, again, the importance of the concept of L-scheme.

We conclude the section by pointing out that each macro grammar can be viewed as a program scheme, called macro scheme.

Intuitively, a procedure parameter scheme consists of a finite set of procedures, of which one is the main procedure. Each procedure consists of a name, a finite (possibly empty) list of formal parameters (of type "procedure without parameters") and a body. The main procedure has no parameters. In the body of a procedure, any procedure name followed by a list of parameters may occur (this is said to be a call of that procedure). Also, of course, any formal parameter of a procedure may occur in the body of that procedure.

Before giving the formal definitions of this section, we first consider two informal examples.

Example 5.1. Let $\Sigma = \{f,g,p,\bar{p}\}$ with $F_\Sigma = \{f,g\}$ and $P_\Sigma = \{p\}$. The

---

† Note that "procedure" is the only type which can be studied without imposing restrictions on the domains of interpretation.

following is an example of a procedure parameter scheme over Σ, consisting of three procedures Z, S and T, of which Z is the main procedure. Z and S have no parameters. T has one (formal) parameter x. The bodies of Z, S and T are

b(Z) = 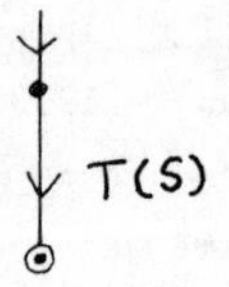

b(S) = 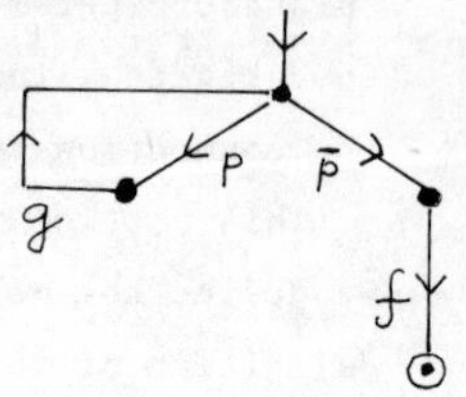

b(T) = 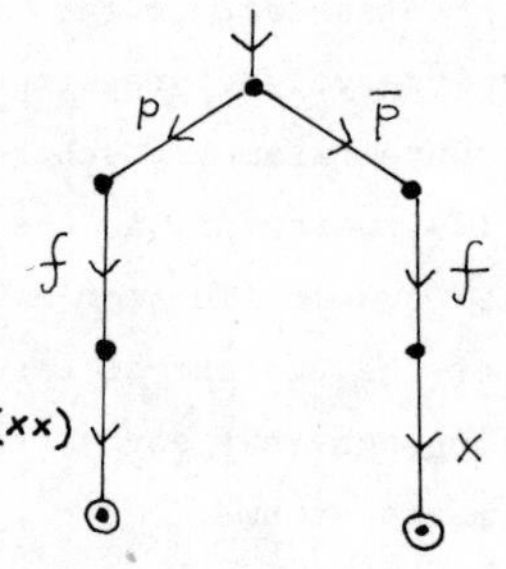

Thus, the arcs in the bodies are labelled by elements of Σ, formal parameters and procedure calls.

Under some interpretation, a call of T with a certain actual parameter results in the execution of the body of T in which the formal parameter x has been replaced by the actual parameter. This will be called the "copy rule". Thus, calls T(S) and T(SS) result in the execution of

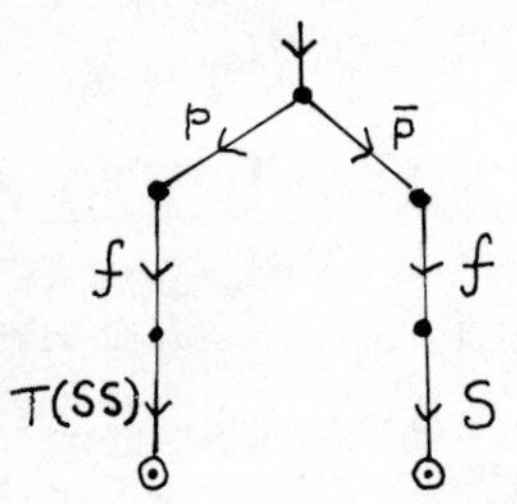

and

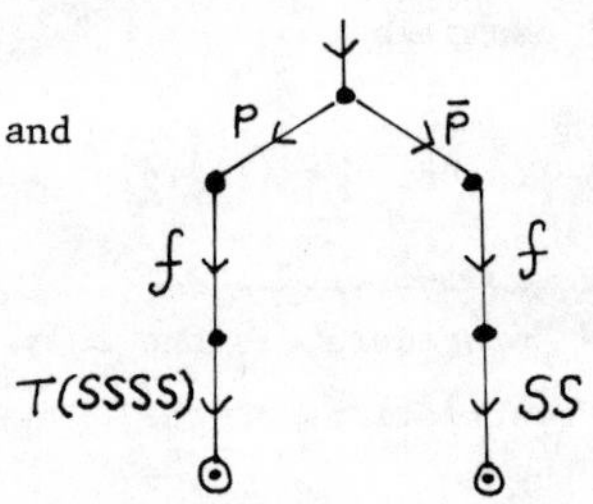

respectively.

The latter Ianov scheme is simply an abbreviation of the following scheme

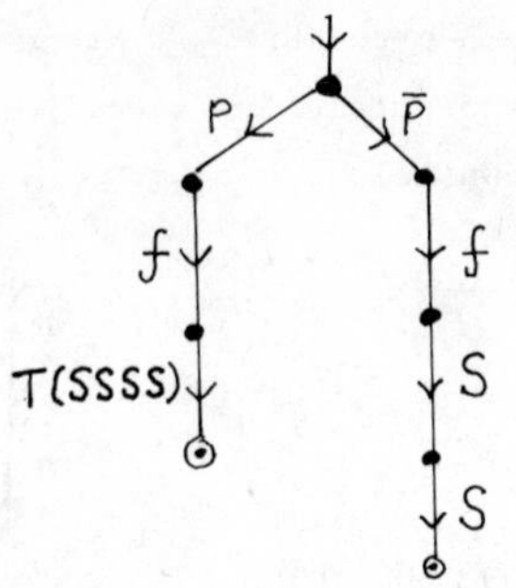

Intuitively, we may regard the procedure parameter scheme of this example as the formal counterpart of the following Algol 60 program:

```
begin procedure S;
      ℓ: if p then begin g; goto ℓ end else f;
    procedure T(x); procedure x;
      begin procedure xx; begin x; x end;
            if p then begin f; T(xx) end
                 else begin f; x end
      end;
    T(S)
end,
```

where it is assumed that Boolean procedure p and procedures f and g (without parameters) have been declared outside the block. ///

In the previous example we have seen that, if A and B are procedures without parameters, then AB ("first A, then B") is also considered to be a procedure without parameters.

In the next example we want to point out two things. Firstly, the elements of F_Σ (where Σ is the alphabet of instruction symbols) are considered as procedures without parameters. Secondly, our procedures with parameters are considered to deliver a value of type "procedure without parameters". More precisely, if T is a procedure with two parameters and A and B are procedures without parameters, then T(A,B) is used as a name for the procedure without parameters, the body of which is obtained from the body of T by the copy rule. Thus, apart from occurring as a procedure call, T(A,B) may also occur as actual parameter of a procedure call.

Example 5.2. Let $\Sigma = \{f,g,p,\bar{p}\}$ with $F_\Sigma = \{f,g\}$ and $P_\Sigma = \{p\}$. Consider the following procedure parameter scheme with three procedures Z, S and T, of which Z is the main procedure. Z has no parameters, S has one parameter x, and T has two parameters x and y (in that order). The bodies of Z, S and T are shown below.

b(Z) =

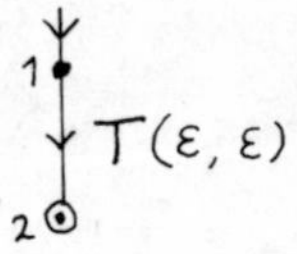

b(S) =

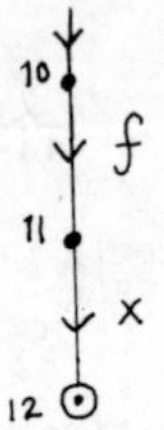

b(T) =

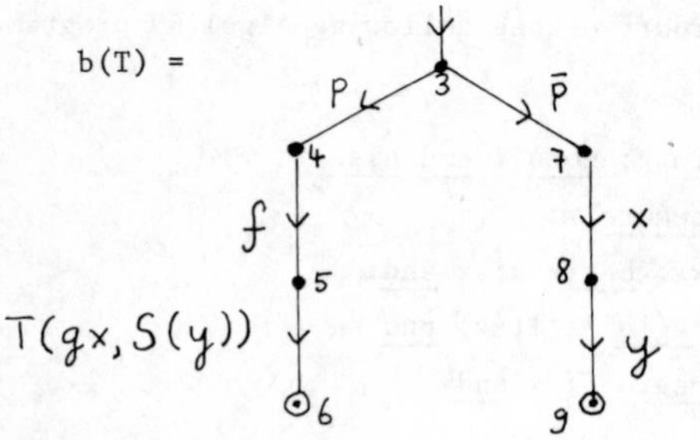

Calls T(ε,ε), T(g,S(ε)) and S(ε) result in the execution of the following programs (note that ε should be considered as a procedure without parameters, with the dummy statement as its body):

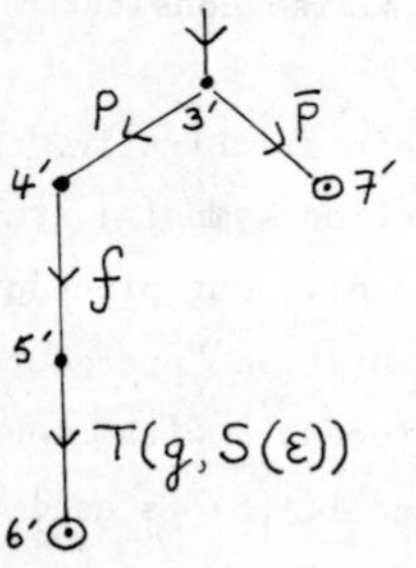

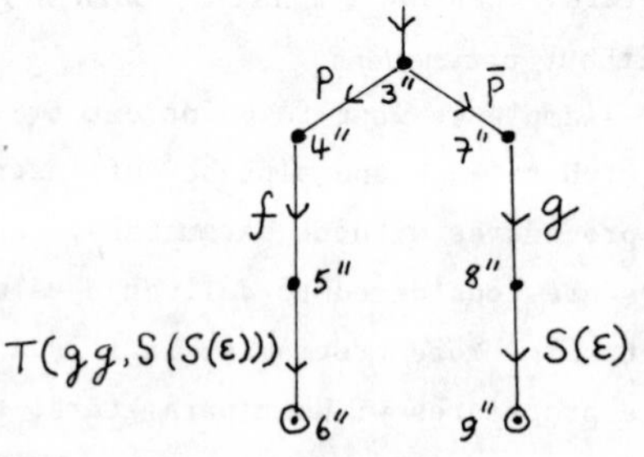

and

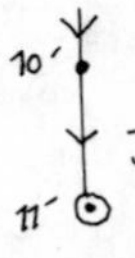

One may view the procedure parameter scheme of this example as representing the control structure of the following Algol 60 program:

```
begin procedure S(x); procedure x; begin f; x end;
      procedure T(x,y); procedure x,y;
        begin procedure gx; begin g; x end;
              procedure Sy; S(y);
              if p then begin f; T(gx,Sy) end
                   else begin x; y end
        end;
      procedure E; ; comment dummy statement;
      T(E,E)
end.
```

It is easy to see that this procedure parameter scheme computes, under any interpretation, the same relation as the L-scheme $\{(pf)^n \bar{p}g^n f^n | n\geq 0\}$. ///

We now start with the formal definitions.

Let Σ be an alphabet (of instruction symbols), and $\mathcal{F}$ an alphabet (of procedure symbols). Let r be a mapping from $\mathcal{F}$ into the set of non-negative integers (for S in $\mathcal{F}$, r(S) is called the rank of S; intuitively, r(S) is the number of parameters of the procedure S). Furthermore, let $X = \{x_1, x_2, x_3, \ldots\}$ be a denumerably infinite set (of formal parameters). Define $X_0 = \emptyset$ and, for $k > 0$, $X_k = \{x_1, x_2, \ldots, x_k\}$. In examples, x, y and z will be used for x_1, x_2 and x_3 respectively.

For each $k \geq 0$, we define the set of terms over X_k, denoted by $T[X_k]$, as follows.

(1) ε is a term, and each element of $\Sigma \cup X_k$ is a term.

(2) If t_1 and t_2 are terms, then $t_1 t_2$ is a term.

(3) If S is in $\mathcal{F}$ and $t_1, t_2, \ldots, t_{r(S)}$ are terms, then $S(t_1, t_2, \cdots, t_{r(S)})$ is a term. If $r(S) = 0$, then we write S instead of S().

The set of simple terms over X_k, denoted by $T_{sm}[X_k]$ is defined by

$$T_{sm}[X_k] = \Sigma \cup X_k \cup \{S(t_1, \cdots, t_{r(S)}) | S \in \mathcal{F} \text{ and } t_1, \ldots, t_{r(S)} \in T[X_k]\}.$$

Thus, intuitively, a simple term is either an instruction symbol, or a formal parameter, or a procedure call. It is easy to show (by induction on the above definition of a term), that each term over X_k can be written uniquely as a product of simple terms over X_k. Thus, if $t \in T[X_k]$, then $t = t_1 t_2 \cdots t_n$ with $n \geq 0$ for certain $t_i \in T_{sm}[X_k]$, $1 \leq i \leq n$.

Using the above terminology and notation we can proceed with defining a nondeterministic procedure parameter scheme.

Definition 5.3. A nondeterministic procedure parameter scheme (abbreviated by npp) is a 5-tuple $U = (\Sigma, \mathcal{F}, r, Z, b)$, where

(1) Σ, $\mathcal{F}$ and r are as above,

(2) Z is a distinguished element of $\mathcal{F}$ (the main procedure symbol), and

(3) b is a mapping from $\mathcal{F}$ into $\bigcup_{k=0}^{\infty}$ NIAN($T_{sm}[X_k]$), such that, for all S in $\mathcal{F}$, b(S) $\in$ NIAN($T_{sm}[X_{r(S)}]$)†. (If S is a procedure symbol, then we say that b(S) is the body of S).

If U is defined as above, then we also say that U is an npp over Σ. In the sequel, the class of all npp's over Σ will be denoted by NPP(Σ), or NPP when Σ is understood.

Notation 5.4. Let $U = (\Sigma, \mathcal{F}, r, Z, b)$ be an npp. For each procedure symbol S, we denote the set of nodes, the start node and the set of final nodes of the nondeterministic Ianov scheme b(S) by N_S, n_S^o and E_S respectively. Furthermore, we denote by N_U and E_U the sets $\bigcup_{S\in\mathcal{F}} N_S$ and $\bigcup_{S\in\mathcal{F}} E_S$ respectively. ///

Example 5.5. Let $\Sigma = \{f,g,p,\bar{p}\}$ with $F_\Sigma = \{f,g\}$ and $P_\Sigma = \{p\}$. Let $\mathcal{F} = \{Z,S,T\}$, and let $r(Z) = r(S) = 0$ and $r(T) = 1$. Then T(S), S, f, ε, T(T(SS)), pf, SS and fT(S) are terms over $\emptyset$ (and, therefore, terms over X_k for any $k \geq 0$). The first five of these terms are simple, the last three are not. Also, xfx, x, T(xx), pxT(x)T(S) are terms over {x}. Finally, $(\Sigma, \mathcal{F}, r, Z, b)$ with b defined as shown in Example 5.1, is a nondeterministic procedure parameter scheme.

Another example of an npp is $(\{f,g,p,\bar{p}\},\{Z,S,T\},r,Z,b)$, where $r(Z) = 0$, $r(S) = 1$, $r(T) = 2$ and b is defined as shown in Example 5.2. ///

To define the relation computed by a nondeterministic procedure

---

† (i) $T_{sm}[X_k]$ is considered to be divided into P_Σ, $\bar{P}_\Sigma$ and $T_{sm}[X_k] - (P_\Sigma \cup \bar{P}_\Sigma)$.

(ii) Strictly speaking, NIAN($T_{sm}[X_k]$) is undefined, since it involves an infinite set of instruction symbols. Henceforth we shall assume that Definition 3.1 is generalized in an obvious way to deal with this situation.

parameter scheme under an interpretation, we first define the nondeterministic Ianov scheme resulting from the application of the copy rule to the body of a procedure.

Definition 5.6. Let $U = (\Sigma, \mathcal{F}, r, Z, b)$ be an npp. Let S be in $\mathcal{F}$ with $r(S) = k$ for some $k \geq 0$. Furthermore, let $t_1, t_2, \ldots, t_k$ be elements of $T[\emptyset]$. Then the actual body of $S(t_1, t_2, \cdots, t_k)$, denoted by $Body(S(t_1, t_2, \cdots, t_k)$ is the nondeterministic Ianov scheme over $T_{sm}[\emptyset]$ defined as follows.

If $k = 0$, then $Body(S) = b(S)$.

If $k > 0$, then $Body(S(t_1, \cdots, t_k))$ is obtained by the following construction:

(1) "Substitute" t_i for x_i everywhere in $b(S)$ for all i, $1 \leq i \leq k$.

(2) "Expand" all terms t_i in the resulting scheme for each i, $1 \leq i \leq k$, in the following sense. Let $t_i = t_{i,1} t_{i,2} \cdots t_{i,m}$ for some $m \geq 0$, where $t_{i,j}$ is a simple term for each j, $1 \leq j \leq m$. Consider an arc leading from node n_1 to node n_2, labelled by t_i. If $m > 0$ then replace this arc by

where the intermediate nodes and arcs are new. If $m = 0$ (that is, $t_i = \varepsilon$) then delete the arc and identify the nodes n_1 and n_2.

Example 5.7.
Consider Example 5.1, in particular its last three pictures. The first one of these pictures represents the actual body of $T(S)$, the second represents the result of step (1) in Definition 5.6 for $T(SS)$, and the third picture is the actual body of $T(SS)$.

The last three pictures of Example 5.2 represent the actual bodies of $T(\varepsilon, \varepsilon)$, $T(g, S(\varepsilon))$ and $S(\varepsilon)$. ///

An easy way to define the relation computed by an npp under an interpretation is to regard the npp as an infinite collection of recursive procedures. Therefore we introduce the following notion.

Definition 5.8. A generalized nrsi is a 4-tuple $(\Sigma, \mathcal{F}, Z, b)$, where $\Sigma, \mathcal{F}, Z$ and b are as defined in Definition 4.1, except that $\mathcal{F}$ does not have to be finite.[†]

Remark 5.9. In order not to bore the reader too much, and to save space, we will not repeat all the definitions and the result from section 4 for the case of generalized nrsi's, but rather note that it suffices to replace the phrase "nrsi" by the phrase "generalized nrsi" in all these definitions and in Theorem 4.11. (The reader should be careful in considering Definition 4.8, where the notion of context-free grammar should be replaced by the notion of "generalized context-free grammar", which differs from a context-free grammar by the fact that the sets of nonterminals and rules are not necessarily finite.) ///

We now define the relation computed by an npp under an arbitrary interpretation.

Definition 5.10. Let $U = (\Sigma, \mathcal{F}, r, Z, b)$ be an npp, and let I be a general interpretation of Σ. Let $Nrsi(U) = (\Sigma, \mathcal{F}_1, Z, b_1)$ be the generalized nrsi with
$\mathcal{F}_1 = \{S(t_1, \cdots, t_{r(S)}) \mid S \in \mathcal{F} \text{ and } t_i \in T[\emptyset] \text{ for all } i, 1 \leq i \leq r(S)\}$, and $b_1(t) = Body(t)$ for all t in $\mathcal{F}_1$. We define I(U), the relation computed by U under I to be I(Nrsi(U)).

Example 5.11. Consider the npp $U = (\Sigma, \mathcal{F}, r, Z, b)$ of Example 5.2, and let $U_1 = Nrsi(U) = (\Sigma, \mathcal{F}_1, Z, b_1)$ be the generalized nrsi associated with U. Then $\mathcal{F}_1$ contains, among others, Z, $T(\varepsilon,\varepsilon)$, $T(g,S(\varepsilon))$ and $S(\varepsilon)$. From Example 5.2 we know the bodies of these elements of $\mathcal{F}_1$. Let I be the pτ-interpretation of Σ with the set of all nonnegative integers as domain,

$I(f) = \{(x,y) \mid x \geq 1 \text{ and } y = x-1\}$,
$I(g) = \{(x,y) \mid y = x+3\}$,
$I(p) = \{(x,x) \mid x > 0\}$, and
$I(\bar{p}) = \{(x,x) \mid x = 0\}$.

---

† Note that the notion of a generalized nrsi involves the notion of a nondeterministic Ianov scheme over an infinite alphabet, see the footnote in Definition 5.3.

Execution of U_1 with input 1 results in†

$$(n_1,1) \vdash (n_3'n_2\ ,1) \vdash (n_4'n_2\ ,1) \vdash (n_5'n_2\ ,0)$$
$$(n_3''n_6'n_2\ ,0) \vdash (n_7''n_6'n_2\ ,0) \vdash (n_8''n_6'n_2\ ,3)$$
$$(n_{10}'n_9''n_6'n_2\ ,3) \vdash (n_{11}'n_9''n_6'n_2\ ,2) \stackrel{*}{\vdash} (\varepsilon,2).$$

Hence, $(1,2) \in I(U_1)$. Therefore, by Definition 5.10, $(1,2) \in I(U)$. Note that the sequence of instruction symbols, encountered during the above execution, is $pf\bar{p}gf$.

It can be shown that $I(U) = \{(x,y) | y=2x\}$. ///

We now show how to associate with each npp an equivalent L-scheme. Intuitively, this L-scheme consists of all sequences of instruction symbols obtained by "following a path through the npp" (see also the informal discussion preceding Definition 3.9).

<u>Definition 5.12.</u> Let $U = (\Sigma,\mathcal{F},r,Z,b)$ be an npp. We define $L(U)$, the <u>L-scheme corresponding to U</u>, to be the language generated by the macro grammar†† $G_U = (N_U,r_1,\Sigma,R,n_Z^o)$, where, for any S in $\mathcal{F}$ and n in N_S, $r_1(n) = r(S)$, and R consists of the following rules.

(1) Let S be in $\mathcal{F}$ with $r(S) = k$ for some $k \geq 0$. Suppose that in $b(S)$ there is an arc leading from n_1 to n_2, labelled by a term t in $T_{sm}[X_k]$. Then the rule $n_1(x_1,\cdots,x_k) \to t'n_2(x_1,\cdots,x_k)$ is in R, where t' is the result of substituting n_T^o for T in t for each T in $\mathcal{F}$.

(2) Let S be in $\mathcal{F}$ with $r(S) = k$ for some $k \geq 0$. Then, for each n in E_S, the rule $n(x_1,\cdots,x_k) \to \varepsilon$ is in R.

<u>Example 5.13.</u> Consider the npp U of Example 5.2. Then, $G_U = (N_U,r_1,\Sigma,R,n_Z^o)$ where $N_U = \{n_1,n_2,\ldots,n_{12}\}$†, $n_Z^o = n_1$ and R contains the rules $n_1 \to n_3(\varepsilon,\varepsilon)n_2$, $n_2 \to \varepsilon$, $n_3(x,y) \to pn_4(x,y)$, $n_3(x,y) \to \bar{p}n_7(x,y)$, $n_4(x,y) \to fn_5(x,y)$, $n_5(x,y) \to n_3(gx,n_{10}(y))n_6(x,y)$, $n_6(x,y) \to \varepsilon$, $n_7(x,y) \to xn_8(x,y)$, $n_8(x,y) \to yn_9(x,y)$, $n_9(x,y) \to \varepsilon$, $n_{10}(x) \to fn_{11}(x)$, $n_{11}(x) \to xn_{12}(x)$, and $n_{12}(x) \to \varepsilon$.

---

† See the footnote of Example 4.7.

†† For the notion of macro grammar, see 1.4.1.5.

The word $pf\bar{p}gf$ is the history of the execution of U with input 1 (see Example 5.11). This word is derivable in G_U as follows:

$$n_1 \Rightarrow n_3(\varepsilon,\varepsilon)n_2 \Rightarrow pn_4(\varepsilon,\varepsilon)n_2 \Rightarrow pfn_5(\varepsilon,\varepsilon)n_2 \Rightarrow pfn_3(g,n_{10}(\varepsilon))n_6(\varepsilon,\varepsilon)n_2 \Rightarrow$$
$$pf\bar{p}n_7(g,n_{10}(\varepsilon))n_6(\varepsilon,\varepsilon)n_2 \Rightarrow pf\bar{p}gn_8(g,n_{10}(\varepsilon))n_6(\varepsilon,\varepsilon)n_2 \Rightarrow$$
$$pf\bar{p}gn_{10}(\varepsilon)n_9(g,n_{10}(\varepsilon))n_6(\varepsilon,\varepsilon)n_2 \Rightarrow pf\bar{p}gfn_{11}(\varepsilon)n_9(g,n_{10}(\varepsilon))n_6(\varepsilon,\varepsilon)n_2 \overset{*}{\Rightarrow}$$
$$pf\bar{p}gf.$$

Obviously, the following smaller set of rules (which can easily be "read off" the bodies of Z, S and T in Example 5.2) generates the same language as G_U:
$Z \rightarrow T(\varepsilon,\varepsilon)$, $T(x,y) \rightarrow pfT(gx,S(y))$, $T(x,y) \rightarrow \bar{p}xy$ and $S(x) \rightarrow fx$. It is easy to see that this set of rules generates the language $\{(pf)^n\,\bar{p}g^nf^n \mid n\geq 0\}$ and so L(U) is equal to this language.

<u>Remark</u>. It can easily be checked that
$(\{f,g,p,\bar{p}\},\{Z,T\},r,Z,b)$ with $r(Z) = 0$, $r(T) = 1$ and

b(Z) = 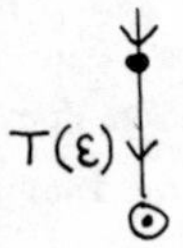

b(T) = 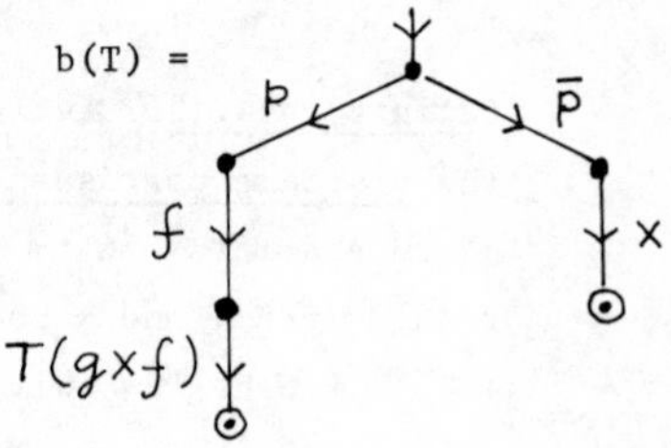

is a simpler npp with the same corresponding L-scheme. ///

We now show that, also in the case of npp's, U and L(U) are equivalent program schemes (recall Theorems 3.11 and 4.11).

<u>Theorem 5.14</u>. For any npp U over Σ and any general interpretation I of Σ, we have $I(L(U)) = I(U)$.

<u>Proof</u>. Let us first remark that, with each macro grammar G, we can associate a generalized context-free grammar † G' generating the same language. In fact, if $G = (N,r,\Sigma,R,Z)$ and if we let $G' = (N',\Sigma,R',Z)$,

---

† For the notion of generalized context-free grammar, see Remark 5.9.

where $N' = \{S(t_1,\cdots,t_{r(S)}) | S \in N$ and $t_i \in T[\emptyset]$ for all $i, 1 \leq i \leq r(S)\}$ †
and $R' = \{S(t_1,\cdots,t_{r(S)}) \rightarrow t' | S(x_1,\cdots,x_{r(S)}) \rightarrow t$ is in R for some t in $T[X_{r(S)}]$, and t' is the result of substituting t_i for x_i everywhere in t, for each $i, 1 \leq i \leq r(S)\}$, then it is easy to see that $L(G') = L(G)$.

To prove the theorem, let $U = (\Sigma, \mathcal{F}, r, Z, b)$ be an npp, and let I be a general interpretation of Σ. Let $V = \mathrm{Nrsi}(U) = (\Sigma, \mathcal{F}_1, Z, b_1)$, recall Definition 5.10. Thus $I(V) = I(U)$. Let W be the generalized nrsi $(\Sigma, \mathcal{F}_1, Z, b_0)$, where, for $S(t_1,\cdots,t_{r(S)})$ in $\mathcal{F}_1$, the body $b_0(S(t_1,\cdots,t_{r(S)}))$ is the result of substituting t_i for x_i everywhere in $b(S)$ for all i, $1 \leq i \leq r(S)$. Thus, b_0 is obtained after step (1) in Definition 5.10, and, therefore, V is obtained by "expanding" W as in step (2) of Definition 5.10. Hence, as can easily be seen, $L(G_W) = L(G_V)$, where G_W and G_V are the generalized context-free grammars associated with W and V by (the generalized) Definition 4.8.

Let G_U be the macro grammar associated with U according to Definition 5.12, and let G_U' be the generalized context-free grammar associated with G_U according to the above remark. Then, obviously, the generalized context-free grammars G_U' and G_W are equal, except for a renaming of nonterminals. This situation is illustrated by the following diagram:

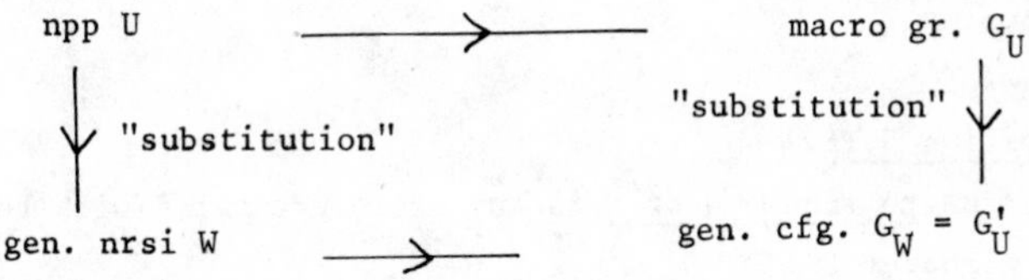

Hence, $L(U) = L(G_U) = L(G_U') = L(G_W) = L(G_V) = L(V)$. Also, by the generalized Theorem 4.11, $I(L(V)) = I(V)$. Consequently, $I(L(U)) = I(L(V)) = I(V) = I(U)$. ///

The above proof shows the usefulness of the generalized notions of

---

† It is the fact that each word over $N' \cup \Sigma$ is uniquely decomposable into a product of elements of $N' \cup \Sigma$, that allows us to treat each element of N' as a single symbol.

the previous section, because all we did was converting the npp notions into the appropriate generalized nrsi notions and applying the generalized Theorem 4.11.

Example 5.15. Consider the derivation of the word $pf\bar{p}gf$ in Example 5.13. This derivation in G_U is also a derivation in G'_U. Furthermore, it is also a derivation in G_W, if we assume that $n_3(\varepsilon,\varepsilon),\ldots,n_9(\varepsilon,\varepsilon)$ are the names of the nodes in $b_o(T(\varepsilon,\varepsilon))$ corresponding to nodes $n_3,\ldots,n_9$ in $b(T)$, $n_3(g,n_{10}(\varepsilon)),\ldots,n_9(g,n_{10}(\varepsilon))$ in $b_o(T(g,S(\varepsilon)))$ correspond to $n_3,\ldots,n_9$ in $b(T)$, and $n_{10}(\varepsilon)$, $n_{11}(\varepsilon)$ are the names of the nodes in $b_o(S(\varepsilon))$ corresponding to nodes n_{10},n_{11} in $b(S)$. ///

As mentioned at the beginning of this section, the definition of a deterministic procedure parameter scheme is omitted. However, it should be clear to the reader how a deterministic procedure parameter scheme can be formally defined. For instance, the npp's in Examples 5.1 and 5.2 are obviously deterministic.

We conclude this section by defining macro schemes. Since by Theorem 5.14 each npp is equivalent to an L-scheme generated by a macro grammar, it is natural to regard every macro grammar as a program scheme, as follows:

Definition 5.16.

(1) A macro scheme over Σ is any macro grammar G with terminal alphabet Σ.

(2) The language L(G) generated by the macro grammar G is also said to be the L-scheme corresponding to the macro scheme G.

(3) Given a general interpretation I of Σ, the relation computed by G under I, denoted by I(G), is defined to be I(L(G)).

We shall denote by MAC(Σ), or MAC when Σ is understood, the class of all macro schemes over Σ.

Note that, as in the case of regular and context-free schemes, it follows directly from Definition 5.16(3), that each macro scheme is equivalent to its corresponding L-scheme.

6. The μ-calculus

As was already pointed out at the beginning of section 4, de Bakker and Scott [1969] proposed a formalism for dealing with recursive program schemes. In this formalism, called the μ-calculus, recursive program schemes are modelled as algebraic terms, called μ-terms. In this section we discuss the nondeterministic extension of the μ-calculus †. The equivalence of the μ-calculus to the formalism of section 4 will be shown in section 8.

This section is organized as follows. First we define the notion of nondeterministic μ-term and the meaning of a μ-term under an arbitrary interpretation. Then we show that with each μ-term we may associate, in a natural manner, a context-free language (Definition 6.8), which, as an L-scheme, is equivalent to that μ-term (Theorem 6.12). Finally, we define the notion of a deterministic μ-term.

Let X be a denumerably infinite set of symbols, called <u>function variables</u>, fixed for the rest of this section.

<u>Definition 6.1.</u> A <u>μ-term</u> is a word over the infinite alphabet $X \cup \{E, \Omega, \underline{or}, ;, \mu, (,)\}$ defined recursively as follows.

(1) Each element of X is a μ-term.

(2) E and Ω are μ-terms.

(3) If t_1 and t_2 are μ-terms, then $(t_1 \ \underline{or} \ t_2)$ and $(t_1 ; t_2)$ are μ-terms.

(4) If x is in X and t is a μ-term, then μx(t) is a μ-term.

Intuitively, μx(t) represents a recursive procedure with name x and body t.

To define the set of μ-terms "over a given finite alphabet Σ", we need the following notions. An occurrence of a function variable x in a

---

† The extension of the μ-calculus by de Bakker and de Roever [1973] is even more general than this.

μ-term t is said to be <u>bound</u> in t, if it occurs in a subterm [†] of t of the form $\mu x(t_1)$ for some μ-term t_1, otherwise the occurrence is said to be <u>free</u> in t. For each μ-term t, let bound(t) (respectively, free(t)) denote the set of all function variables which have bound (respectively, free) occurrences in t.

If Σ is a (finite) alphabet included in X, then we say that t is a μ-term <u>over</u> Σ if free(t) ⊂ Σ and bound(t) ∩ Σ = ∅. In the sequel, the class of all μ-terms over Σ will be denoted by NμCAL(Σ), or NμCAL when Σ is understood.

<u>Example 6.2</u>. Let $\Sigma = \{f,g,p,\bar{p},q,\bar{q}\}$, and suppose that $\Sigma \cup \{x,y\} \subset X$. Then both

$\mu x($ ($(((p;f);x);g)$ <u>or</u> $\bar{p}$)) and

$\mu x($ ($(p;g)$ <u>or</u> $(\bar{p};(\mu y(((q;(f;x))$ <u>or</u> $(\bar{q};y)));x))$))

are μ-terms belonging to NμCAL(Σ). ///

We now define the relation computed by a μ-term under an arbitrary interpretation.

<u>Definition 6.3</u>. For a μ-term t and a general interpretation I = (D,h) of X [††], the <u>relation computed by t under I</u>, denoted by I(t), is defined recursively as follows.

(1) For x in X, I(x) = h(x).

(2) $I(E) = id_D$ and $I(\Omega) = \emptyset$.

(3) For μ-terms t_1 and t_2, $I((t_1$ <u>or</u> $t_2)) = I(t_1) \cup I(t_2)$ and $I((t_1;t_2)) = I(t_1) \circ I(t_2)$.

(4) Let $t = \mu x(t_1)$, where x is a function variable and t_1 is a μ-term. For $n \geq 0$ we define relations w_n over D and general interpretations $I_n = (D,h_n)$ of X as follows: [†††]

(i) $w_o = \emptyset$ and $w_{n+1} = I_n(t_1)$

(ii) for y in X, $h_n(y) = \begin{cases} w_n & \text{if } y = x \\ h(y) & \text{if } y \neq x. \end{cases}$

The relation computed by t under I is now defined by $I(t) = \bigcup_{n=0}^{\infty} w_n$.

---

† If t_1 and t_2 are μ-terms, then t_1 is said to be a subterm of t_2 if there exist words φ and ψ, such that $t_2 = \phi t_1 \psi$.

†† The reader shouldn't be bothered by the fact that X is an infinite alphabet. As in the finite case (Definition 2.1), D is a set and h is a mapping from X into $P(D \times D)$.

††† Note that w_n and I_n depend on t.

Intuitively, the relations w_n in Definition 6.3(4) are the so called n-truncations[†] of the relation I(t). This means that, for any $n \geq 0$, and for any d_1 and d_2 in D, (d_1,d_2) is in w_n if, and only if, d_1 can be transformed into d_2 by the recursive procedure x while the depth of recursion (i.e. the number of nested calls of x) is smaller than n at any moment.

Remark 6.4. It is easy to see, that, for a μ-term t and a general interpretation I of X, the relation I(t) depends in fact only on the relations h(x) with x in free(t). Thus, if Σ is an alphabet included in X, and t is an element of NμCAL(Σ), then, to obtain I(t), it suffices to specify a general interpretation of Σ. ///

Example 6.5. Let $\Sigma = \{f,g,p,\bar{p}\}$, and suppose that $\Sigma \cup \{x\} \subset X$. Consider the μ-term $t = \mu x(((((p;f);x);g)$ or $\bar{p}$)). Let I = (D,h) be the general interpretation of X, such that D is the set of all integers,

$h(f) = \{(d_1,d_2) | d_2=d_1-1\}$,

$h(g) = \{(d_1,d_2) | d_2=d_1+1\}$,

$h(p) = \{(d,d) | d>0\}$,

$h(\bar{p}) = \{(d,d) | d\leq 0\}$,

and h is defined in an arbitrary manner for the elements of X - Σ.

Let us compute the relations w_n and the general interpretations I_n, according to Definition 6.3(4). Since $w_o = \emptyset$, $I_o(x) = \emptyset$ and $I_o(y) = I(y)$ for all y, $y \neq x$. Now $w_1 = (I(p)\circ I(f)\circ I_o(x)\circ I(g)) \cup I(\bar{p})$, so $w_1 = I(\bar{p}) = \{(d,d) | d\leq 0\}$, and $I_1(x) = \{(d,d) | d\leq 0\}$. It follows that $w_2 = (I(p)\circ I(f)\circ I_1(x)\circ I(g)) \cup I(\bar{p}) = \{(1,1)\} \cup I(\bar{p}) = \{(d,d) | d\leq 1\}$. It is easy to show by induction on n that, for $n \geq 0$, $w_{n+1} = \{(d,d) | d\leq n\}$. Consequently, $I(t) = \bigcup_{n=0}^{\infty} w_n = id_D$.

The reader may compare this example with Example 4.7. ///

There is a natural way of defining the L-scheme corresponding to a given μ-term. It uses the following operation on languages.[††]

---

† See Morris [1971].

†† This operation was introduced in Gruska [1971, Definition 2.3].

Definition 6.6. Let A and B be languages and let σ be a symbol. If s is the substitution with $s(\sigma) = B$ and $s(\sigma_1) = \sigma_1$ for all σ_1, $\sigma_1 \neq \sigma$, then we denote the language s(A) by $A \overset{\sigma}{\uparrow} B$. The σ-iteration of A, denoted by A^σ, is defined to be the language $\bigcup_{n=0}^{\infty} A_n$, where $A_o = \emptyset$ and, for $n \geq 0$, $A_{n+1} = A \overset{\sigma}{\uparrow} A_n$.

Example 6.7. Let f, g, p, $\bar{p}$ and x be symbols, and consider the language $A = \{pfxg, \bar{p}\}$. Let us compute the x-iteration A^x of A:

$A_1 = A \overset{x}{\uparrow} A_o = A \overset{x}{\uparrow} \emptyset = \{\bar{p}\}$,

$A_2 = A \overset{x}{\uparrow} A_1 = \{pf\bar{p}g, \bar{p}\}$,

$A_3 = A \overset{x}{\uparrow} A_2 = \{pfpf\bar{p}gg, pf\bar{p}g, \bar{p}\}$, etcetera.

It is easy to show by induction on n, that, for $n \geq 0$, $A_{n+1} = \{(pf)^k \, \bar{p}g^k \mid 0 \leq k \leq n\}$. Consequently, $A^x = \bigcup_{n=0}^{\infty} A_n = \{(pf)^k \, \bar{p}g^k \mid k \geq 0\}$. ///

We now define the L-scheme corresponding to a μ-term.

Definition 6.8. For a μ-term t, the L-scheme corresponding to t, denoted by L(t), is the language over free(t) defined recursively as follows.

(1) For x in X, $L(x) = x$.

(2) $L(E) = \varepsilon$ and $L(\Omega) = \emptyset$.

(3) For μ-terms t_1 and t_2, $L((t_1 \text{ or } t_2)) = L(t_1) \cup L(t_2)$ and $L((t_1;t_2)) = L(t_1) \cdot L(t_2)$.

(4) For any function variable x and any μ-term t, $L(\mu x(t)) = (L(t))^x$.

Thus, the L-scheme corresponding to $\mu x(t)$ is the x-iteration of the L-scheme corresponding to t.

Remark 6.9. Note that, if Σ is an alphabet included in X and t is an element of $N\mu CAL(\Sigma)$, then L(t) is a language over Σ. ///

Example 6.10. Consider the μ-term t of Example 6.5. It follows easily from Example 6.7 that $L(t) = \{(pf)^k \, \bar{p}g^k \mid k \geq 0\}$. ///

The main result of Gruska [1971] is stated without proof in the following proposition. †

---

† Gruska [1971, Theorem 2.7 and Corollary 2.8].

Proposition 6.11. Let Σ be an alphabet. For each t in NμCAL(Σ), L(t) is a context-free language over Σ. Conversely, for each context-free language A over Σ there is a μ-term t in NμCAL(Σ) such that L(t) = A.

This result means that the μ-terms of NμCAL(Σ) can be viewed as "context-free expressions", in analogy with the notion of regular expression. Each context-free expression (that is, μ-term) shows how a context-free language can be built up from the languages ε, $\emptyset$ and σ, for σ in Σ, by the operations of union, product and x-iteration.

The next theorem shows that, for any μ-term t, t and L(t) compute the same relation under all interpretations.

† Theorem 6.12. For any μ-term t and any general interpretation I of X, we have I(L(t)) = I(t).

Proof. The proof is by induction on the definition of the μ-term t (Definition 6.1). We restrict ourselves to the case that $t = \mu x(t_1)$, where x is in X and t_1 is a μ-term. All other cases may easily be verified by the reader.

Recall that by Definition 6.3(4), $I(t) = \bigcup_{n=0}^{\infty} w_n$.

By Definition 6.8(4), $L(t) = (L(t_1))^x$. Thus, by Definition 6.6, there exist languages A_n, $n \geq 0$, such that $L(t) = \bigcup_{n=0}^{\infty} A_n$, $A_o = \emptyset$ and $A_{n+1} = s_n(L(t_1))$, where s_n is the substitution with $s_n(x) = A_n$ and $s_n(y) = y$ for all y in X, such that $y \neq x$. It follows that $I(L(t)) = \bigcup_{n=0}^{\infty} I(A_n)$.

Consequently, it remains to show that $\bigcup_{n=0}^{\infty} I(A_n) = \bigcup_{n=0}^{\infty} w_n$. In fact, it is even true that, for $n \geq 0$, $I(A_n) = w_n$. We show this by induction on n.

For n = 0, $I(A_o) = I(\emptyset) = \emptyset = w_o$.

Now assume that $I(A_n) = w_n$. Then $h_n(x) = w_n = I(A_n) = I(s_n(x))$; recall Definition 6.3 (4) for the definition of the general interpretations $I_n = (D_I, h_n)$. Also, for all y such that $y \neq x$, $h_n(y) = h_I(y) = I(s_n(y))$. Application of Lemma 2.12 shows that $I_n(A) = I(s_n(A))$ for all L-schemes A.

---

† This theorem is strongly related to the "union theorem" of de Bakker and Meertens [1973, Theorem 3.1].

Hence

$$\begin{aligned} I(A_{n+1}) &= I(s_n(L(t_1))) && \text{by the definition of } A_{n+1} \\ &= I_n(L(t_1)) && \text{by the above} \\ &= I_n(t_1) && \text{by the inductive hypothesis (in the induction on the definition of t)} \\ &= w_{n+1} && \text{by the definition of } w_{n+1}. \end{aligned}$$

///

Example 6.13. Consider the μ-term t and the general interpretation I from Example 6.5. The μ-term t is of the form $\mu x(t_1)$. It was shown in Example 6.5 that, for $n \geq 0$, $w_{n+1} = \{(d,d) | d \leq n\}$. It was shown in Examples 6.7 and 6.10 that, for $n \geq 0$, $A_{n+1} = \{(pf)^k \bar{p}g^k | 0 \leq k \leq n\}$. It is easy to see that, for $n \geq 0$, $I(A_{n+1}) = w_{n+1}$. ///

The next corollary follows immediately from Theorem 6.12.

Corollary 6.14. Let Σ be an alphabet included in X. For any μ-term t over Σ and any general interpretation I of Σ, we have I(L(t)) = I(t).

We conclude this section by defining deterministic μ-terms.

Definition 6.15. Let Σ be an alphabet included in X. The set of Σ-deterministic μ-terms is defined recursively as follows.

(1) Each element of $X - (P_\Sigma \cup \bar{P}_\Sigma)$ is Σ-deterministic.

(2) E and Ω are Σ-deterministic.

(3) If t_1 and t_2 are Σ-deterministic μ-terms, and p is in P_Σ, then $((p;t_1)$ or $(\bar{p};t_2))$ and $(t_1;t_2)$ are Σ-deterministic.

(4) If t is a Σ-deterministic μ-term and x is in X, then μx(t) is Σ-deterministic.

Furthermore, a μ-term is said to be a deterministic μ-term over Σ if it is Σ-deterministic and element of NμCAL(Σ).

We shall denote the class of all deterministic μ-terms over Σ by μCAL(Σ), or μCAL when Σ is understood.

Example 6.16. The second μ-term of Example 6.2 belongs to μCAL(Σ). The first does not belong to μCAL(Σ), however the equivalent μ-term μx(((p;((f;x);g)) or $(\bar{p}$;E))) does.

Note that in de Bakker and Scott [1969] the μ-term $((p;t_1)$ <u>or</u> $(\bar{p};t_2))$ is written as $(p \rightarrow t_1,t_2)$. In this notation, the second μ-term of Example 6.2 can be written as $\mu x((p \rightarrow g,(\mu y((q \rightarrow (f;x),y));x)))$. ///

7. L-schemes viewed as infinite trees

In sections 3, 4 and 5 we have been concerned with associating L-schemes with graph-like program schemes. In this section we show that it is possible to associate with each L-scheme an equivalent graph-like program scheme, namely a (possibly) infinite nondeterministic Ianov scheme which has the form of a (possibly) infinite tree (Definition 7.4 and Theorem 7.7). Since this correspondence is one-to-one (Theorem 7.8), L-schemes may be viewed as trees. One of the consequences of this viewpoint is, that with each graph-like program scheme from the previous sections an equivalent infinite tree can be associated - a fact well known from the literature †. Another consequence is, that certain concepts concerning nondeterministic Ianov schemes (like those of "execution" and determinism) can be carried over to L-schemes; see Theorem 7.11 and Definition 7.13.

So let us start with defining the notion of a generalized nondeterministic Ianov scheme (where "generalized" stands for the fact that the Ianov scheme considered may be infinite; cf. Definition 5.8 of a generalized nrsi).

Definition 7.1. A generalized nondeterministic Ianov scheme (over an alphabet Σ) is a 7-tuple $(\Sigma, N, n^o, E, A, e, \ell)$, where Σ, N, n^o, E, A, e and ℓ are as defined in Definition 3.1, except that N, E and A do not have to be finite.

The class of all generalized nondeterministic Ianov schemes over an alphabet Σ will be denoted by $NIAN^{\infty}(\Sigma)$.

---

† This idea seems to be due to Scott [1971]. (In fact, the lattice $P(\Sigma^*)$ of L-schemes over Σ can be viewed as a nondeterministic variant of Scott's "lattice of flowdiagrams", which consists, intuitively, of all deterministic finite and infinite trees over Σ). It is also considered in Kfoury [1973, § 1.4], Rosen [1972, section 2] and Engelfriet [1972 b, § 5b].

Remark 7.2. By replacing the phrase "nondeterministic Ianov scheme" by "generalized nondeterministic Ianov scheme" in all definitions of section 3, one obtains all appropriate generalized definitions. (Thus, for any generalized nondeterministic Ianov scheme U, the definitions of execution of U under a general interpretation, of the relation I(U) computed by U under a general interpretation, of the L-scheme L(U) corresponding to U, and of a generalized deterministic Ianov scheme are obtained. Note that, in Definition 3.9, the notion of regular grammar should be replaced by the notion of "generalized regular grammar", which differs from a regular grammar by the fact that the sets of nonterminals and rules are not necessarily finite). Also, after the same replacement, Theorem 3.11 remains valid. (In fact, the proof given for Theorem 3.11 also holds in the generalized case). ///

Example 7.3. Let $\Sigma = \{f,p,\bar{p}\}$. Let N be the set of all positive integers, $n^o = 1$, and $E = N - \{3n|n\geq 1\}$. Then the 7-tuple $U = (\Sigma,N,n^o,E,A,e,\ell)$, where, for each $n \geq 0$, there is an arc from 3n+1 to 3n+2 labelled by $\bar{p}$, an arc from 3n+1 to 3n+3 labelled by p, and an arc from 3n+3 to 3n+4 labelled by f, is a generalized nondeterministic Ianov scheme. A necessarily unfinished picture of U is given below.

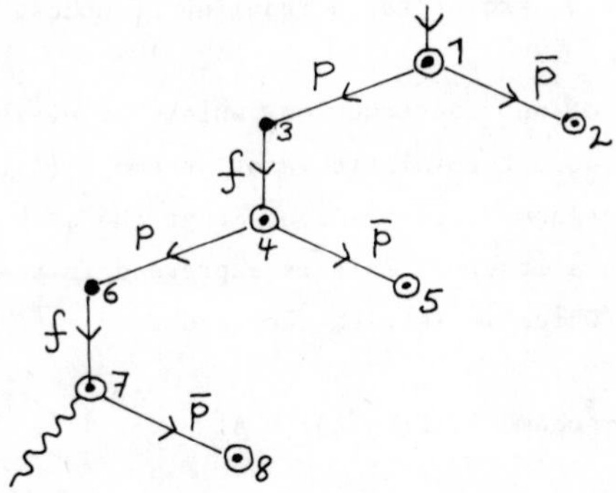

The L-scheme L(U) is generated by the generalized regular grammar $G_U = (N,\{f,p,\bar{p}\},R,1)$, where R consists of all rules $[3n+1] \rightarrow \bar{p}[3n+2]$, $[3n+1] \rightarrow p[3n+3]$, $[3n+3] \rightarrow f[3n+4]$, $[3n+1] \rightarrow \varepsilon$ and $[3n+2] \rightarrow \varepsilon$, for all $n \geq 0$. It is easy to see that $L(U) = (pf)^*\bar{p} \cup (pf)^*$. ///

We now show how to associate with each L-scheme a generalized nondeterministic Ianov scheme, equivalent to the L-scheme.

<u>Definition 7.4.</u> Let B be an L-scheme over an alphabet Σ. The <u>generalized nondeterministic Ianov scheme corresponding to the L-scheme B</u>, denoted by $U_\infty(B)$, is defined as follows.

(1) If $B = \emptyset$, then $U_\infty(B) = (\Sigma,\{n^o\}, n^o,\emptyset,\emptyset,\emptyset,\emptyset)$.

(2) If $B \neq \emptyset$, then $U_\infty(B) = (\Sigma,N,n^o,E,A,e,\ell)$, where N is the set of all prefixes of words in B, $n^o = \varepsilon$, $E = B$, and, if, for ϕ in Σ^* and $\sigma \in \Sigma$, both ϕ and $\phi\sigma$ are in N, then there is an arc leading from node ϕ to node $\phi\sigma$, labelled by σ.

Note that $U_\infty(B)$ is an ordinary nondeterministic Ianov scheme if, and only if, B is a finite L-scheme.

For every alphabet Σ, $U_{\Sigma,\infty}$ will denote the mapping from $P(\Sigma^*)$ into $NIAN^\infty(\Sigma)$, associating $U_\infty(B)$ with each L-scheme B. Whenever Σ is understood, we write U_∞ rather than $U_{\Sigma,\infty}$.

<u>Example 7.5.</u> Let $\Sigma = \{f,p,\bar{p}\}$. Consider the L-scheme $B = (pf)^*\bar{p} \cup (pf)^*$. The corresponding generalized nondeterministic Ianov scheme is $U_\infty(B) = (\{f,p,\bar{p}\},N,\varepsilon,B,A,e,\ell)$, where $N = (pf)^* \cup (pf)^*p \cup (pf)^*\bar{p}$, and, for $n \geq 0$, there is an arc from $(pf)^n$ to $(pf)^n\bar{p}$ labelled by $\bar{p}$, an arc from $(pf)^n$ to $(pf)^n p$ labelled by p, and an arc from $(pf)^n p$ to $(pf)^{n+1}$ labelled by f. Note that $U_\infty(B)$ is equal to the generalized nondeterministic Ianov scheme of Example 7.3, except for a renaming of nodes. ///

The important feature of our construction, which for every L-scheme A provides a generalized nondeterministic Ianov scheme $U_\infty(A)$, is the fact that it preserves L-schemes, in the sense that the L-scheme corresponding to $U_\infty(A)$ is A itself. This is expressed in the following lemma, the easy proof of which is left to the reader.

<u>Lemma 7.6.</u> For any L-scheme A, $L(U_\infty(A)) = A$.

It is easy to see that, for every L-scheme A, $U_\infty(A)$ has the form of a tree (which may be finite or infinite, depending on the fact whether A is finite or infinite). Therefore we shall use the natural notation $TREE(\Sigma)$ for the set $\{U_\infty(A) \mid A \subset \Sigma^*\}$. Consequently, for every alphabet Σ, the mapping $U_{\Sigma,\infty}$ can be considered as a mapping from $P(\Sigma^*)$ onto $TREE(\Sigma)$. (Note that $TREE(\Sigma)$ is a proper subset of $NIAN^\infty(\Sigma)$).

The next two theorems are immediate consequences of Lemma 7.6. The first shows that, for any L-scheme A, $U_\infty(A)$ and A are equivalent program schemes. The second shows that, for every Σ, $U_{\Sigma,\infty}$ is a one-to-one mapping.

Theorem 7.7. For any L-scheme A over an alphabet Σ and any general interpretation I of Σ, we have $I(U_\infty(A)) = I(A)$.

Proof. Immediate from Lemma 7.6 and the generalized Theorem 3.11. ///

Theorem 7.8. For every alphabet Σ, the mapping $U_{\Sigma,\infty}$ is one-to-one and onto TREE(Σ).

Proof. Immediate from Lemma 7.6. ///

It follows from these two theorems that L-schemes may be viewed as generalized nondeterministic Ianov schemes in the form of trees. In the rest of this section we discuss two of the consequences of this point of view.

Firstly, let U be a program scheme over an alphabet Σ belonging to one of the classes of program schemes introduced in the previous sections. Let T(U) denote $U_\infty(L(U))$. Then, for any general interpretation I of Σ, $I(T(U)) = I(U)$. (Proof: $I(U_\infty(L(U))) = I(L(U))$ by Theorem 7.7, and $I(L(U)) = I(U)$ by Theorems 3.11, 4.11, 5.14 and 6.12). Thus, for each program scheme from one of these classes there is an equivalent infinite or finite tree.

Example 7.9. Let $\Sigma = \{f,p,\bar{p}\}$, and let U be the nondeterministic Ianov scheme shown below.

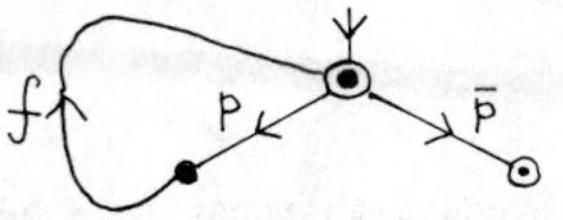

It is easy to see that $L(U) = (pf)^*\bar{p} \cup (pf)^*$. Hence, by Example 7.5, T(U) is the infinite tree shown in Example 7.3. ///

Secondly, concepts connected with nondeterministic Ianov schemes may be carried over to L-schemes (see Remark 7.2). Here are two examples of this.

Given an L-scheme A over an alphabet Σ and a general interpretation I of Σ, one may consider the "execution" of A under I, which is simply the "execution" of $U_\infty(A)$ under I (see the remarks preceding Definition 3.5). Formally, "using" Definitions 3.5 and 7.4, such an execution may be defined as follows.

Definition 7.10. Let A be an L-scheme over an alphabet Σ and let I be a general interpretation of Σ. Let N_A denote the set of all prefixes of words in A. If, for ϕ in Σ^* and σ in Σ, ϕ and $\phi\sigma$ are in N_A, and if (x_1,x_2) is in $I(\sigma)$, then we write $(\phi,x_1) \vdash_{A,I} (\phi\sigma,x_2)$, thus defining the relation $\vdash_{A,I}$ on $N_A \times D_I$. Furthermore, $\vdash^*_{A,I}$ denotes the transitive-reflexive closure of $\vdash_{A,I}$.

The relation computed by A under I can be characterized as follows (cf. Definition 3.6).

Theorem 7.11. For any nonempty L-scheme A over an alphabet Σ and any general interpretation I of Σ, we have $I(A) = \{(x,y) \mid (\varepsilon,x) \vdash^*_{A,I} (\phi,y)$ for some ϕ in A$\}$.

Proof. By directly using Definition 2.7 of I(A), the proof is straightforward. ///

Example 7.12. Let $\Sigma = \{f,p,\bar{p}\}$. Consider the L-scheme $A = (pf)^*\bar{p} \cup (pf)^*$. Then $N_A = (pf)^* \cup (pf)^*p \cup (pf)^*\bar{p}$. Consider the general interpretation I = (D,h), where D is the set of nonnegative integers,

$h(f) = \{(x,y) \mid x\geq 1 \text{ and } y=x-1\}$,

$h(p) = \{(x,x) \mid x>0\}$ and

$h(\bar{p}) = \{(0,0)\}$.

Then, under the interpretation I and with input 1, A has the following three executions:

$(\varepsilon,1)$,

$(\varepsilon,1) \vdash (p,1) \vdash (pf,0)$ and

$(\varepsilon,1) \vdash (p,1) \vdash (pf,0) \vdash (pf\bar{p},0)$.

Thus, I(A) has the values 1 and 0 for the argument 1. It is easy to see that $I(A) = \{(x,y) | 0 \le y \le x\}$. ///

Another concept which can be carried over to L-schemes is that of determinism.

† Definition 7.13. Let A be an L-scheme over an alphabet Σ. We say that A is syntactically deterministic (abbreviated by syntdet), if, for each ϕ in Σ^*, either $A \cap \phi\Sigma^* = \emptyset$, or $A \cap \phi\Sigma^* = \{\phi\}$, or $A \cap \phi\Sigma^* \subset \phi\sigma\Sigma^*$ for some σ in Σ, or $A \cap \phi\Sigma^* \subset \phi(p \cup \bar{p})\Sigma^*$ for some p in P_Σ.

The reader may easily see that an L-scheme A is syntactically deterministic, if and only if $U_\infty(A)$ is a generalized deterministic Ianov scheme (see Remark 7.2).

Example 7.14. Let $\Sigma = \{f,p,\bar{p}\}$ with $F_\Sigma = \{f\}$ and $P_\Sigma = \{p\}$. The L-scheme $A = (pf)^*\bar{p} \cup (pf)^*$ is not syntdet. To see this, note that, for $\phi = \varepsilon$, A contains both ϕ and $\phi\bar{p}$, and consequently $A \cap \phi\Sigma^*$ does not satisfy any of the conditions in Definition 7.13. (This corresponds to the fact that $U_\infty(A)$ does not satisfy requirement (3) of Definition 3.13, which is clear from Examples 7.5 and 7.3).

The L-scheme $B = (pf)^*\bar{p}$ is syntdet, which can be checked as follows. For ϕ in $(pf)^*$, $B \cap \phi\Sigma^* = \phi(pf)^*\bar{p} = \phi pf(pf)^*\bar{p} \cup \phi\bar{p} \subset \phi(p \cup \bar{p})\Sigma^*$, and for ϕ in $(pf)^*p$, $B \cap \phi\Sigma^* = \phi f(pf)^*\bar{p} \subset \phi f\Sigma^*$, and for ϕ in $(pf)^*\bar{p}$, $B \cap \phi\Sigma^* = \{\phi\}$, and for all other ϕ, $B \cap \phi\Sigma^* = \emptyset$. ///

The notion of a syntdet L-scheme is of importance, because, as will be shown later, it computes a partial function under all pπ-interpretations (see Lemma 14.3 and Lemma 14.13).

---

† The phrase "syntactically" is used to distinguish the above notion of determinism from another one, to be introduced in section 14.

8. Program scheme systems

So far, in discussing a class θ of program schemes, we were proceeding in a uniform manner (see sections 3 to 6). We first defined the program schemes of the class θ. (Note that such a program scheme always involved an alphabet of instruction symbols). Then we provided a mechanism which, for every program scheme from θ and every general interpretation of the alphabet of instruction symbols of the program scheme, gave us the object we are really interested in: the relation computed by the program scheme under the interpretation. On the other hand, based on the language theoretic point of view (fundamental to this whole work), we presented a mechanism which, for each program scheme in θ, yielded us a language over the alphabet of instruction symbols of the program scheme. (Such a language represented the set of all possible "histories of computation" of the program scheme). The so obtained language was always representative for the given program scheme, in the sense that to obtain the relation computed by the program scheme under an interpretation, it was sufficient to interprete the language. (This fact was expressed in the "main theorems" of sections 3 to 6 in the following form: "For any program scheme U in θ and any general interpretation I of the alphabet of instruction symbols of U, we have $I(L(U)) = I(U)$").

In this section we introduce the notion of a "program scheme system" as the natural abstraction of the situation described above.

Since languages are sufficient for obtaining the relations computed by elements of a given program scheme system, it is natural to regard the program scheme system as specifying a class of languages. Thus, we shall say that one program scheme system is "ℓ-included" in another, if the class of languages specified by the former is included in that specified by the latter. Also, program scheme systems specifying the same class of languages will be called "ℓ-equal" (Definition 8.8). Results concerning ℓ-inclusion and ℓ-equality of various program scheme systems are stated in Theorems 8.13 and 8.14, and are illustrated in the diagram at the end of this section.

We define a program scheme system as a four-tuple satisfying a specific condition.

Definition 8.1. A program scheme system (abbreviated by pss) is a 4-tuple $\mathcal{L} = (\Sigma, \theta, \mathcal{R}, L)$, where

(1) Σ is an alphabet (of instruction symbols),

(2) θ is a set (of program schemes),

(3) $\mathcal{R}$ is a rule which assigns to each program scheme U in θ and each general interpretation I of Σ a relation $\mathcal{R}(U,I)$ on D_I. ($\mathcal{R}(U,I)$ is always denoted by $I(U)$, and is called the relation computed by U under I),

(4) L is a mapping from θ into $P(\Sigma^*)$. (For any program scheme U in θ, $L(U)$ is called the L-scheme corresponding to U, or the language generated by U),

and

(5) $\mathcal{R}$ and L are related by the following condition: for any program program scheme U in θ and any general interpretation I of Σ, $\mathcal{R}(U,I) = I(L(U))$, that is, $I(U) = I(L(U))$.

If $\mathcal{L} = (\Sigma, \theta, \mathcal{R}, L)$ is a pss, then we say that $\mathcal{L}$ is a pss over Σ, and any element of θ is called a program scheme over Σ.

Notation 8.2

(1) Note that, by the above definition, the rule $\mathcal{R}$ is uniquely determined by the mapping L, and so, in the sequel, we shall often write "$\mathcal{L} = (\Sigma, \theta, L)$" rather than "$\mathcal{L} = (\Sigma, \theta, \mathcal{R}, L)$"

(2) For specific pss's $\mathcal{L} = (\Sigma, \theta, \mathcal{R}, L)$, we shall use the name of the class θ to denote $\mathcal{L}$. ///

Before presenting some examples of pss's, we introduce the obvious notion of a "sub-pss".

Definition 8.3. Let $\mathcal{L}_1 = (\Sigma, \theta_1, \mathcal{R}_1, L_1)$ and $\mathcal{L}_2 = (\Sigma, \theta_2, \mathcal{R}_2, L_2)$ be pss's. Then, $\mathcal{L}_1$ is a sub-pss of $\mathcal{L}_2$ if $\theta_1 \subset \theta_2$ and, for every U in θ_1, $L_1(U) = L_2(U)$.

Note that, by Definition 8.1(5), the above condition automatically implies that, for any U in θ_1 and any general interpretation I of Σ, $\mathcal{R}_1(U,I) = \mathcal{R}_2(U,I)$.

Remark 8.4. If $\mathcal{L} = (\Sigma,\theta,\mathcal{R},L)$ is a pss and θ_1 is a subset of θ, then it should be clear that $(\Sigma,\theta_1,\mathcal{R}_1,L_1)$, where $\mathcal{R}_1$ and L_1 are equal to $\mathcal{R}$ and L restricted to θ_1, is a sub-pss of $\mathcal{L}$. In the sequel, $(\Sigma,\theta_1,\mathcal{R}_1,L_1)$ is referred to as "the sub-pss θ_1 of $\mathcal{L}$". We also use phrases like "the sub-pss of $\mathcal{L}$ consisting of all elements of θ satisfying such and such property" to indicate the sub-pss θ_1 of $\mathcal{L}$, where θ_1 is the set of all elements of θ satisfying the property. ///

We now give some examples of program scheme systems.

Example 8.5

(1) In Theorem 3.11 we have shown that, for every alphabet Σ, the 4-tuple $(\Sigma,NIAN(\Sigma),\mathcal{R},L)$, where $\mathcal{R}$ and L are defined in Definitions 3.6 and 3.9 respectively, is a pss. According to Notation 8.2(2), this pss is denoted by NIAN(Σ). Note that IAN(Σ) denotes the sub-pss of NIAN(Σ) consisting of all deterministic Ianov schemes over Σ.

In the same way, for any alphabet Σ, the following are pss's over Σ: REG(Σ), NRSI(Σ), RSI(Σ), CFG(Σ), NPP(Σ), MAC(Σ), NμCAL(Σ), μCAL(Σ) and $NIAN^{\infty}(\Sigma)$.

(2) If Σ is an alphabet, then $(\Sigma,P(\Sigma^*),\mathcal{R},L)$ where $\mathcal{R}$ is defined in Definition 2.7 and L is the identity mapping on $P(\Sigma^*)$, is clearly a pss. This pss is denoted by $P(\Sigma^*)$ and is called the pss of all L-schemes over Σ.

(3) For any alphabet Σ, let FIN(Σ) denote the set of all finite L-schemes over Σ. FIN(Σ) is a sub-pss of $P(\Sigma^*)$. (Note that FIN(Σ) is the set of all L-schemes corresponding to some "cycle-free" nondeterministic Ianov scheme over Σ. Note also that FIN(Σ) is in one-to-one correspondence with the set of all finite trees over Σ; see section 7).

(4) For a given alphabet Σ, let TYPE-0(Σ) be the set of all type 0 grammars with terminal alphabet Σ. Let L be the mapping from TYPE-0(Σ) into $P(\Sigma^*)$, such that, for any type 0 grammar G, L(G) is the language generated by G (as defined in 1.4.1.1). Furthermore, for every type 0 grammar G with terminal alphabet Σ and every general interpretation I of Σ, let $\mathcal{R}(G,I)$ be the relation I(L(G)) on D_I. Then $(\Sigma,\text{TYPE-0}(\Sigma),\mathcal{R},L)$

is a pss.[†] ///

To each program scheme system corresponds a class of L-schemes defined as follows.

<u>Definition 8.6</u>. Let $\mathcal{L} = (\Sigma,\theta,L)$ be a pss. We define Lang($\mathcal{L}$), the <u>class of L-schemes corresponding to $\mathcal{L}$</u>, by

$$\text{Lang}(\mathcal{L}) = \{A\in P(\Sigma^*) \mid A=L(U) \text{ for some } U \text{ in } \theta\}.$$

<u>Example 8.7</u>. Let Σ be an alphabet. Then Lang(REG(Σ)) is equal to the class of all regular languages over Σ. Also, by Definition 3.9, Lang(NIAN(Σ)) $\subset$ Lang(REG(Σ)). It will be shown in Theorem 8.14 that Lang(NIAN(Σ)) = Lang(REG(Σ)). ///

Definition 8.1(5) shows that, in a pss, every program scheme is equivalent to the L-scheme corresponding to it. Consequently, when investigating semantic properties (that is properties defined in terms of interpretations) of program schemes from a pss $\mathcal{L}$, we are justified to deal with Lang($\mathcal{L}$) rather than $\mathcal{L}$ itself. This leads to "identifying" pss's with identical classes of L-schemes corresponding to them.

<u>Definition 8.8</u>. Let $\mathcal{L}_1$ and $\mathcal{L}_2$ be pss's over the same alphabet. We say that $\mathcal{L}_1$ is <u>ℓ-included</u> in $\mathcal{L}_2$, denoted by $\mathcal{L}_1 \subset_\ell \mathcal{L}_2$, if Lang($\mathcal{L}_1$) $\subset$ Lang($\mathcal{L}_2$). We say that $\mathcal{L}_1$ and $\mathcal{L}_2$ are <u>ℓ-equal</u>, denoted by $\mathcal{L}_1 =_\ell \mathcal{L}_2$, if Lang($\mathcal{L}_1$) = Lang($\mathcal{L}_2$).

<u>Example 8.9</u>. Every pss $\mathcal{L}$ over an alphabet Σ is ℓ-equal to the sub-pss Lang($\mathcal{L}$) of $P(\Sigma^*)$. Less trivial examples will be given in Theorems 8.13 and 8.14. ///

<u>Remark 8.10</u>. Observe that if pss $\mathcal{L}_1$ is ℓ-included in pss $\mathcal{L}_2$, then

---

† In Ito [1968, section IV], TYPE-0 is called the class of "production-type" program schemes. In Kfoury [1973, §1], the class of generalized nondeterministic Ianov schemes associated with TYPE-0 according to section 7, is called the class of (monadic, single-variable) "effective schemas". TYPE-0 can also be viewed as the monadic, single-variable case of the class of "effective functionals" in Strong [1971a].

$\mathcal{L}_1$ has "less or equal computing power" than $\mathcal{L}_2$, in the sense that for each program scheme from $\mathcal{L}_1$ there is an equivalent program scheme in $\mathcal{L}_2$. (This is shown as follows. Let U be a program scheme in $\mathcal{L}_1$. Since $\mathrm{Lang}(\mathcal{L}_1) \subset \mathrm{Lang}(\mathcal{L}_2)$, there is a program scheme V in $\mathcal{L}_2$ such that L(V) = L(U). Also, by Definition 8.1(5), U is equivalent to L(U) and V to L(V). Hence V is equivalent to U).

Thus, ℓ-equal pss's have "the same computing power". As can easily be seen, the converse of this statement is false. ///

It is quite often that the effectiveness of ℓ-inclusion and ℓ-equality of pss's is of interest (as usual we say that ℓ-inclusion of one pss in another is effective if, for each program scheme from the first pss, a program scheme from the other pss can effectively be found, such that the L-schemes corresponding to them are the same). Typically this is the case, when the decidability of a semantic property in a pss $\mathcal{L}_1$ may be inferred from the decidability of this property in a pss $\mathcal{L}_2$ and the effective ℓ-inclusion of $\mathcal{L}_1$ in $\mathcal{L}_2$.

<u>Definition 8.11</u>. Let $\mathcal{L}_1 = (\Sigma,\theta_1,L_1)$ and $\mathcal{L}_2 = (\Sigma,\theta_2,L_2)$ be pss's. We say that $\mathcal{L}_1$ is <u>effectively ℓ-included</u> in $\mathcal{L}_2$, denoted by $\mathcal{L}_1 \subseteq_{\ell(\mathrm{eff})} \mathcal{L}_2$, if there is an algorithm which, given a program scheme U_1 in θ_1, produces a program scheme U_2 in θ_2 such that $L_2(U_2) = L_1(U_1)$. We say that $\mathcal{L}_1$ and $\mathcal{L}_2$ are <u>effectively ℓ-equal</u>, denoted by $\mathcal{L}_1 =_{\ell(\mathrm{eff})} \mathcal{L}_1$, if $\mathcal{L}_1 \subseteq_{\ell(\mathrm{eff})} \mathcal{L}_2$ and $\mathcal{L}_2 \subseteq_{\ell(\mathrm{eff})} \mathcal{L}_1$.

<u>Remark 8.12</u>. The above definition is only meaningful if θ_1 and θ_2 both consist of "constructive" objects. Thus, for example, the the definition cannot be applied to the pss $P(\Sigma^*)$. ///

Note that $\subseteq_{\ell(\mathrm{eff})}$ is a partial ordering, and so $=_{\ell(\mathrm{eff})}$ is an equivalence relation.

The rest of this section is devoted to the investigation of ℓ-inclusion and ℓ-equality between most of the pss's which have been discussed so far. The results are formulated in two theorems.

Theorem 8.13. For any alphabet Σ,

(1) $FIN(\Sigma) \subset_{\ell(eff)} REG(\Sigma)$,

(2) $REG(\Sigma) \subset_{\ell(eff)} CFG(\Sigma)$,

(3) $CFG(\Sigma) \subset_{\ell(eff)} MAC(\Sigma)$,

(4) $MAC(\Sigma) \subset_{\ell(eff)} TYPE\text{-}0(\Sigma)$,

(5) $IAN(\Sigma) \subset_{\ell(eff)} RSI(\Sigma)$,

(6) $IAN(\Sigma) \subset_{\ell(eff)} NIAN(\Sigma)$, and

(7) $RSI(\Sigma) \subset_{\ell(eff)} NRSI(\Sigma)$.

Proof. Let Σ be an arbitrary alphabet. Note first that if $\mathcal{L}_1$ is a sub-pss of $\mathcal{L}_2$, then $\mathcal{L}_1$ is effectively ℓ-included in $\mathcal{L}_2$. This leaves us with the following cases.

(1) For each finite language, a regular grammar generating it can effectively be found (see, e.g. Hopcroft and Ullman [1969, Theorems 3.7 and 3.5]). Consequently $FIN \subset_{\ell(eff)} REG$.

(3) Given a context-free scheme $G = (N,\Sigma,R,Z)$, let G_1 be the macro scheme (N,r,Σ,R,Z) with $r(S) = 0$ for all S in N. Clearly, $L(G_1) = L(G)$. So, $CFG \subset_{\ell(eff)} MAG$.

(4) It is shown in Fischer [1968, Corollary 5.5] that to each macro grammar a type 0 grammar, generating the same language, can effectively be found. Hence, $MAC \subset_{\ell(eff)} TYPE\text{-}0$.

(5) Given a deterministic Ianov scheme U over Σ, let V be the deterministic recursive system of Ianov schemes $(\Sigma,\mathcal{F},Z,b)$ with $\mathcal{F} = \{Z\}$ and $b(Z) = U$. Obviously, $L(V) = L(U)$. Thus $IAN \subset_{\ell(eff)} RSI$. ///

Theorem 8.14. For any alphabet Σ,

(1) $NIAN(\Sigma) =_{\ell(eff)} REG(\Sigma)$,†

(2) $NRSI(\Sigma) =_{\ell(eff)} CFG(\Sigma)$,†

(3) $NPP(\Sigma) =_{\ell(eff)} MAC(\Sigma)$,

(4) $N\mu CAL(\Sigma) =_{\ell(eff)} CFG(\Sigma)$, and

(5) $\mu CAL(\Sigma) =_{\ell(eff)} RSI(\Sigma)$.

Proof. Let Σ be an arbitrary alphabet.

(1) It follows immediately from Definition 3.9 that $NIAN \subset_{\ell(eff)} REG$. To show the converse, let $G = (N,\Sigma,R,Z)$ be a regular grammar. Without loss of generality we assume that each rule of R has one of the forms $S \to \sigma T$ or $S \to \varepsilon$, where S and T are in N and σ in Σ ††. Let U be the nondeterministic Ianov scheme (Σ,N,Z,E,A,e,ℓ), where E is the set of all nonterminals S such that $S \to \varepsilon$ is in R, A is the set of all rules of the form $S \to \sigma T$, and the arc $S \to \sigma T$ leads from S to T and is labelled by σ. Then it is easy to see that $G_U = G$ (for the definition of G_U, see Definition 3.9). Hence, $L(U) = L(G_U) = L(G)$.

(2) It follows directly from Definition 4.8 that $NRSI \subset_{\ell(eff)} CFG$. To show that $CFG \subset_{\ell(eff)} NRSI$, let $G = (N,\Sigma,R,Z)$ be a context-free grammar. Let U be the nrsi (Σ,N,Z,b), where, for each S in N, the nondeterministic Ianov scheme $b(S)$ over $\Sigma \cup N$ is constructed in such a way that $L(b(S)) = \{\alpha \mid (S \to \alpha) \in R\}$. It follows from Theorem 8.13(1) and point (1) of this theorem that such an nrsi U can be constructed. One may easily show that $L(U) = L(G)$.

(3) As the proof is similar to the proof of (2), we leave it to the reader.

---

† By a reasoning analogous to that in Remark 8.10, it easily follows from (1) and (2), that, for any general interpretation I of Σ, $\{I(U) \mid U \in NIAN\} = \{I(G) \mid G \in REG\}$ and $\{I(U) \mid U \in NRSI\} = \{I(G) \mid G \in CFG\}$. The latter two results were shown in Mazurkiewicz [1972 b].

†† See for instance Salomaa [1973, the proof of Theorem II 6.1].

(4) This is an alternative way of expressing (effectively) Proposition 6.11.

(5) We shall not give a proof of the fact that $\mu CAL =_{\ell(eff)} RSI$. With the help of a characterization of Lang(RSI) to be given in section 18, it would be easy to adapt the proof of Proposition 6.11 given in Gruska [1971] to the deterministic case. ///

Note that by (2) and (4) of the above theorem, for any alphabet Σ, the pss's NRSI(Σ) and NμCAL(Σ) are ℓ-equal, and so, by Remark 8.10, they are equivalent. (Recall that this was announced in the introduction to section 6).

Another way of formulating results (1), (2) and (3) of Theorem 8.14 (without mentioning effectiveness) is given in the following corollary.

Corollary 8.15. For any alphabet Σ,

(1) Lang(NIAN(Σ)) is the set of all regular languages over Σ,

(2) Lang(NRSI(Σ)) is the set of all context-free languages over Σ, and

(3) Lang(NPP(Σ)) is the set of all macro languages over Σ.

Remark 8.16. In view of the above, we shall henceforth talk about REG, RSI, CFG and MAC rather than about NIAN, μCAL, NRSI (or NμCAL) and NPP respectively. ///

To conclude this section (and Part I) we summarize Theorems 8.13 and 8.14 in the following diagram, where an alphabet Σ is understood.

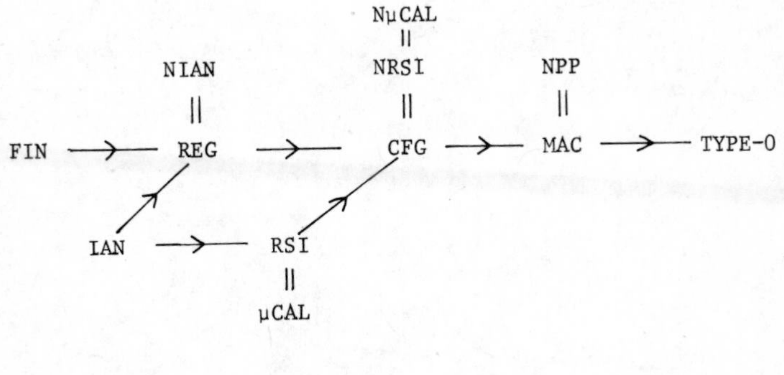

In this diagram, " = " stands for " $=_{\ell(eff)}$ ",and " $\longrightarrow$ " means "effectively ℓ-included, but not ℓ-equal". The fact that the pss's connected by $\longrightarrow$ are not ℓ-equal, is well known from formal language theory for the horizontal row from FIN to TYPE-0. For all other cases it will follow from the characterizations of Lang(IAN) and Lang(RSI), which will be given in Corollaries 18.9 and 18.19.

PART II

GENERAL PROPERTIES

OF PROGRAM SCHEMES

Survey of Contents

A property of a program scheme is called "semantic", if it can be defined in terms of the relations computed by the program scheme under arbitrary interpretations. It was shown in Part I that, in many cases, the investigation of a semantic property of a program scheme may be carried out by considering the same property for the corresponding L-scheme.

In this Part we consider essentially three semantic properties of program schemes: equivalence, "semantic determinism" and "semantic regularity". Each of these properties is defined by requiring that for all admissible interpretations a certain property holds for the relation (relations) computed by the program scheme (schemes) involved.(In the case of equivalence the property of the relations is equality, in the case of semantic determinism the property of the relation is being a partial function and in the case of semantic regularity the property of the relation is being "regular in the basic instructions").

The main results are the following.

(1) Each of these semantic properties can be expressed as a syntactic property. In fact we define a mapping, called the "standard mapping", from languages into languages. The image of an L-scheme under this mapping is called its "standard form". It turns out that each of the above semantic properties of a program scheme can be expressed as a syntactic property of the standard form of its L-scheme. (In the case of equivalence the syntactic property is equality, in the case of semantic determinism it is syntactic determinism and in the case of semantic regularity it is regularity).

(2) Each of these semantic properties can be tested with the use of a "universal interpretation". Thus, for example, there exists an interpretation such that if two program schemes compute the same relation under this particular interpretation, then they compute the same relation under all interpretations. Hence this particular(universal) interpretation is sufficient for testing equivalence of program schemes.

The following describes the contents of the sections of this Part.

In section 9, choosing various classes of admissible interpretations, we obtain several notions of equivalence of program schemes.

It will turn out in section 11 that it is only essential in our choice of admissible interpretation whether predicate symbols are interpreted as partial or as total predicates. In this work we are mainly concerned with the latter case.

In section 10 we define the standard mapping,which transforms each L-scheme into its standard form. We prove that two program schemes equivalent if and only if the standard forms of their L-schemes are identical (the "standard form theorem"). We also provide an algebraic characterization of equivalence of L-schemes.

Section 11 discusses the existence of universal interpretations.

In section 12 we consider interpretations with partial predicates. Results analogous to those of sections 10 and 11 turn out to be valid.

Section 13 is concerned with restricting the class of admissible interpretations. It is shown that for a particular kind of restriction (called generalized shift distribution) a standard form theorem holds and a universal interpretation exists.

In section 14 the property of semantic determinism of program schemes is defined and a "determinism theorem" is proved.

In section 15 the property of semantic regularity of program schemes is defined and a "regularity theorem" is proved.

Diagram of Sections

Below we give a rough diagram of the interrelations between the sections of Part II. In this diagram, "x→y" means that some knowledge of section x is required to be able to understand (a part of) section y.

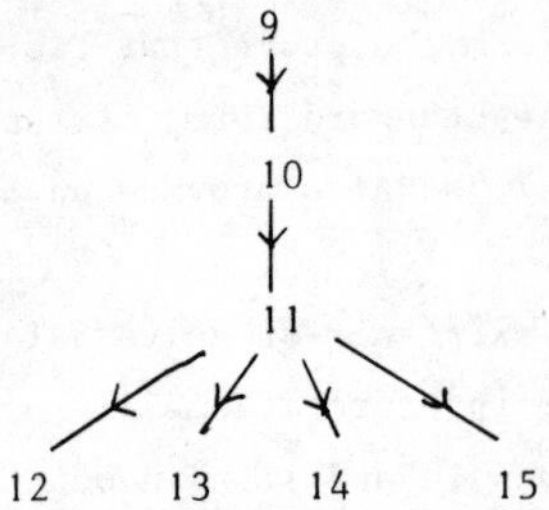

9. Equivalence of program schemes.
10. The standard form theorem.
11. Universal interpretations.
12. Equivalence with partial predicates.
13. Generalized shift distributions.
14. Semantic determinism of program schemes.
15. Semantic regularity of program schemes.

The dependency of sections 12 - 15 on section 11 is not so crucial. In fact the reader may start to read any of the sections 12 - 15 without first reading section 11. Which parts of section 11 will be needed in any particular case, will be clear from the text.

Sections 12 and 13 are "optional" in the sense that, if the reader decides to skip section 12 and/or section 13, then he will find that (provided he will later on skip appropriate parts of the text) it will not effect his understanding of the rest of this work.

We would like to point out that, as far as Part I is concerned, it is only its section 2 which is needed for understanding this Part.

More Terminology

Convention. In the sequel, Σ will denote a fixed, but arbitrary alphabet of instruction symbols. Whenever a concept or notation involves an alphabet of instruction symbols, it will be understood that this alphabet is Σ. In this sense, we shall use F, P and $\overline{P}$ rather than F_Σ, P_Σ and $\overline{P}_\Sigma$; also, all mentioned general interpretations are understood to be "of Σ", and all program schemes are understood of be "over Σ". ///

Convention. For reasons which will become clear in section 10, it will be assumed in the sequel that the elements of P have an arbitrary, but fixed order. Whenever we write "let $P = \{p_1, p_2, \ldots, p_m\}$" or something similar, the order of the elements of P is assumed to be as indicated, that is $p_1, p_2, \ldots, p_m$. ///

Notation. We shall often use letters a and b to denote elements of $P \cup \overline{P}$. Furthermore, if a denotes the positive (or negative) predicate symbol p (or $\bar{p}$), then $\bar{a}$ is used to denote $\bar{p}$ (or p). ///

Notation. The set $(P \cup \overline{P})^*$ will be denoted by T. Elements of T will be called tests. ///

Example. If $P = \{p,q\}$ (and so $\overline{P} = \{\bar{p},\bar{q}\}$), then p, $\bar{p}\bar{q}$, $qq\bar{p}q$, ε, $q\bar{q}p$ are tests. ///

We now introduce a special use of the term "program scheme".

Terminology. (For those readers who studied section 8; readers who did not, should consult the next paragraph).

In what follows we shall use the phrase "program scheme (over Σ)" as a generic term to talk about any element of any pss over Σ. (Note that this terminology is already implicit in Definition 8.1). If U is a program scheme in this sense, then we shall use L(U) to denote the L-scheme corresponding to U, and, for any general interpretation I, we shall use I(U) to denote the relation computed by U under I. Thus, when for instance two program schemes U and V are discussed, these program schemes do not necessarily belong to the same pss.

Note that, in particular, L-schemes are program schemes and, for each

L-scheme A, L(A) = A (see Example 8.5(2)). ///

<u>Terminology</u>. (For those readers who skipped section 8).

In what follows we shall use the word "<u>program scheme (over Σ)</u>" to denote an arbitrary mathematical object U with the following properties:

(1) For each general interpretation I of Σ , there is associated with U a relation on D_I, denoted by I(U) and called the relation computed by U under I.

(2) There is associated with U an L-scheme over Σ, denoted by L(U) and called the L-scheme corresponding to U.

(3) For any general interpretation I of Σ, I(L(U)) = I(U).

It was shown in sections 3 to 7 that many well known mathematical objects are program schemes in this sense. For instance, in section 3, it was shown that nondeterministic Ianov schemes are program schemes in this sense.

We now define, for each L-scheme A, L(A) = A. From this definition, and Definition 2.7, it follows that L-schemes are program schemes in the above sense. ///

9. Equivalence of program schemes

One of the main concepts in the theory of program schemes is that of equivalence (two program schemes are equivalent, if they compute the same relation under any interpretation). A related concept is that of covering † : a program scheme is covered by another program scheme, if, for all interpretations, the relation computed by the former is included in the relation computed by the latter. Equivalence and covering of program schemes were introduced in Ianov [1960] and de Bakker and Scott [1969] respectively.

In this section we first define the notions of equivalence and covering. As an immediate consequence of our L-scheme point of view it is shown that two program schemes are equivalent if and only if they have equivalent L-schemes corresponding to them (Lemma 9.5). Moreover it is shown, that, in the special case that the alphabet of instruction symbols contains no predicate symbols, two program schemes are equivalent if and only if the L-schemes corresponding to them are the same (Theorem 9.6).

Then we show that several set-theoretic and language-theoretic operations on L-schemes preserve equivalence and covering (Lemma 9.7 and Theorem 9.11). Part of these results may be expressed by saying that the set of equivalence classes of L-schemes constitutes a cslm (Theorem 9.9).

Since we have defined various types of interpretations (Definition 2.3), it is natural to consider various types of equivalences of program schemes, depending on the class of interpretations under which the relations computed by the program schemes are compared.

In the following definition the prefix x should be replaced consistently by any of the prefixes π, τ, $p\pi$, $p\tau$, $t\pi$ or $t\tau$.

---

† The term "covering" is nonstandard. In de Bakker and Scott [1969] the more natural term "inclusion" is used. We decided to use "covering" rather than "inclusion", since the latter may easily be confused with inclusion of sets (in particular L-schemes).

Definition 9.1. Let U and V be program schemes †. We say that U is x-equivalent to V, denoted by $U \equiv_x V$, if, for all x-interpretations I, $I(U) = I(V)$. We say that U is x-covered by V, denoted by $U \leq_x V$, if, for all x-interpretations I, $I(U) \subset I(V)$.

Thus, we have π-equivalence and π-covering, denoted by $\equiv_\pi$ and $\leq_\pi$ respectively, we have τ-equivalence and τ-covering, denoted by $\equiv_\tau$ and $\leq_\tau$ respectively, etcetera.

Note that, as one would expect, $\leq_x$ is a reflexive and transitive relation, and $\equiv_x$ is an equivalence relation. Also, for any program schemes U and V, $U \equiv_x V$ if and only if both $U \leq_x V$ and $V \leq_x U$. Note finally that simple properties like the following hold: for any pair of program schemes U and V, if $U \leq_\pi V$ then $U \leq_\tau V$.

Before proceeding with an example, we introduce a notational convention, followed by an important remark on it.

Notation 9.2. In the sequel we shall omit the symbol τ, whenever no confusion can result. Thus we shall use "≡" and "≤" rather than "$\equiv_\tau$" and "$\leq_\tau$", "equivalent" and "covered" rather than "τ-equivalent" and "τ-covered", and "interpretation" rather than "τ-interpretation". ///

Remark 9.3. The reason for introducing the above convention is the fact that, in the sequel, we shall be mainly concerned with τ-equivalence and τ-covering.

Those readers who are primarily concerned with tτ-equivalence (that is, those who interpret function and predicate symbols as total functions and predicates), may be interested to know in advance that the relations $\equiv_\tau$, $\equiv_{p\tau}$ and $\equiv_{t\tau}$ will turn out to be equal (Theorem 11.13).

Apart from τ-equivalence we shall also investigate π-equivalence and π-covering. In fact, whenever possible, we shall formulate definitions and results for equivalence in such a way, that only slight changes are needed to convert them into the appropriate definitions and results for π-equivalence. In the rest of this section and in the next two sections we

---

† Note that the term "program scheme" is used in a technical sense, explained in the introduction to Part II.

discuss the τ-case only. The π-case will be discussed in section 12.

For those readers whose main concern is with pπ-equivalence (that is, those who interpret function and predicate symbols as partial functions and predicates), we note that the relations $\equiv_{\pi}$, $\equiv_{p\pi}$ and $\equiv_{t\pi}$ will turn out to be equal (see section 12). ///

We now give some examples of equivalent L-schemes. These examples will be quite useful later on.

Example 9.4. If a and b are predicate symbols, then the following equivalences hold:

(1) $a \cup \bar{a} \equiv \varepsilon$,†

(2) $a\bar{a} \equiv \emptyset$,

(3) $ab \equiv ba$, and

(4) $aa \equiv a$.

To prove these equivalences note that, if D is a set, and p and q are relations on D included in id_D, then $p \circ q = p \cap q$. From this, equivalences (3) and (4) follow directly. Equivalences (1) and (2) follow from the fact that, for any p in P, the pair $(p,\bar{p})$ is always interpreted as a total predicate. ///

The following result is an immediate consequence of the definitions.

Lemma 9.5. If U and V are arbitrary program schemes, then

(1) $U \equiv L(U)$,

(2) $U \leq V$ if and only if $L(U) \leq L(V)$, and

$U \equiv V$ if and only if $L(U) \equiv L(V)$.

Proof. (1) follows immediately from the fact that U is a program scheme (recall the Terminology from the introduction to Part II). The first part of (2) follows from (1) and elementary properties of $\equiv$ and $\leq$. The second part of (2) is a direct consequence of the first part. ///

The first statement of the above lemma expresses in a short way the

---

† For the meaning of $\bar{a}$, see the introduction to this Part.

"fundamental law of program schemes": for every program scheme U and every interpretation I, I(U) = I(L(U)).

The second statement shows that, in the general study of equivalence and covering of program schemes, one may restrict oneself to L-schemes.

A consequence of Lemma 9.5(2) is that, for any program schemes U and V, if L(U) = L(V), then $U \equiv V$. Thus, a simple sufficient condition for the equivalence of program schemes is the equality of the L-schemes corresponding to them †. We now show that this condition is also necessary in the case that Σ contains no predicate symbols. This result will in fact follow from a more general one in the next section (Theorem 10.23). However, it is proved here in order to introduce the reader to the techniques of the next section.

Theorem 9.6. If $P = \emptyset$ ††, then, for every pair of program schemes U and V,

$U \leq V$ if and only if $L(U) \subset L(V)$, and

$U \equiv V$ if and only if $L(U) = L(V)$.

Proof. The second part of the theorem is a direct consequence of the first part. Furthermore, by Lemma 9.5, it is sufficient to prove the first part for L-schemes (recall also that, for all L-schemes A, L(A) = A). So let us consider arbitrary L-schemes A and B. We have to show that $A \leq B$ if and only if $A \subset B$. The if part follows from Lemma 2.9(2), and the only-if part is proved as follows.

Let us assume that $A \leq B$. Let I be the interpretation (D,h), such that $D = F^*$ and, for any f in F, $h(f) = \{(f\phi,\phi) \mid \phi \in F^*\}$. Then one can easily show (by induction on the length of ω) that, for any ϕ, ψ and ω in F^*,

(*) $(\phi,\psi) \in I(\omega)$ if and only if $\phi = \omega\psi$.

To show that $A \subset B$, let ϕ be an arbitrary element of A. Then, by (*), $(\phi,\varepsilon) \in I(\phi)$. Thus, by Definition 2.7(4), $(\phi,\varepsilon) \in I(A)$. Consequently, since $A \leq B$, $(\phi,\varepsilon) \in I(B)$. Hence, again by Definition 2.7(4), there is a word ω in B, such that $(\phi,\varepsilon) \in I(\omega)$. And so, by (*), $\phi = \omega$ and thus ϕ is an element of B. Hence $A \subset B$. ///

---

† In the case of Ianov schemes, this is shown in Kaplan [1969, Theorem 2].

†† Note that, if $P = \emptyset$, then $\overline{P} = \emptyset$ and $\Sigma = F$.

The above theorem shows that, in the case that Σ contains function symbols only, equivalence of program schemes can be treated by traditional techniques from formal language theory. (In fact, if $P = \emptyset$, then program schemes U and V are equivalent if and only if grammars G_U and G_V generate the same language, where we assume that G_U generates L(U) and G_V generates L(V), as in Definition 3.9. The problem of investigating whether two grammars generate the same language is one of the traditional topics in formal language theory †). It is easy to see that, in the case that Σ does contain predicate symbols, the theorem does not hold (for example, for every p in P, the L-schemes pp and p are equivalent, but not the same). Nevertheless, it will be shown in the next section that a theorem, similar to the above, can be established for the general case.

In the next lemma we show the effect which the usual operations on L-schemes have on covering and equivalence of L-schemes.

Lemma 9.7. Let A, B, A_1 and B_1 be L-schemes. Also, for every j in some index set J, let A_j and B_j be L-schemes. Finally, let p be a positive predicate symbol. Then the following statements are true.

(1) $A \leq B$ if and only if $A \cup B \equiv B$

(2) If $A \subset B$, then $A \leq B$.

(3) If, for all j in J, $A_j \leq B_j$, then $\bigcup_{j\in J} A_j \leq \bigcup_{j\in J} B_j$.

(4) If $A \leq A_1$ and $B \leq B_1$, then $AB \leq A_1B_1$.

(5) If $A \leq A_1$ and $B \leq B_1$, then $(p \rightarrow A,B) \leq (p \rightarrow A_1,B_1)$.

(6) If $A \leq B$, then $A^* \leq B^*$.

Proof. We first note that (1) follows easily from (2) and (3). Statements (2) to (6) can easily be proved from statements (2) to (6) of Lemma 2.9 and known properties of relations. As an example, we prove (4). So let us assume that $A \leq A_1$ and $B \leq B_1$. Let I be an arbitrary interpretation.

---

† For instance, since NIAN $=_{\ell(\text{eff})}$ REG, it follows from a well known fact in formal language theory that, if $P = \emptyset$, equivalence of nondeterministic Ianov schemes is decidable.

Then, by the definition of covering, $I(A) \subset I(A_1)$ and $I(B) \subset I(B_1)$. Thus, obviously, $I(A) \circ I(B) \subset I(A_1) \circ I(B_1)$. Hence by Lemma 2.9(4), $I(AB) \subset I(A_1B_1)$. Consequently, since I was arbitrarily chosen, $AB \leq A_1B_1$. ///

It is easy to see that statements (3) to (6) of the above lemma also hold when "≤" is replaced by "≡".

We use Lemma 9.7 in the following example, taken from McCarthy [1963, § 7].

Example 9.8. Let A, B and C be L-schemes, and let p be in P, then,

(1) $(p \to (p \to A,B),C) \equiv (p \to A,C)$, and

(2) $(p \to A,A) \equiv A$.

The first equivalence is proved as follows:

$(p \to (p \to A,B),C)$

$= p(pA \cup \bar{p}B) \cup \bar{p}C$ by the definition of conditional composition

$= ppA \cup p\bar{p}B \cup \bar{p}C$

$\equiv pA \cup \emptyset B \cup \bar{p}C$ by Example 9.4 and Lemma 9.7

$= pA \cup \bar{p}C$

$= (p \to A,C)$

The second equivalence can be proved similarly. ///

It follows from Lemma 9.7(3) and (4) that equivalence is a cslm-congruence † on the cslm $P(\Sigma^*)$. Therefore, the algebraic structure of the set of all equivalence classes of L-schemes can be expressed as follows.

†† Theorem 9.9. $P(\Sigma^*)/\equiv$ is a cslm.

Proof. See 1.3.6. in section 1. ///

---

† For the notion of cslm-congruence, see 1.3.6.

†† $P(\Sigma^*)/\equiv$ is related to the quotient algebra $E/\equiv$ in Scott [1971,§ 8] (recall also the introduction to section 7).

We comment the following on the "lattice-structure" of $P(\Sigma^*)/\equiv$.

Remark 9.10. In the cslm $P(\Sigma^*)/\equiv$, the cslm-operations $*$, $\bigvee$ and the cslm-constant e are defined in the usual way: for any L-schemes A and B, $[A] * [B] = [AB]$ † ; if, for each j in some index set J, A_j is an L-scheme, then $\bigvee_{j\in J} [A_j] = [\bigcup_{j\in J} A_j]$; $e = [\varepsilon]$.

Since $P(\Sigma^*)$ is a complete semi-lattice, it is even a complete lattice (see 1.3.3 in section 1)††. Hence a "meet-operation" $\bigwedge$ with the usual properties can be defined. However, one has to be careful, since it is not true that, for all L-schemes A and B, $[A] \wedge [B] = [A \cap B]$. (This can be seen as follows. Let $A = pp$ and $B = p$. Then $[A \cap B] = [\emptyset]$, but, since $pp \equiv p$, $[A] \wedge [B] = [p] \wedge [p] = [p] \neq [\emptyset]$). We postpone the discussion of this matter to section 10, where a specific element of the equivalence class $[A] \wedge [B]$ will be indicated (Remark 10.26). ///

We end this section by considering the effect of the operation of substitution on the equivalence and covering of L-schemes. It will be shown that substitution preserves equivalence, in the sense that, if s is a restricted substitution, and A and B are equivalent L-schemes, then s(A) and s(B) are equivalent L-schemes. Since only τ-interpretations are involved, it should be obvious that the above is not necessarily true if we allow substitutions that are unrestricted for predicate symbols. So, in the next theorem, we require that all predicate symbols remain unchanged by the substitution.

Theorem 9.11. Let s be a substitution on Σ such that, for all p in P, $s(p) = p$ and $s(\bar{p}) = \bar{p}$. Then, for arbitrary L-schemes A and B,

if $A \leq B$, then $s(A) \leq s(B)$, and

if $A \equiv B$, then $s(A) \equiv s(B)$.

Proof. Obviously, the second statement follows directly from the first. The first statement is proved as follows. Let us assume that $A \leq B$,

---

† $[A]$ denotes $\{B \in P(\Sigma^*) \mid B \equiv A\}$.

†† In fact, as will be shown later (Theorem 10.25), it turns out that $P(\Sigma^*)/\equiv$ is a complete Boolean algebra.

and let I be an arbitrary (τ-)interpretation. Let $I_s = (D_s, h_s)$ be the general interpretation such that $D_s = D_I$, and, for each σ in Σ, $h_s(\sigma) = I(s(\sigma))$. The fact that predicate symbols remain unchanged by s, implies that I_s is a τ-interpretation. And so, since $A \leq B$, $I_s(A) \subset I_s(B)$. Also by Lemma 2.12, $I_s(A) = I(s(A))$ and $I_s(B) = I(s(B))$. Consequently $I(s(A)) \subset I(s(B))$. Since I was arbitrarily chosen, it follows that $s(A) \leq s(B)$. ///

Intuitively, the above theorem shows that equivalent program schemes remain equivalent, when function symbols are viewed as (nonrecursive) procedure calls (see the intuitive discussion of substitution at the end of section 2).

10. The standard form theorem

In this section we "solve" the problem of equivalence of program schemes. We show that with each program scheme an equivalent "standard" L-scheme can be associated in such a way, that two program schemes are equivalent if and only if the corresponding standard L-schemes are the same (Theorem 10.24). This theorem, to be called the "standard form theorem", will play a central role in the further development of the theory of L-schemes.

This section is divided into three parts.

First, we define the notion of a "standard" L-scheme (Definition 10.4) and prove that standard L-schemes are equivalent if and only if they are the same (Lemma 10.12).

Then the so called standard mapping S is defined (Definition 10.17). It transforms each L-scheme into an equivalent standard one (Corollary 10.22). From this we obtain the following special case of the standard form theorem: "two L-schemes are equivalent if and only if they are transformed into the same standard L-scheme by the mapping S" (Theorem 10.23). The standard form theorem itself is a direct consequence of this special case.

Finally, two algebraic characterizations of the equivalence relation between L-schemes are proved (Theorems 10.27 and 10.29).

In the previous section we have shown that, if Σ contains no predicate symbols, then two program schemes are equivalent if and only if they are equal (recall Theorem 9.6). We have also shown that if Σ does contain predicate symbols, then different L-schemes may very well be equivalent (see Example 9.4). Nevertheless, even if $P \neq \emptyset$, we can define a natural class of L-schemes such that any two different L-schemes of this class are nonequivalent. Each L-scheme A from this class has the property that, in each word of A, a so called "standard" test † occurs between any two consecutive function symbols (and also at the beginning and at the end of the word). Intuitively, a standard test is a test, which, under any

---

† Recall from the introduction to this Part that a test is an element of $(P \cup \overline{P})^*$.

interpretation I, computes the values of the predicates $(I(p), I(\bar{p}))$ for all p in P, exactly once and in a fixed order.

Definition 10.1. Let $P = \{p_1, p_2, \ldots, p_m\}$†. Let, for all i in $\{1,2,\ldots,m\}$, P_i denote $\{p_i, \bar{p}_i\}$.
A standard test is any element of $P_1 \cdot P_2 \cdots P_m$ (where for m = 0, we assume that $P_1 \cdot P_2 \cdots P_m = \{\varepsilon\}$).

We shall use T_S to denote the set of all standard tests. (Recall that T denotes the set of all tests).

Example 10.2. If $P = \{p,q\}$, then $T_S = \{pq, p\bar{q}, \bar{p}q, \bar{p}\bar{q}\}$. If $P = \{p\}$, then $T_S = \{p, \bar{p}\}$. If $P = \emptyset$, then $T_S = \{\varepsilon\}$. ///

Before defining the notion of a standard word, we note that each word ϕ in Σ^* can be written uniquely as $\phi = t_1 f_1 t_2 f_2 \cdots t_k f_k t_{k+1}$, where $k \geq 0$ ††, $t_1, t_2, \ldots, t_{k+1} \in T$ and $f_1, f_2, \ldots, f_k \in F$. We define ϕ to be standard if all tests t_i are standard.

Definition 10.3. A standard word is any element of $(T_S \cdot F)^* \cdot T_S$.

We shall use W_S to denote the set of all standard words.

We now define a L-scheme to be standard if all its words are standard.

Definition 10.4. A standard L-scheme is any element of $P(W_S)$.

The following terminology will also be used.

---

† Recall that, according to the second Convention in the introduction to this Part, the elements of P have the ordering $p_1, p_2, \ldots, p_m$.

†† Note that if k = 0, then "$t_1 f_1 t_2 f_2 \cdots t_k f_k t_{k+1}$" stands for "$t_1$".

Definition 10.5. A program scheme U is said to be standard if L(U) is a standard L-scheme. A program scheme V is said to be a standard form of a program scheme V_1 if V is standard and equivalent to V_1.

Example 10.6. Let $P = \{p,q\}$ and $F = \{f\}$. Consider the L-schemes $A = (qpf)^*(\bar{q} \cup q\bar{p})$ and $B = (pqf)^*(\bar{p}q \cup \bar{p}\bar{q} \cup p\bar{q})$. It is easy to see that B is a standard L-scheme, while A is not. Also, it follows from Example 9.4 and Lemma 9.7, that $B \equiv A$. Hence B is a standard form of A. ///

It will be shown in Lemma 10.12, that standard L-schemes are equivalent if and only if they are the same. In the proof of this lemma, just as in the proof of the related Theorem 9.6, we shall make use of a particular interpretation, which we now define.

Definition 10.7. The general interpretation $I_o = (D_o, h_o)$ is defined as follows.

(1) $D_o = W_S$.

(2) For each f in F, $h_o(f) = \{(tf\phi,\phi) \mid t \in T_S \text{ and } \phi \in W_S\}$.

(3) For each a in $P \cup \bar{P}$,

$h_o(a) = \{(t\phi,t\phi) \mid t \in T_S, \phi \in (F \cdot T_S)^* \text{ and a } \underline{\underline{in}} \text{ t}\}$ †.

Lemma 10.8. I_o is a pτ-interpretation.

Proof. It is clear that, for each f in F, $h_o(f)$ is a partial function. To see that, for each p in P, $(h_o(p), h_o(\bar{p}))$ is a total predicate, we note the following: for any standard test t and any p in P, either p in t or $\bar{p}$ in t, but not both. ///

In the next lemma we describe the relation computed by an arbitrary word in Σ^* under the interpretation I_o.

---

† For the definition of "in", see 1.2.1.

Lemma 10.9. Let ω be in Σ^*, and ϕ, ψ in W_S with $\phi = t_1 f_1 t_2 f_2 \cdots t_k f_k t_{k+1}$ (where $k \geq 0$, $t_1, \ldots, t_{k+1} \in T_S$ and $f_1, \ldots, f_k \in F$). Then, $(\phi,\psi) \in I_o(\omega)$ if and only if there is an integer n ($0 \leq n \leq k$) such that

(1) $\psi = t_{n+1} f_{n+1} \cdots t_k f_k t_{k+1}$, and

(2) there are tests t_i' ($1 \leq i \leq n+1$) such that t_i' in t_i and $\omega = t_1' f_1 t_2' f_2 \cdots t_n' f_n t_{n+1}'$.

Proof. The straightforward proof is left to the reader. ///

Remark 10.10. In what follows we shall use the above lemma only in the case that ω is also in W_S. In that case, property (2) may be replaced by the following property (2'):

(2') $\omega = t_1 f_1 t_2 f_2 \cdots t_n f_n t_{n+1}$.

To see this, note that if t_1 and t_2 are standard tests and t_1 in t_2, then $t_1 = t_2$. ///

Example 10.11. Let $P = \{p,q\}$ and $F = \{f,g\}$. Then $I_o(qppfg\bar{q}\bar{q})$ contains the pairs $(pqf\bar{p}qgp\bar{q}fpq, p\bar{q}fpq)$ and $(pqfpqg\bar{p}\bar{q}, p\bar{q})$, but is undefined for the arguments pqfpq, pqgpq and pqfpqgpq. ///

We now show that, if standard L-schemes are equivalent, then they are the same. To this aim we prove that, if standard L-schemes compute the same relation under I_o, then they are the same.

Lemma 10.12.† Let A and B be standard L-schemes. Then the following three statements are equivalent.

(1) $A \leq B$,

(2) $I_o(A) \subset I_o(B)$, and

(3) $A \subset B$.

---

† For Ianov schemes, a result similar to this was first shown in Rutledge [1964, p.8]. In fact, in that paper, it was shown that, for any two standard Ianov schemes U and V, $U \equiv V$ if and only if $L(U) = L(V)$.

<u>Proof</u>

(1) ⇒ (2). By the definition of $\leq$.

(3) ⇒ (1). By Lemma 9.7(2).

(2) ⇒ (3). Let us assume that $I_o(A) \subset I_o(B)$. Let ϕ be an arbitrary word in A. Let $\phi = t_1 f_1 t_2 f_2 \cdots t_k f_k t_{k+1}$, where $k \geq 0$, $t_1, t_2, \ldots, t_{k+1} \in T_S$ and $f_1, f_2, \ldots, f_k \in F$. Then, by Lemma 10.9, $(\phi, t_{k+1}) \in I_o(\phi)$. Thus $(\phi, t_{k+1}) \in I_o(A)$. Consequently, since $I_o(A) \subset I_o(B)$, $(\phi, t_{k+1}) \in I_o(B)$. Hence there is a word ω in B, such that $(\phi, t_{k+1}) \in I_o(\omega)$. It follows from Lemma 10.9 and Remark 10.10 that $\phi = \omega$, and thus ϕ is an element of B. Hence $A \subset B$. ///

It is easy to see that this lemma also holds when " $\leq$ " and " $\subset$ " are replaced by " $\equiv$ " and " $=$ " respectively.

It follows from the above lemma, that each L-scheme A has at most one standard form in $P(\Sigma^*)$. (Proof: if B and C are both standard L-schemes equivalent to A, then $B \equiv C$, and so, by Lemma 10.12, $B = C$). Our aim in the next part of this section is to show that each L-scheme has a unique standard form in $P(\Sigma^*)$. (This implies the standard form theorem: two L-schemes are equivalent if and only if their unique standard forms are the same). To show this, we have to define for each L-scheme A an equivalent standard L-scheme S(A). Since this mapping will be defined (Definition 10.17) as a cslm morphism from $P(\Sigma^*)$ into $P(W_S)$, we first provide $P(W_S)$ with a cslm-structure. (Note that $P(W_S)$ is not closed under product of languages, and so $P(W_S)$ is not a "sub-cslm" of $P(\Sigma^*)$!).

<u>Definition 10.13</u>. Let A and B be standard L-schemes. Then the <u>standard product</u> of A and B, denoted by $A * B$, is defined to be the standard L-scheme $\{\phi t \psi \mid t \in T_S, \phi \in (T_S \cdot F)^*, \psi \in (F \cdot T_S)^*, \phi t \in A \text{ and } t\psi \in B\}$.

We have called $A * B$ the standard product of A and B because, as will be shown in Example 10.25, it is equivalent to the product AB.

<u>Example 10.14</u>. Let $P = \{p,q\}$ and $F = \{f\}$. Consider the standard L-schemes $A = (p(q \cup \bar{q})f)^* \bar{p}(q \cup \bar{q})$ and $B = (p \cup \bar{p})q(fpq)^*$. It is easy to see that $A * B = (p(q \cup \bar{q})f)^* \bar{p}q(fpq)^*$. ///

With standard product as product operation, T_S as unity with respect to this operation and union as join operation, $P(W_S)$ is a cslm.

Lemma 10.15. $(P(W_S),*,T_S,\subset,\bigcup)$ is a cslm.

Proof. The proof is left to the reader. ///

Remark 10.16. We note here that the cslm $P(W_S)$ is a special case of the cslm's discussed in Example 1.3.4.4. In fact, consider the following category. The set of objects is T_S and the set of morphisms is W_S. For t_1 and t_2 in T_S, the set of morphisms from t_1 to t_2 is $t_1(F\cdot T_S)^* \cap (T_S\cdot F)^* t_2$. The identity morphism on the object t is t itself. Finally, the composition of the morphisms ϕt and $t\psi$ (with $t \in T_S$, $\phi \in (T_S F)^*$ and $\psi \in (FT_S)^*$) is $\phi t \psi$. Then $P(W_S)$ is the cslm of all sets of morphisms of this category, as defined in Example 1.3.4.4. ///

The mapping S, called the "standard mapping", is now defined.

Definition 10.17.† The standard mapping S from $P(\Sigma^*)$ into $P(W_S)$ is defined as follows.

(1) For each f in F, $S(f) = T_S\cdot f\cdot T_S$.

(2) For each a in $P \cup \overline{P}$, $S(a) = \{t\epsilon T_S | a \text{ in } t\}$.††

(3) S is a cslm-morphism.

Recall that $P(\Sigma^*)$ is the free cslm generated by Σ (Remark 1.3.5.1). Hence S is uniquely determined by the above definition.

Example 10.18. Let $P = \{p,q\}$ and $F = \{f\}$. Then
$S(p) = \{pq,p\overline{q}\}$, $S(pf) = S(p) * S(f) = \{pq,p\overline{q}\} * (T_S f T_S) =$
$= p(q \cup \overline{q})fT_S$, $S(pff) = p(q \cup \overline{q})fT_S fT_S$, and $S(pp) = S(p) * S(p) = S(p)$. ///

---

† In Kaplan [1969, pp. 372-373], S(A) is defined for each regular L-scheme A, and is called a "K-event".

†† For the definition of "in", see 1.2.1.

Before showing that, for each L-scheme A, S(A) is equivalent to A, we now present some useful properties of S.

Lemma 10.19.

(1) For each t in T, $S(t) = \{t_1 \in T_S \mid t \text{ \underline{in} } t_1\}$.

(2) Let $\phi = t_1 f_1 t_2 f_2 \cdots t_k f_k t_{k+1}$, where $k \geq 0$, $t_1, \ldots, t_{k+1} \in T$ and $f_1, \ldots, f_k \in F$. Then $S(\phi) = S(t_1) \cdot f_1 \cdot S(t_2) \cdot f_2 \cdots S(t_k) \cdot f_k \cdot S(t_{k+1})$.

(3) For each L-scheme A, $S(A) = \bigcup_{\phi \in A} S(\phi)$.

(4) For each standard L-scheme A, S(A) = A.

Proof. From the definition of "cslm-morphism", it follows that S has the following properties: $S(\varepsilon) = T_S$; for any L-schemes A and B, $S(AB) = S(A) * S(B)$; if, for each j in some index set J, A_j is an L-scheme then $S(\bigcup_{j \in J} A_j) = \bigcup_{j \in J} S(A_j)$.

From these properties, statements (1), (2) and (3) can easily be proved. Statement (4) follows from (1), (2), (3) and the definition of standard L-scheme. The proofs are left to the reader. ///

Example 10.20. Let P = {p,q} and F = {f}. Consider the L-scheme $A = (qpf)^*(\bar{q} \cup q\bar{p})$ of Example 10.6. Let us determine S(A). Since S(qp) = pq, it is easy to show, by induction on n, that $S((qpf)^n) = (pqf)^n \cdot T_S$. Hence $S((qpf)^*) = (pqf)^* \cdot T_S$, and so $S(A) = (pqf)^*(p\bar{q} \cup \bar{p}\bar{q} \cup \bar{p}q)$. Thus S(A) equals the L-scheme B of Example 10.6. ///

We now show that, for each L-scheme A, $S(A) \equiv A$. In fact, for the sake of a later theorem (Theorem 10.29), we prove the following slightly more general result.

Lemma 10.21. Let $\sim$ be a cslm-congruence on $P(\Sigma^*)$, such that, for each a in $P \cup \bar{P}$,

(1) $a \cup \bar{a} \sim \varepsilon$, and (2) $a\bar{a} \sim \emptyset$.

Then, for every L-scheme A, $S(A) \sim A$.

Proof. From Lemma 10.19 ((2) and (3)), and the fact that $\sim$ is a cslm-congruence, it follows that it suffices to prove that, for any test t, $S(t) \sim t$. Before doing so, we note firstly that, for any a in $P \cup \bar{P}$,

(3) $aa \sim a$

(Proof: $a \sim a(a \cup \bar{a}) = (aa \cup a\bar{a}) \sim aa$),

and secondly that, for any a and b in $P \cup \bar{P}$,

(4) $ab \sim ba$

(Proof: $ab\bar{a} \sim (ab\bar{a} \cup a\bar{a}) \sim (ab\bar{a} \cup a(b\cup\bar{b})\bar{a}) = (ab\bar{a} \cup ab\bar{a} \cup a\bar{b}\bar{a}) = (ab\bar{a} \cup a\bar{b}\bar{a}) = a(b\cup\bar{b})\bar{a} \sim a\bar{a} \sim \emptyset$. So $ab\bar{a} \sim \bar{a}ba$, since both are equivalent to $\emptyset$. Then, $ab \sim ab(a\cup\bar{a}) = (aba \cup ab\bar{a}) \sim (aba \cup \bar{a}ba) = (a\cup\bar{a})ba \sim ba$).

We now give a sketch of the proof that, for an arbitrary test t, $S(t) \sim t$. The following two cases can be distinguished.

Case 1. There is some p in P, such that p and $\bar{p}$ both occur in t. Then, by "repeated application of (4)", p and $\bar{p}$ can be "brought together". Hence, by (2), $t \sim \emptyset$. Also, by Lemma 10.19(1), $S(t) = \emptyset$. Thus $S(t) \sim t$.

Case 2. There is no p in P such that both p and $\bar{p}$ occur in t. Suppose that $P = \{p_1,p_2,\dots,p_m\}$. By "repeated application" of (3) and (4), it can be shown, that $t \sim \phi_1\phi_2\cdots\phi_m$ for certain words $\phi_1,\phi_2,\dots,\phi_m$ with $\phi_i \in \{p_i,\bar{p}_i,\varepsilon\}$ for all i, $1 \le i \le m$. Since, during the application of (3) and (4), the set of symbols occurring in the test does not change, it follows from Lemma 10.19(1) that $S(t) = S(\phi_1\phi_2\cdots\phi_m)$. Let A be the set $A_1A_2\cdots A_m$, where, for $1 \le i \le m$, if $\phi_i \neq \varepsilon$ then $A_i = \{\phi_i\}$, and if $\phi_i = \varepsilon$ then $A_i = \{p_i,\bar{p}_i\}$. By (1), $\phi_1\phi_2\cdots\phi_m \sim A$. Also, by Lemma 10.19(1), $S(\phi_1\phi_2\cdots\phi_m) = A$. It now follows that $S(t) = S(\phi_1\phi_2\cdots\phi_m) = A \sim \sim \phi_1\phi_2\cdots\phi_m \sim t$, and the lemma is proved. ///

Corollary 10.22. For each L-scheme A, $S(A) \equiv A$.

Proof. Immediate from Theorem 9.9, Example 9.4 and the previous lemma. ///

The above corollary, together with Lemma 10.12, implies the main theorem of this section.

Theorem 10.23. Let A and B be L-schemes. Then,

$A \le B$ if and only if $S(A) \subset S(B)$, and

$A \equiv B$ if and only if $S(A) = S(B)$.

Proof. Immediate from Corollary 10.22 and Lemma 10.12. ///

As a corollary we obtain the following result on program schemes.

Theorem 10.24. Let U and V be program schemes. Then,

$U \leq V$ if and only if $S(L(U)) \subset S(L(V))$, and

$U \equiv V$ if and only if $S(L(U)) = S(L(V))$.

Proof. Immediate from Theorem 10.23 and Lemma 9.5. ///

In the sequel, Theorems 10.23 and 10.24 will both be referred to as the standard form theorem.†

Example 10.25. Let A and B be arbitrary standard L-schemes. Then, by the definition of S, $S(AB) = S(A) * S(B)$. Using Lemma 10.19 (4), it follows that $S(AB) = A * B = S(A*B)$. Hence, by the standard form theorem, $A * B \equiv AB$. ///

In the following corollary we express the standard form theorem in a slightly different way.

Corollary 10.26. Let U and V be program schemes. Then

(1) U is a standard form of V if and only if $L(U) = S(L(V))$,

(2) if U_S and V_S are standard forms of U and V respectively, then $U \equiv V$ if and only if $L(U_S) = L(V_S)$.

Proof. (1) Immediate from Definition 10.5, the standard form theorem and Lemma 10.19(4).

(2) Immediate from (1) and the standard form theorem. ///

In the last part of this section it is shown that the standard form theorem implies two characterizations of the relation of equivalence in $P(\Sigma^*)$.

The first theorem is a result on the "lattice structure" of $P(\Sigma^*)/\equiv$ (see Theorem 9.9).

Theorem 10.27. $P(\Sigma^*)/\equiv$ is a complete Boolean algebra.

---

† A theorem similar to this one has been shown in Garland and Luckham [1973, Theorem 2.7].

Proof. By definition, the standard mapping S is a cslm-morphism from $P(\Sigma^*)$ into $P(W_S)$. By Lemma 10.19(4), S is even onto $P(W_S)$. Also, by the standard form theorem, $\equiv$ is the "kernel congruence" of S. Hence $P(\Sigma^*)/\equiv$ and $P(W_S)$ are isomorphic cslm's (see 1.3.6 in section 1). The theorem now follows from the obvious fact that $P(W_S)$ is a complete Boolean algebra. ///

We note the following properties of the Boolean operations in $P(\Sigma^*)/\equiv$ (see Remark 9.10).

Remark 10.28. Let A and B be arbitrary L-schemes. Then, in $P(\Sigma^*)/\equiv$, $[A] \wedge [B] = [S(A) \cap S(B)]$. (Proof: Since $S(A) \cap S(B) \subset S(A)$ and $S(A) \equiv A$, it follows that $S(A) \cap S(B) \leq A$. Similarly, $S(A) \cap S(B) \leq B$. Now suppose that C is an L-scheme such that $C \leq A$ and $C \leq B$. By the standard form theorem, $S(C) \subset S(A)$ and $S(C) \subset S(B)$. Hence $S(C) \subset S(A) \cap S(B)$. And so $C \leq S(A) \cap S(B)$). Similarly, it can be shown that the Boolean complement of [A] in $P(\Sigma^*)/\equiv$ is $[W_S - S(A)]$. ///

The second theorem charactizes the relation $\equiv$ as the smallest cslm-congruence on $P(\Sigma^*)$ of a certain type.

Theorem 10.29. The relation $\equiv$ is the smallest cslm-congruence on $P(\Sigma^*)$ such that, for all a in $P \cup \bar{P}$, $a \cup \bar{a} \equiv \varepsilon$ and $a\bar{a} \equiv \emptyset$.

Proof. Firstly, $\equiv$ is a cslm-congruence on $P(\Sigma^*)$ with the above properties (Theorem 9.9 and Example 9.4).

Secondly, let $\sim$ be a cslm-congruence on $P(\Sigma^*)$ such that, for all a in $P \cup \bar{P}$, $a \cup \bar{a} \sim \varepsilon$ and $a\bar{a} \sim \emptyset$. (Then, by Lemma 10.21, $S(A) \sim A$ for all L-schemes A). We have to show that $\equiv$ is smaller than $\sim$, that is, for any L-schemes A and B, if $A \equiv B$ then $A \sim B$. So let us assume that $A \equiv B$. Then, by the standard form theorem, $S(A) = S(B)$. Hence, by Lemma 10.21, it follows that $A \sim B$, and the theorem is proved. ///

The above theorem can be interpreted as follows. For any L-schemes A and B, A and B are equivalent if and only if the equivalence "$A \equiv B$" can be "derived" from the "axioms" $a \cup \bar{a} \equiv \varepsilon$ and $a\bar{a} \equiv \emptyset$, for all a in $P \cup \bar{P}$, by a finite number of "applications" of the cslm-properties of $P(\Sigma^*)$ and the properties of $\equiv$ as a cslm-congruence. (Note however that this "axiomatic system" is not constructive, since it uses the infinitary join operation). †

---

† In Kaplan [1969] a constructive axiomatic system for the class of regular L-schemes, resembling the above "axiomatic system" for L-schemes, is presented. It is shown that, for any regular L-schemes A and B, $A \equiv B$ if and only if "$A \equiv B$" is derivable in that system. Thus, Theorem 10.29 may be viewed as a generalization of Theorem 6 of Kaplan's paper.

11. Universal interpretations

It is well known that, when considering equivalence of program schemes, one may often restrict oneself to a proper subset of the set of all interpretations [†]. In this section we show that even one single interpretation suffices to decide whether two program schemes are equivalent or not. That is, we show the existence of an interpretation I such that any two program schemes are equivalent if they compute the same relation under I. Such an interpretation will be called "universal".

This section is organized as follows.

First we define the notion of a universal interpretation and prove that the interpretation I_o, defined in the previous section, is universal (Theorem 11.3). We also show the existence of a universal $t\tau$-interpretation (Theorem 11.12). This implies that the equivalence relations $\equiv_\tau$, $\equiv_{p\tau}$ and $\equiv_{t\tau}$ are all the same (Theorem 11.13).

Next it is shown that there is a universal interpretation in the class of free or Herbrand interpretations (Theorem 11.15).

Then, a theorem is proved which says that, in considering equivalence, one may restrict oneself to $t\tau$-interpretations with a finite domain (Theorem 11.17). However, there is no universal interpretation with a finite domain (Theorem 11.18).

Finally, we introduce a generalized notion of interpretation (called "cat-interpretation", where "cat" stands for "categorical") and show that the corresponding notion of equivalence coincides with that of τ-equivalence (Theorem 11.27). The standard mapping S turns out to be a cat-interpretation which is universal with respect to the class of all cat-interpretations (Remark 11.28).

Universal interpretations are formally defined as follows:

Definition 11.1. An interpretation I is said to be *universal* if, for all program schemes U and V, $U \equiv V$ if and only if $I(U) = I(V)$. [††]

Algebraically, an interpretation is universal if its kernel congruence

----

† See, for instance, Ashcroft, Manna and Pnueli [1973, § 2] and the discussion in Chandra and Manna [1972, § 1].

†† It is straightforward to show that, if I is universal, then for all program schemes U and V, $U \leq V$ if and only if $I(U) \subset I(V)$.

is the relation $\equiv$ (recall that, by Definition 2.10, an interpretation is a cslm-morphism).

The next lemma will be used to establish universality of interpretations.

<u>Lemma 11.2.</u> Let I be an interpretation. Then, I is universal if and only if, for all standard L-schemes A and B, if $I(A) \subset I(B)$ then $A \subset B$.

<u>Proof.</u> The if part is proved as follows. Let us assume that, for all standard L-schemes A and B, if $I(A) \subset I(B)$, then $A \subset B$. Then, for arbitrary L-schemes A and B, $A \equiv B$ if and only if $I(A) = I(B)$. (Proof: If $A \equiv B$, then, by the definition of equivalence, $I(A) = I(B)$. If $I(A) = I(B)$, then, since each L-scheme is equivalent to its standard form, $I(S(A)) = I(S(B))$. Hence, by our assumption, $S(A) = S(B)$, and so, by the standard form theorem, $A \equiv B$). From this, it easily follows that, for arbitrary program schemes U and V, $U \equiv V$ if and only if $I(U) = I(V)$.

The easy only-if part of the proof is left to the reader. ///

The existence of universal interpretations is shown in the next theorem†.

<u>Theorem 11.3.</u> I_o is a universal interpretation.

<u>Proof.</u> The theorem follows directly from Lemma 10.12 and Lemma 11.2. ///

It is easy to see that, since I_o is a pτ-interpretation (Lemma 10.8), the above theorem implies that the equivalence relations $\equiv_{p\tau}$ and $\equiv$ are the same. Note however, that I_o is not a tτ-interpretation. Thus, in order to show that the equivalence relations $\equiv_{t\tau}$ and $\equiv$ are the same (see Remark 9.3), we have to find a universal tτ-interpretation.

For later use, we first define a universal pτ-interpretation I_1, related to I_o. Then we define a universal tτ-interpretation I_2.

---

† For the definition of I_o, see Definition 10.7.
The existence of a universal interpretation was suggested to the author by P. van Emde Boas (personal communication).

Definition 11.4. The general interpretation $I_1 = (D_1, h_1)$ is defined as follows.

(1) $D_1 = (T_S \cdot F)^* \times W_S$.

(2) For each f in F,

$h_1(f) = \{((\psi, tf\phi), (\psi tf, \phi)) \mid \psi \in (T_S \cdot F)^*, t \in T_S \text{ and } \phi \in W_S\}$.

(3) For each a in $P \cup \overline{P}$,

$h_1(a) = \{((\psi, t\phi), (\psi, t\phi)) \mid \psi \in (T_S \cdot F)^*,\ t \in T_S, \phi \in (F \cdot T_S)^* \text{ and } a \text{ \underline{in} } t\}$.†

Lemma 11.5. I_1 is a pτ-interpretation.

Proof. Similar to the proof of Lemma 10.8. ///

Example 11.6 (See Example 10.11). Let $P = \{p,q\}$ and $F = \{f,g\}$. Then $I_1(qppfg\overline{q}\overline{q})$ contains the pairs of pairs $((\varepsilon, pqf\overline{p}qgp\overline{q}fpq), (pqf\overline{p}qg, p\overline{q}fpq))$ and $((\overline{p}qg, pqfpqgp\overline{q}), (\overline{p}\overline{q}gpqfqg, p\overline{q}))$. ///

Intuitively, I_1 imitates the interpretation I_0 on the second coordinate of an element of D_1, and remembers the history of its computation in the first coordinate of that element. This is expressed formally in the following lemma, the proof of which is left to the reader.

Lemma 11.7. Let A be an L-scheme, and let (ϕ_1, ψ_1) and (ϕ_2, ψ_2) be elements of D_1. Then, $((\phi_1, \psi_1), (\phi_2, \psi_2)) \in I_1(A)$ if and only if $(\psi_1, \psi_2) \in I_0(A)$ and $\phi_1 \psi_1 = \phi_2 \psi_2$.

This implies that I_1 is universal.

Lemma 11.8. I_1 is a universal interpretation.

Proof. By Lemma 11.2 and the universality of I_0, it suffices to show that, for any L-schemes A and B, if $I_1(A) \subset I_1(B)$, then $I_0(A) \subset I_0(B)$. So let us assume that $I_1(A) \subset I_1(B)$, and let (ψ_1, ψ_2) be an arbitrary element of $I_0(A)$. Then, by Lemma 10.9, there is a ψ in $(T_S F)^*$ such that

---

† For the definition of "<u>in</u>", see 1.2.1.

$\psi_1 = \psi\psi_2$. Hence, by Lemma 11.7, $((\varepsilon,\psi_1),(\psi,\psi_2)) \in I_1(A)$. Consequently, since $I_1(A) \subset I_1(B)$, $((\varepsilon,\psi_1),(\psi,\psi_2)) \in I_1(B)$, and so, again by Lemma 11.7, $(\psi_1,\psi_2) \in I_o(B)$. Thus $I_o(A) \subset I_o(B)$ and the lemma is proved. ///

Using the interpretation I_1, we define the tτ-interpretation I_2, and prove that it is universal.

Definition 11.9. The general interpretation $I_2 = (D_2,h_2)$ is defined as follows.

(1) D_2 is the set of all finite subsets of D_1.

(2) For each f in F,
$h_2(f) = \{(X,Y) \mid Y=\{y \in D_1 \mid (x,y) \in h_1(f) \text{ for some x in } X\}\}$.

(3) For each p in P,
$h_2(p) = \{(X,X) \mid \text{ for each x in X, } (x,x) \in h_1(p)\}$, and
$h_2(\bar{p}) = \{(X,X) \mid \text{ there exists x in X such that } (x,x) \in h_1(\bar{p})\}$.

Lemma 11.10. I_2 is a tτ-interpretation.

The proof of this lemma is left to the reader.

Example 11.11 (See Examples 11.6 and 10.11). Let $P = \{p,q\}$ and $F = \{f,g\}$. Then, for the argument $\{(\varepsilon,pqf\bar{p}qgp\bar{q}fpq),(\bar{p}\bar{q}g,pqfpqgpq)\}$, the partial function $I_2(qppfg\bar{q}\bar{q})$ has the value
$\{(pqf\bar{p}qg,p\bar{q}fpq),(\bar{p}\bar{q}gpqfpqg,pq)\}$. ///

Theorem 11.12. I_2 is a universal interpretation.

Proof. By Lemma 11.2 and the universality of I_1, it suffices to show that, for all L-schemes A and B, if $I_2(A) \subset I_2(B)$, then $I_1(A) \subset I_1(B)$. But this easily follows from the following obvious fact: for all x and y in D_1 and each L-scheme A, $(x,y) \in I_1(A)$ if and only if $(\{x\},\{y\}) \in I_2(A)$. ///

Note that Definition 11.9, Lemma 11.10 and Theorem 11.12 do not use specific properties of I_1, but only the fact that I_1 is a universal interpretation. The specific properties of I_1 will be used in section 14.

The next theorem shows that equivalence of program schemes does not depend on whether function symbols are interpreted in the class of relations, or in the class of partial functions or in the class of total functions.

Theorem 11.13. For all program schemes U and V , $U \equiv V$ if and only if $U \equiv_{t\tau} V$. †

Proof. Let U and V be arbitrary program schemes. Obviously, if $U \equiv V$, then $U \equiv_{t\tau} V$. If $U \equiv_{t\tau} V$, then, since I_2 is a $t\tau$-interpretation, $I_2(U) = I_2(V)$ and so, by the universality of I_2, $U \equiv V$. ///

In other words, the equivalence relations $\equiv_{t\tau}$, $\equiv_{p\tau}$ and $\equiv_{\tau}$ are all the same.

We now briefly discuss "free" interpretations.††

Definition 11.14. An interpretation I is said to be free if $D_I = F^*$ and, for each f in F, $I(f) = \{(\phi, \phi f) | \phi \epsilon F^*\}$.

Thus, free interpretations differ only in the interpretation of the predicate symbols.

In the next theorem it is shown that free interpretations can be universal.

---

† See Remark 9.3.

†† Free interpretations were introduced in Luckham, Park and Paterson [1970, p.225]. In Ashcroft, Manna and Pnueli [1973, § 2] , they are called "Herbrand" interpretations.

† Theorem 11.15. If F is nonempty, then there are universal free interpretations.

Proof. It is easy to see that a free interpretation I exists, satisfying the following requirement: for every $k \geq 0$, every sequence of standard tests $t_1, t_2, \ldots, t_{k+1}$ and every sequence of function symbols $f_1, f_2, \ldots, f_k$, there is a word ω in D_I such that $(\omega,\omega) \in I(t_1)$, $(\omega f_1, \omega f_1) \in I(t_2)$, $(\omega f_1 f_2, \omega f_1 f_2) \in I(t_3), \ldots,$ $(\omega f_1 f_2 \cdots f_k, \omega f_1 f_2 \cdots f_k) \in I(t_{k+1})$. Let I_H be any such interpretation. We claim that I_H is universal. This is proved using Lemma 11.2 as follows. Let A and B be standard L-schemes such that $I_H(A) \subset I_H(B)$. We have to show that $A \subset B$. Let ϕ be an arbitrary element of A. Then ϕ is of the form $t_1 f_1 t_2 f_2 \cdots t_k f_k t_{k+1}$, where $k \geq 0$, $t_1, \ldots, t_{k+1} \in T_S$ and $f_1, \ldots, f_k \in F$. Hence, by the definition of I_H, there is a word ω in F^* such that for all i $(0 \leq i \leq k)$, $(\omega f_1 \cdots f_i, \omega f_1 \cdots f_i) \in I_H(t_{i+1})$. This implies that $(\omega, \omega f_1 f_2 \cdots f_k) \in I_H(\phi)$. Consequently, since $I_H(A) \subset I_H(B)$, there is a word ψ in B such that $(\omega, \omega f_1 f_2 \cdots f_k) \in I_H(\psi)$. Clearly, this is possible only if $\psi = \phi$, and so ϕ is an element of B. Thus the theorem holds. ///

It follows from Theorem 11.12 (and also from Theorem 11.15) that there are universal $t\tau$-interpretations with a countable domain. Thus, two program schemes are equivalent if they compute the same relation under all $t\tau$-interpretations with a countable domain. The question arises

---

† In Luckham, Park and Paterson [1970, p.225] it is shown that two program schemes are equivalent if they compute the same relation under all free interpretations. Hence, Theorem 11.15 looks like a stronger result. However, in the literature (and in particular in Luckham, Park and Paterson [1970]), an interpretation is frequently defined as a triple (D,h,x), where (D,h) is an interpretation in our sense and x in D is the input. A free interpretation is then defined as a triple (D,h,ε), where (D,h) is a free interpretation as defined above. Hence, in the literature, the input is fixed and the predicates vary. In this theorem we show that we can fix the predicates, when the input is allowed to vary.

whether the same is true for tτ-interpretations with a finite domain (the answer will be "yes"), and, in particular, whether a universal interpretation with a finite domain exists (the answer will be "no").

Definition 11.16. Let U and V be program schemes. We write $U \le_{fin} V$ if, for all tτ-interpretations I with finite domain, $I(U) \subset I(V)$. Also, we write $U \equiv_{fin} V$ if $U \le_{fin} V$ and $V \le_{fin} U$.

In the next theorem it is shown that any two program schemes are equivalent if they compute the same relation under all tτ-interpretations with a finite domain.

† Theorem 11.17. Let U and V be program schemes. Then, $U \equiv_{fin} V$ if and only if $U \equiv V$.

Proof. The if part of the proof is trivial. To prove the only-if part, we first consider the case of standard L-schemes, and prove that

(*) for any standard L-schemes A and B, if $A \le_{fin} B$, then $A \subset B$.

Let A and B be arbitrary standard L-schemes such that $A \le_{fin} B$, and let ϕ be an arbitrary element of A. We have to show that $\phi \in B$. The standard word ϕ is of the form $t_1 f_1 t_2 f_2 \cdots t_k f_k t_{k+1}$, for some $k \ge 0$, $t_1, \dots, t_{k+1} \in T_S$ and $f_1, \dots, f_k \in F$. Let $I = (D,h)$ be the following interpretation:

(1) $D = \{0,1,2,\dots,k+1\}$.

(2) For each f in F,
$h(f) = \{(i,i+1) \mid 1 \le i \le k \text{ and } f = f_i\} \cup \{(i,0) \mid 1 \le i \le k \text{ and } f \ne f_i\} \cup \{(0,0)\} \cup \{k+1,0\}$.

(3) For each p in P,
$h(p) = \{(i,i) \mid 1 \le i \le k+1 \text{ and } p \text{ \underline{in} } t_i\} \cup \{(0,0)\}$, and
$h(\bar{p}) = \{(i,i) \mid 1 \le i \le k+1 \text{ and } \bar{p} \text{ \underline{in} } t_i\}$.††

---

† This is called the "compactness" property of equivalence. See Luckham, Park and Paterson [1970, Theorem 2.2] and Milner [1970, Theorem 6.2].

†† For the definition of "in", see 1.2.1.

Clearly, $(1,k+1) \in I(\phi)$. Hence, since I is obviously a $t\tau$-interpretation with a finite domain, there is a word ψ in B such that $(1,k+1) \in I(\psi)$. From this, it easily follows that $\psi = \phi$, and so ϕ is an element of B.

We leave it to the reader to prove that the theorem follows from (*).

///

We now show that, in general, there are no universal interpretations with a finite domain.

Theorem 11.18. If F is nonempty, then there is no universal interpretation with a finite domain.

Proof. Let us assume, to the contrary, that I is a universal interpretation with finite domain. Then, for all L-schemes A and B, $A \equiv B$ if and only if $I(A) = I(B)$. Consequently, the number of equivalence classes in $P(\Sigma^*)$ is finite. By the standard form theorem, it follows that $P(W_S)$ is a finite set (see also the proof of Theorem 10.27). Clearly, this is possible only if F is empty. Hence no such interpretation exists. ///

Note that, if F is empty, then I_2 is a universal $t\tau$-interpretation with a finite domain.

So far we have considered classes of interpretations properly included in the class of τ-interpretations, and we have proved that the resulting notions of equivalence coincide with τ-equivalence. In the rest of this section we propose a generalization of the notion of τ-interpretation (which we call cat-interpretation), and show that the corresponding notion of equivalence coincides with τ-equivalence. It is also shown that the standard mapping S can be viewed as a cat-interpretation which is universal with respect to the class of all cat-interpretations.

Readers who are not familiar with the notion of category may skip the rest of this section.

Definition 11.19. A cat-cslm is a cslm consisting of all sets of morphisms of a category, as defined in Example 1.3.4.4.

Example 11.20. It was shown in Example 1.3.4.4 that $P(\Sigma^*)$ is a cat-cslm, and also that, for any set D, $P(D \times D)$ is a cat-cslm.

By Remark 10.16, $P(W_S)$ is a cat-cslm. ///

Note that a cat-cslm is a natural generalization of a cslm $P(D \times D)$, where D is any set of objects. In fact, the notion of a set of morphisms is a natural generalization of the notion of a relation, since a morphism may be regarded as a pair of objects, together with a way of computing the second object from the first.

In the next definition we generalize the notion of predicate.

Definition 11.21. Let $C = (P(M), \star, \{e_A | A \in K\}, \subset, \bigcup)$ be a cat-cslm (for the notation used, see Example 1.3.4.4). A pair (p,q) with p and q in $P(M)$ is called a total predicate of C if $p \cup q = \{e_A | A \in K\}$ and $p \cap q = \emptyset$.

Note that, if (p,q) is a total predicate of C as above, then (p,q) can be viewed as a total predicate on the set K of objects.

Example 11.22. For any set D, the total predicates of the cat-cslm $P(D \times D)$ are precisely the total predicates on D. In the cat-cslm $P(\Sigma^\star)$ there are two total predicates, namely $(\varepsilon, \emptyset)$ and $(\emptyset, \varepsilon)$. In the cat-cslm $P(W_S)$, a total predicate is a pair (A,B) with $A \cup B = T_S$ and $A \cap B = \emptyset$. ///

The obvious generalization of the notion of interpretation is defined as follows.†

Definition 11.23. A cat-interpretation is a cslm-morphism I from $P(\Sigma^\star)$ into some cat-cslm C such that, for each p in P, $(I(p), I(\bar{p}))$ is a total predicate of C.

Example 11.24. By its definition, the standard mapping S is a cat-interpretation from $P(\Sigma^\star)$ into the cat-cslm $P(W_S)$.
Note also that each τ-interpretation is a cat-interpretation. ///

---

† See Definition 2.10.

Finally, we define cat-equivalence of L-schemes.

Definition 11.25. Let A and B be L-schemes. We say that A and B are cat-equivalent, denoted by $A \equiv_{cat} B$, if, for all cat-interpretations I, I(A) = I(B).

The following lemma summarizes the elementary properties of cat-equivalence. Its proof, which is similar to the proofs of Lemma 9.7 and Example 9.4, is left to the reader.

Lemma 11.26. The relation $\equiv_{cat}$ is a cslm-congruence on $P(\Sigma^*)$, such that, for all a in $P \cup \overline{P}$, $a \cup \bar{a} \equiv_{cat} \varepsilon$ and $a\bar{a} \equiv_{cat} \emptyset$.

We are now in a position to prove that cat-equivalence and τ-equivalence are identical relations.

Theorem 11.27. For any two L-schemes A and B, $A \equiv_{cat} B$ if and only if $A \equiv B$.

Proof. The only-if part follows directly from the fact that each τ-interpretation is a cat-interpretation. The if part is a direct consequence of Lemma 11.26 and Theorem 10.29. ///

Remark 11.28. It follows from Theorem 11.27 and the standard form theorem that the standard mapping S is a "cat-universal" cat-interpretation, meaning that, for any two L-schemes A and B, $A \equiv_{cat} B$ if and only if S(A) = S(B). ///

Note that Definition 11.25, Theorem 11.27 and Remark 11.28 are not formulated for arbitrary program schemes. This is because we did not define "the set of morphisms I(U) computed by program scheme U under cat-interpretation I". It should be clear to the reader that a natural definition of this concept could be given for the program schemes discussed in Part I, in such a way that, for any program scheme U and any cat-interpretation I, I(L(U)) = I(U). From this the general versions of Definition 11.25, Theorem 11.27 and Remark 11.28 would follow.

12. Equivalence with partial predicates

In this section we consider π-equivalence.[†]

As already explained in Remark 9.3, we have tried to formulate our definitions and results on τ-equivalence (in sections 9, 10 and 11) in such a way, that only slight changes are needed to convert them into the appropriate definitions and results on π-equivalence. It turns out that all theorems concerning τ-equivalence (except for Theorem 10.27) have obvious counterparts for the case of π-equivalence.

We now discuss the alterations which have to be made to sections 9, 10 and 11 in order to obtain a theory of π-equivalence.

First of all, the symbol τ should be replaced by the symbol π everywhere in these three sections (except for Definition 9.1, Notation 9.2 and Remark 9.3). This should be done also whenever τ occurs "implicitly" (recall Notation 9.2), meaning that, for example, "$\equiv$" and "$\leq$" should be replaced by "$\equiv_\pi$" and "$\leq_\pi$" respectively, "equivalent" by "π-equivalent", and "interpretation" by "π-interpretation". Also the phrase "total predicate" should be replaced by the phrase "partial predicate".

All other changes will now be discussed systematically section by section.

Section 9. We only consider the introduction and the text from Example 9.4 onwards.

- Example 9.4(1) should be replaced by "$a \leq_\pi \varepsilon$" (or what amounts to the same, "$a \cup \varepsilon \equiv_\pi \varepsilon$").
- Example 9.8(2) should be replaced by "$(p \to A, A) \leq_\pi A$".

---

† Note that, for all program schemes U and V, if $U \equiv_\pi V$, then $U \equiv_\tau V$. Note also that the relations $\equiv_\pi$ and $\equiv_\tau$ are not the same (for instance, for any p in P, $p \cup \bar{p}$ and ε are τ-equivalent, but not π-equivalent. For these reasons, in McCarthy [1963, section 7], the relations $\equiv_\tau$ and $\equiv_\pi$ are called "weak" and "strong" equivalence respectively.

No other changes are needed.

We note the following about the π-versions of the theorems of this section. The π-version of Theorem 9.6 has the same content as its τ-version, since it is assumed that P is empty. The π-version of Theorem 9.9 states that $P(\Sigma^*)/\equiv_\pi$ is a cslm. The π-version of Theorem 9.11 states that substitution preserves π-equivalence.

Section 10

The first pages of section 10, from Definition 10.1 to Example 10.6 should be replaced by the text below (included between the words begin and end). This text introduces all the essential changes, which have to be made when considering π-equivalence.

begin

Definition 10.1 (π). Let $P = \{p_1, p_2, \ldots, p_m\}$. Let, for all i in $\{1,2,\ldots,m\}$, P_i' denote $\{p_i, \bar{p}_i, \varepsilon\}$. A π-standard test is any element of $P_1' \cdot P_2' \cdots P_m'$ (where for m = 0 we assume that $P_1' \cdot P_2' \cdots P_m' = \{\varepsilon\}$).

We shall use T_S^π to denote the set of all π-standard tests.

Example 10.2 (π). If $P = \{p,q\}$, then $T_S^\pi = \{\varepsilon, p, \bar{p}, q, \bar{q}, pq, p\bar{q}, \bar{p}q, \bar{p}\bar{q}\}$. If $P = \{p\}$, then $T_S^\pi = \{\varepsilon, p, \bar{p}\}$. If $P = \emptyset$, then $T_S^\pi = \{\varepsilon\}$. ///

Intuitively, a π-standard test is a test which, under any π-interpretation I, computes the values of the predicates $(I(p), I(\bar{p}))$ for some of the p in P, exactly once and in a fixed order.

Definition 10.3 (π). A π-standard word is any element of $(T_S^\pi \cdot F)^* \cdot T_S^\pi$.

We shall use W_S^π to denote the set of all π-standard words.

Definition. Let ϕ and ψ be in Σ^*. We write ϕ cont ψ, if the following holds: there exist $k \geq 0$, $t_1, t_2, \ldots, t_{k+1}$ and $t_1', t_2', \ldots, t_{k+1}'$ in T, and $f_1, f_2, \ldots, f_k$ in F, such that

(1) for all i ($1 \leq i \leq k+1$), t_i in t_i',

(2) $\phi = t_1 f_1 t_2 f_2 \cdots t_k f_k t_{k+1}$, and

(3) $\psi = t_1' f_1 t_2' f_2 \cdots t_k' f_k t_{k+1}'$.

Definition 10.4 (π). A π-standard L-scheme A is an element of $P(W_S^\pi)$ such that, for all ϕ and ψ in Σ^*, if $\phi \epsilon A$ and ϕ cont ψ, then $\psi \epsilon A$.

The set of all π-standard L-schemes will be denoted by $P_\pi(W_S^\pi)$.

Definition 10.5 (π). A program scheme U is said to be π-standard if L(U) is a π-standard L-scheme. A program scheme V is said to be a π-standard form of a program scheme V_1 if V is standard and π-equivalent to V_1.

Example 10.6 (π). Let P = {p,q} and F = {f}. Then, $pqf\bar{q}$ cont $pqfp\bar{q}$. The L-scheme $A = (pqf)^*(\bar{p}q \cup \bar{q})$ is not a π-standard L-scheme, but all elements of A are π-standard words. The L-scheme $B = (pqf)^*(\bar{p}q \cup \bar{q} \cup p\bar{q} \cup \bar{p}\bar{q})$ is π-standard. Note that $A \equiv_\pi B$. ///

end

In the rest of section 10 and in section 11, the following replacements should be made:

standard	by	π-standard
T_S, W_S, $P(W_S)$	by	T_S^π, W_S^π, $P_\pi(W_S^\pi)$ respectively
I_o, D_o, h_o	by	I_o^π, D_o^π, h_o^π respectively
S	by	S_π.

Apart from these replacements, the following changes should be made in the rest of section 10.

- All Examples should be skipped.
- The proof of Lemma 10.8 should be adapted in an obvious way.
- Remark 10.10 should be skipped.
- In the proof of Lemma 10.12, the last two sentences should be replaced by the following: "It follows from Lemma 10.9 that ω cont ϕ, and thus, since ω is in B, it follows from the definition of π-standard L-scheme that ϕ is an element of B. Hence $A \subset B$."
- In Definition 10.13 and 10.17, it should be checked that the π-standard L-schemes involved, really are π-standard.
- The statement of Lemma 10.21 should be as follows: "Let $\sim$ be a cslm-congruence on $P(\Sigma^*)$ such that, for all a and b in $P \cup \bar{P}$, (1) $a \cup \varepsilon \sim \varepsilon$, (2) $a\bar{a} \sim \emptyset$, (3) $aa \sim a$, and (4) $ab \sim ba$. Then, for any L-scheme A, $S_\pi(A) \sim A$."

In the proof of this lemma, the proofs of (3) and (4) should be skipped, and, in the case that $\phi_i = \varepsilon$, the set A_i (where $1 \le i \le m$) should be defined as $\{p_i, \bar{p}_i, \varepsilon\}$.

- Theorem 10.27 should be skipped, since its π-version is not true. $P(\Sigma^*)/\equiv_\pi$ is a complete lattice (since it is a cslm), but not a Boolean algebra. (To see this, note that the cslm's $P(\Sigma^*)/\equiv_\pi$ and $P_\pi(W_S^\pi)$ are isomorphic, and, obviously, $P_\pi(W_S^\pi)$ is not a Boolean algebra).
- In Remark 10.28 the last sentence should be skipped.
- The statement of Theorem 10.29 should be as follows: "The relation $\equiv_\pi$ is the smallest cslm-congruence on $P(\Sigma^*)$ such that, for all a and b in $P \cup \bar{P}$, $a \cup \varepsilon \equiv_\pi \varepsilon$, $a\bar{a} \equiv_\pi \emptyset$, $aa \equiv_\pi a$ and $ab \equiv_\pi ba$."

The proof of Theorem 10.29 should be adapted accordingly.

We note the following about the π-versions of the theorems of Section 10. The <u>π-standard form theorem</u> says that, for all program schemes U and V, $U \le_\pi V$ if and only if $S_\pi(L(U)) \subset S_\pi(L(V))$, and $U \equiv_\pi V$ if and only if $S_\pi(L(U)) = S_\pi(L(V))$. The π-version of Theorem 10.29 is stated above.

<u>Section 11</u>. We only consider section 11 up to (and including) Theorem 11.18. Apart from the replacements mentioned before, the following should be made:

universal	by	π-universal
I_1, D_1, h_1	by	I_1^π, D_1^π, h_1^π respectively
I_2, D_2, h_2	by	I_2^π, D_2^π, h_2^π respectively
$\le_{fin}$, $\equiv_{fin}$	by	$\le_{\pi fin}$, $\equiv_{\pi fin}$ respectively

Furthermore, the following changes should be made:

- All Examples should be skipped.
- The proof of Theorem 11.15 should be adapted in an obvious way, left to the reader.
- In the proof of Theorem 11.17, the sentence before the last one should be replaced by "From this it easily follows that ψ <u>cont</u> φ, and so φ is an element of B".

The π-versions of the theorems in this part of section 11 are listed below.

I_1^π is a π-universal π-interpretation.

I_2^π is a π-universal tπ-interpretation.

For all program schemes U and V, $U \equiv_\pi V$ if and only if $U \equiv_{t\pi} V$.

If F is nonempty, then there are π-universal free π-interpretations.

For all program schemes U and V, $U \equiv_{\pi\mathrm{fin}} V$ if and only if $U \equiv_{\pi} V$.

If F is nonempty, then there is no π-universal π-interpretation with a finite domain.

13. Generalized shift distributions

It is often useful to postulate certain connections between the instruction symbols, and to consider only those interpretations which satisfy these postulates. For instance, in Ianov [1960] the so called shift distributions were introduced. In a shift distribution one associates with each function symbol f a set P_f of positive predicate symbols, and one restricts attention to interpretations I such that the application of I(f) changes only the values of predicates $(I(p), I(\bar{p}))$ with p in P_f. The following extension of the notion of shift distribution was introduced by Rutledge [1964] and investigated by Kaplan [1969]. With each function symbol f one associates a subset A_f of $T_S \times T_S$, and one restricts attention to interpretations I such that application of I(f) changes the predicate values only as allowed by A_f (more precisely: if $(x,y) \in I(f)$, then there should be a pair (t_1,t_2) in A_f such that $(x,x) \in I(t_1)$ and $(y,y) \in I(t_2)$).

In this section we first define the very general notion of "hypothesis". Given a set H of hypotheses, two program schemes are defined to be H-equivalent if they compute the same relation under all interpretations which satisfy the hypotheses in H. It is shown that H-equivalence is a cslm-congruence on $P(\Sigma^*)$ (Theorem 13.8).

Then we introduce the notion of generalized shift distribution (which lies between the notion of shift distribution, as described above, and the notion of a set of hypotheses). For a given generalized shift distribution H, an "H-standard mapping" S_H is defined, and it is shown that an "H-standard form theorem" holds: for all program schemes U and V, U and V are H-equivalent if and only if the mapping S_H transforms their L-schemes into the same L-scheme (Theorem 13.24). We also prove two algebraic characterizations of the H-equivalence relation (Theorems 13.25 and 13.26).

Finally, for a given generalized shift distribution H, it is shown that an "H-universal" interpretation exists, that is, an interpretation I, satisfying H, such that two program schemes are H-equivalent if and only if they compute the same relation under I (Theorem 13.28).

Since the definitions and results of this section will develop along the same lines as those in sections 9, 10 and 11, they will be given with a few comments only.

We first define the notion of hypothesis, and that of an interpretation satisfying a set of hypotheses.

Definition 13.1. A hypothesis is any pair of program schemes. An L-scheme hypothesis is any pair of L-schemes.

Definition 13.2. Let H be a set of hypotheses, and let I be an interpretation. We say that I is an H-interpretation, or that I satisfies H, if, for all hypotheses (U,V) in H, I(U) = I(V).

Thus the use of a hypothesis (U,V) indicates that one is only interested in those interpretations, under which U and V compute the same relation.

Example 13.3. Let F = {f} and P = {p}. Consider the L-scheme hypothesis $(pf\bar{p} \cup \bar{p}fp, \emptyset)$, and let H be the set consisting of this hypothesis only. Then an interpretation I satisfies H, if application of the relation I(f) does not change the value of the predicate $(I(p), I(\bar{p}))$. Let, for instance, I be the interpretation with the set of integers as its domain, $I(f) = \{(x,y) \mid y=x+2\}$, $I(p) = \{(x,x) \mid x \text{ is even}\}$ and $I(\bar{p}) = \{(x,x) \mid x \text{ is odd}\}$. Obviously, $I(pf\bar{p}) = I(\bar{p}fp) = \emptyset$, and so I is an H-interpretation. ///

Next, we define equivalence of program schemes under the assumption of a set of hypotheses.

† Definition 13.4. Let H be a set of hypotheses, and let U and V be program schemes. We say that U is H-equivalent to V, denoted by $U \equiv_H V$,

---

† The general notion of H-equivalence was introduced in de Bakker and Scott [1969]. In that paper, an equivalence "$U \equiv_H V$", where $H = \{(U_1,V_1),\ldots,(U_n,V_n)\}$, is written as "$U_1 = V_1, \ldots, U_n = V_n \vdash U = V$", and is called an "implication" (the notation is obviously borrowed from logic). In de Bakker [1971, Definition 3.2] it is called an "assertion". In the latter monograph, many examples of specific sets of hypotheses can be found.

if, for all H-interpretations I, I(U) = I(V). We say that U is <u>H-covered</u> by V, denoted by $U \leq_H V$, if, for all H-interpretations I, $I(U) \subset I(V)$.

<u>Example 13.5</u>. Consider the set H of Example 13.3. Obviously, $f \equiv_H pfp \cup \bar{p}f\bar{p}$ and $pff\bar{p} \equiv_H \emptyset$. ///

Again, as a consequence of our L-scheme point of view, it suffices to consider the case of L-schemes. This is shown in the next lemma. First, a definition is needed.

<u>Definition 13.6</u>. Let H be a set of hypotheses. The <u>set of L-scheme hypotheses corresponding to H</u>, denoted by L(H), is defined by $L(H) = \{(A,B) \mid L(U)=A \text{ and } L(V)=B \text{ for some axiom } (U,V) \text{ in } H\}$.

<u>Lemma 13.7</u>. For each set H of hypotheses, and each pair of program schemes U and V,

$U \leq_H V$ if and only if $L(U) \leq_{L(H)} L(V)$, and

$U \equiv_H V$ if and only if $L(U) \equiv_{L(H)} L(V)$.

<u>Proof</u>. Since, for each program scheme W, $L(W) \equiv W$, it follows that the class of H-interpretations coincides with the class of L(H)-interpretations. It also follows that $U \leq_H V$ if and only if $L(U) \leq_H L(V)$. From this, the lemma can easily be proved. ///

The elementary properties of H-equivalence of L-schemes are expressed in the following theorem.

<u>Theorem 13.8</u>. Let H be a set of L-scheme hypotheses. Then $\equiv_H$ is a cslm-congruence on $P(\Sigma^*)$ †, such that, for any L-schemes A and B,

(1) if $(A,B) \in H$, then $A \equiv_H B$, and

(2) if $A \equiv B$, then $A \equiv_H B$.

The easy proof of this theorem is left to the reader.

---

† Consequently, $P(\Sigma^*)/\equiv_H$ is a cslm (c.f. Theorem 9.9).

Remark 13.9. It is an open problem whether, for each set H of L-scheme hypotheses, $\equiv_H$ is the smallest cslm-congruence on $P(\Sigma^*)$ satisfying (1) and (2) in the above theorem. In Theorem 13.26 this problem is solved for the special case of generalized shift distributions. ///

In the rest of this section, the so called generalized shift distributions will be discussed. Let us first recall the notion of shift distribution as it occurs in the literature.

Definition 13.10. A Rutledge shift distribution is a set of hypotheses consisting of one hypothesis of the form $(Q,\emptyset)$, where Q is a subset of $T_S \cdot F \cdot T_S$.[†]

Intuitively, a Rutledge shift distribution determines the predicate values which cannot, and which can, occur after application of some I(f), with f in F, to an argument with given predicate values.

Example 13.11. Let $P = \{p,q\}$ and $F = \{f,g\}$. Consider the Rutledge shift distribution $H = \{(Q,\emptyset)\}$, where $Q = T_S f(p\bar{q} \cup \bar{p}q \cup \bar{p}\bar{q}) \cup T_S g T_S$. Then, an interpretation I satisfies H if, firstly, $I(g) = \emptyset$, and secondly, after application of I(f) to any argument, the predicates $(I(p), I(\bar{p}))$ and $(I(q), I(\bar{q}))$ have the value true for the result. ///

It should be clear that the notion of shift distribution introduced by Ianov [1960], as discussed in the introduction to this section, can be viewed as a special case of a Rutledge shift distribution[††]. An example of such a shift distribution was given in Example 13.3.

We now generalize the notion of shift distribution.

---

† If with each function symbol f a subset A_f of $T_S \times T_S$ is associated, as explained in the introduction to this section, then it should be clear to the reader that the corresponding Rutledge shift distribution consists of the hypothesis $(Q,\emptyset)$, where $Q = \{t_1 f t_2 \mid (t_1,t_2) \text{ is not in } A_f\}$.

†† See Rutledge [1964, footnote on p.2].

Definition 13.12. A generalized shift distribution (abbreviated by gsd) is a set of hypotheses, consisting of one hypothesis of the form $(Q,\emptyset)$, where Q is any L-scheme.†

In the sequel we shall write $H = (Q,\emptyset)$ rather than $H = \{(Q,\emptyset)\}$.

Thus, a generalized shift distribution $H = (Q,\emptyset)$ forces us to consider only interpretations I such that, for all ϕ in Q, $I(\phi) = \emptyset$.

Example 13.13. Let $F = \{f\}$ and $P = \{p\}$. Consider the gsd $H = (fff^{*}p,\emptyset)$. The H-interpretations are those interpretations I such that, if one applies I(f) two or more times to any element of D_I, then the predicate $(I(p), I(\bar{p}))$ is false for the result. ///

An example of the use of generalized shift distributions will be given in Example 17.2.

Convention 13.14. In the rest of this section, Q will denote an arbitrary, but fixed L-scheme. Furthermore, H will denote the corresponding gsd $(Q,\emptyset)$. ///

In order to prove a lemma (Lemma 13.18) which is basic to the proof of the "H-standard form theorem", we first introduce a particular interpretation, related to the interpretation I_o of section 10, and show that it is an H-interpretation.

Definition 13.15. The general interpretation $I_o^H = (D_o^H, h_o^H)$ is defined as follows.

(1) $D_o^H = W_S - S(\Sigma^{*}\cdot Q\cdot\Sigma^{*})$.

(2) For each σ in Σ, $h_o^H(\sigma) = h_o(\sigma) \cap (D_o^H \times D_o^H)$.

In the next lemma we describe the relation computed by an L-scheme under I_o^H.

---

† Obviously we might assume without loss of generality that Q is standard. Such generalized shift distributions were briefly considered in Kaplan [1969, bottom of p.384].

Lemma 13.16. For each L-scheme A, $I_o^H(A) = I_o(A) \cap (D_o^H \times W_S)$.

Proof. It is a direct consequence of the definition of D_o^H that, for any ϕ and ψ in Σ^*, and any σ in Σ, if $\phi \in D_o^H$ and $(\phi,\psi) \in h_o(\sigma)$, then $\psi \in D_o^H$. From this, the lemma easily follows. ///

The next lemma shows that I_o^H satisfies H.

Lemma 13.17. I_o^H is an H-interpretation.

Proof. It suffices to show that, for each ω in S(Q), $I_o^H(\omega) = \emptyset$. (Then $I_o^H(S(Q)) = \emptyset$. Thus $I_o^H(Q) = \emptyset$ and the lemma is proved).

Let us suppose, to the contrary, that there are ω in S(Q) and ϕ,ψ in D_o^H, such that $(\phi,\psi) \in I_o^H(\omega)$. Then, by Lemma 13.16 and Lemma 10.9 (and Remark 10.10), ω is a prefix of ϕ. Hence, since $S(\Sigma^*Q\Sigma^*) = (T_S F)^* \cdot S(Q) \cdot (FT_S)^*$, ϕ is an element of $S(\Sigma^*Q\Sigma^*)$. This contradicts the fact that ϕ is in D_o^H. ///

Now we can prove the basic lemma.

Lemma 13.18. Let A and B be standard L-schemes included in D_o^H. Then the following three statements are equivalent.

(1) $A \leq_H B$,

(2) $I_o^H(A) \subset I_o^H(B)$, and

(3) $A \subset B$.

Proof.

(1) ⇒ (2). By the definition of $\leq_H$, and Lemma 13.17.

(3) ⇒ (1). By Theorem 13.8(2).

(2) ⇒ (3), Using Lemma 13.16, it is easy to give a proof similar to the proof of Lemma 10.12. ///

Next, the "H-standard mapping" is defined.

Definition 13.19. The H-standard mapping S_H from $P(\Sigma^*)$ into $P(D_o^H)$ is defined as follows: for every L-scheme A, $S_H(A) = S(A) - S(\Sigma^* \cdot Q \cdot \Sigma^*)$.

In other words, for every L-scheme A, $S_H(A) = S(A) \cap D_o^H$.

Example 13.20. Consider the gsd $H = (fff^*p, \emptyset)$ of Example 13.13. Then $S_H((pf)^*\bar{p}) = \{\bar{p}, pf\bar{p}, pfpf\bar{p}\}$. ///

The next lemma will be used to show that, for every L-scheme A, $S_H(A) \equiv_H A$.

Lemma 13.21. Let $\sim$ be a cslm-congruence on $P(\Sigma^*)$ such that $Q \sim \emptyset$ and, for all a in $P \cup \bar{P}$, $a \cup \bar{a} \sim \varepsilon$ and $a\bar{a} \sim \emptyset$. Then, for any L-scheme A, $S_H(A) \sim A$.

Proof. It follows from Lemma 10.21 that, for every L-scheme B, $S(B) \sim B$. Thus, since $Q \sim \emptyset$, it follows that $S(Q) \sim \emptyset$. Hence, since $\sim$ is a cslm-congruence and $S(\Sigma^* Q \Sigma^*) = (T_S F)^* \cdot S(Q) \cdot (FT_S)^*$, we have that $S(\Sigma^* Q \Sigma^*) \sim \emptyset$.

Let A be an arbitrary L-scheme. By Lemma 10.21, $S(A) \sim A$. Also, since $S(\Sigma^* Q \Sigma^*) \sim \emptyset$,

$$\begin{aligned} S_H(A) &= S(A) - S(\Sigma^* Q \Sigma^*) \\ &\sim (S(A) - S(\Sigma^* Q \Sigma^*)) \cup S(\Sigma^* Q \Sigma^*) \\ &= S(A) \cup S(\Sigma^* Q \Sigma^*) \\ &\sim S(A). \end{aligned}$$

Hence $S_H(A) \sim A$, and the lemma is proved. ///

Corollary 13.22. For each L-scheme A, $S_H(A) \equiv_H A$.

Proof. Immediate from the previous lemma and Theorem 13.8. ///

The above corollary, together with Lemma 13.18, implies the following two theorems. Both will be called the H-standard form theorem.

Theorem 13.23. Let A and B be L-schemes. Then,

$A \leq_H B$ if and only if $S_H(A) \subset S_H(B)$, and

$A \equiv_H B$ if and only if $S_H(A) = S_H(B)$.

Proof. Immediate from Lemma 13.18 and Corollary 13.22. ///

Theorem 13.24. Let U and V be program schemes. Then,

$U \leq_H V$ if and only if $S_H(L(U)) \subset S_H(L(V))$, and

$U \equiv_H V$ if and only if $S_H(L(U)) = S_H(L(V))$.

Proof. Immediate from Theorem 13.23 and Lemma 13.7. ///

The next two results provide a characterization of the H-equivalence relation (note the analogy with Theorems 10.27 and 10.29).

Theorem 13.25. $P(\Sigma^*)/\equiv_H$ is a complete Boolean algebra.

Proof. Although S_H is, in general, not a cslm-morphism from $P(\Sigma^*)$ into $P(D_o^H)$ (see Remark 13.29), it is obviously a morphism with respect to the lattice structure of $P(\Sigma^*)$ and $P(D_o^H)$. By the H-standard form theorem, it follows that $P(\Sigma^*)/\equiv_H$ and $P(D_o^H)$ are isomorphic complete lattices. The theorem now follows from the fact that $P(D_o^H)$ is a Boolean algebra. ///

Theorem 13.26. The relation $\equiv_H$ is the smallest cslm-congruence on $P(\Sigma^*)$ such that $Q \equiv_H \emptyset$ and, for all a in $P \cup \overline{P}$, $a \cup \bar{a} \equiv_H \varepsilon$ and $a\bar{a} \equiv_H \emptyset$.

Proof. Firstly, $\equiv_H$ is a cslm-congruence on $P(\Sigma^*)$ with the above properties (Theorem 13.8).

Secondly, let $\sim$ be a cslm-congruence on $P(\Sigma^*)$ such that $Q \sim \emptyset$ and, for all a in $P \cup \overline{P}$, $a \cup \bar{a} \sim \varepsilon$ and $a\bar{a} \sim \emptyset$. Then, by Lemma 13.21, $S_H(A) \sim A$ for all L-schemes A. Consequently, if A and B are L-schemes such that $A \equiv_H B$, then, by the H-standard form theorem, $S_H(A) = S_H(B)$, and so $A \sim B$. Thus $\equiv_H$ is smaller than $\sim$. ///

The last result of this section is on "H-universality".

Definition 13.27. An H-interpretation I is said to be H-universal if, for all program schemes U and V, $U \equiv_H V$ if and only if $I(U) = I(V)$.

The existence of H-universal interpretations is established in the following theorem.

Theorem 13.28. I_o^H is an H-universal H-interpretation.

Proof. Let U and V be arbitrary program schemes. Then,

$U \equiv_H V$

$\Longleftrightarrow L(U) \equiv_H L(V)$ by Lemma 13.7

$\Longleftrightarrow S_H(L(U)) = S_H(L(V))$ by Theorem 13.23

$\Longleftrightarrow I_o^H(S_H(L(U))) = I_o^H(S_H(L(V)))$ by Lemma 13.18

$\Longleftrightarrow I_o^H(U) = I_o^H(V)$ by Corollary 13.22. ///

It is left to the reader to show that there are H-universal H-interpretations which are tτ-interpretations. This implies that, in the definition of H-equivalence, one may restrict oneself to tτ-interpretations.

We also leave it to the reader to show that the definitions and results of this section may easily be converted into analogous definitions and results for the case of π-interpretations.

We conclude this section with an algebraic remark and a definition.

Remark 13.29. It is easy to see, that in general $P(D_o^H)$ is not closed under standard product (Definition 10.13). Thus, for arbitrary gsd's H, it seems that there is no natural way to view S_H as a cslm-morphism.

Now let $H = (Q,\emptyset)$, with $Q \subset T_S \cdot F \cdot T_S$, be a Rutledge shift distribution (Definition 13.10). One can easily show that in this case $P(D_o^H)$ is a cslm with standard product and union as its cslm-operations. Also, one can show that S_H is a cslm-morphism. In fact, S_H is the unique cslm-morphism from $P(\Sigma^*)$ into $P(D_o^H)$, such that

(1) for each f in F, $S_H(f) = S(f) - Q$, and

(2) for each a in $P \cup \overline{P}$, $S_H(a) = S(a)$.† ///

We note here that the notion of cslm will play no role in the rest of this work.

The following definition will be needed in the sequel.

---

† In Kaplan [1969, p.381], $S_H(A)$ is defined for each Rutledge shift distribution H and each regular L-scheme A, and is called a "shift K-event".

<u>Definition 13.30</u>. A <u>regular shift distribution</u> is a generalized shift distribution $H = (Q,\emptyset)$ such that Q is a regular language.

Whenever effectiveness is discussed, it will be assumed that a regular shift distribution $H = (Q,\emptyset)$ is effectively given by a regular grammar G such that $L(G) = Q$.

14. Semantic determinism of program schemes

In this section we investigate determinism of program schemes. The term "deterministic" has already been used several times in Part I (see for instance Definitions 3.13, 4.13, 6.15 and 7.13). In all these cases a class of (nondeterministic) program schemes was given, and a program scheme from this class was defined to be "deterministic" if it satisfied certain syntactic restrictions (that is, restrictions pertaining to its "form"). Obviously, such a concept of determinism varies with the specific class of program schemes under consideration, and therefore it cannot belong to a general theory of program schemes. However, the syntactic restrictions were always chosen in such a way, that one could intuitively be sure that, under all pτ-interpretations, the program scheme would have a "deterministic execution", and thus would compute a partial function (see Definition 3.13 and the remark following it). For this reason, it is natural to investigate the following semantic concept of determinism which is applicable to any kind of program scheme: a program scheme will be called "semantically deterministic" if it computes a partial function under all pτ-interpretations (Definition 14.1).

The main results of this section (stated in Theorem 14.7) are the following †. Firstly, a program scheme is semantically deterministic if and only if its L-scheme has a certain syntactic property (its standard form is syntactically deterministic). Secondly, there exists an interpretation I which is "universal with respect to semantic determinism", in the sense that a program scheme is semantically deterministic if and only if it computes a partial function under the interpretation I.

At the end of the section we briefly discuss the case of π-interpretations (Lemma 14.13 and Theorem 14.14).

We start with the definition of semantic determinism.

Definition 14.1. A program scheme U is called semantically deterministic (abbreviated by semdet) if, for all pτ-interpretations I, I(U) is a partial function.

---

† Note the analogy with the results in sections 10 and 11.

Note that, for any two program schemes U and V, if $U \equiv V$ and U is semdet, then V is semdet. In particular, for each program scheme U, U is semdet if and only if L(U) is semdet. Therefore, in the general study of semantic determinism, we shall concentrate on L-schemes (cf. Lemma 9.5).

Example 14.2. Let $F = \{f,g\}$ and $P = \{p\}$. Then fg, $fpg \cup f\bar{p}f$, $(\bar{p}f)^*p$ and $pf \cup ppf$ are semdet, but $pf \cup ppg$ and $(pf)^*$ are not. ///

Recall from section 7 that an L-scheme is called syntactically deterministic (abbreviated by syntdet) if it corresponds to a generalized deterministic Ianov scheme (see Definition 7.13). In what follows it will be proved that an L-scheme is semantically deterministic if and only if its standard form is syntactically deterministic (Theorem 14.6). To show this, we first prove the intuitively obvious fact that each syntdet L-scheme computes a partial function under all pτ-interpretations.

Lemma 14.3. Each syntdet L-scheme is semdet.

Proof. Let us first remark that, for every pτ-interpretation I and every ϕ in Σ^*, $I(\phi)$ is a partial function. (This follows from the obvious facts that, for each σ in Σ, $I(\sigma)$ is a partial function, and that the composition of partial functions is a partial function).

Let A be a syntdet L-scheme, let I be a pτ-interpretation, and let x, y and z be elements of D_I such that $(x,y) \in I(A)$ and $(x,z) \in I(A)$. Thus, there are ϕ and ψ in A such that $(x,y) \in I(\phi)$ and $(x,z) \in I(\psi)$. We shall prove that $\phi = \psi$. (Then, by the above remark, $y = z$. Hence I(A) is a partial function, and the lemma is proved). Suppose, to the contrary, that $\phi \neq \psi$. Let ω be the longest common prefix of ϕ and ψ (that is, any other common prefix of ϕ and ψ is also a prefix of ω). By the syntactic determinism of A, $A \cap \phi\Sigma^* = \{\phi\}$ and $A \cap \psi\Sigma^* = \{\psi\}$. Hence there are nonempty words ϕ_1 and ψ_1 such that $\phi = \omega\phi_1$ and $\psi = \omega\psi_1$. Moreover, by the definition of ω, ϕ_1 and ψ_1 have different first symbols. Thus, by the syntactic determinism of A, there is a p in P, such that $A \cap \omega\Sigma^* \subset \omega(p \cup \bar{p})\Sigma^*$. Consequently, there are ϕ_2 and ψ_2 in Σ^* such that $\phi = \omega p\phi_2$ and $\psi = \omega\bar{p}\psi_2$ (or vice versa). Since $(x,y) \in I(\phi)$, there exists x_1 in D_I such that $(x,x_1) \in I(\omega)$ and $(x_1,x_1) \in I(p)$. Similarly, there exists x_2 in D_I such that $(x,x_2) \in I(\omega)$ and $(x_2,x_2) \in I(\bar{p})$. Since, by the remark from the beginning of this proof, $I(\omega)$ is a partial function, $x_1 = x_2$. This contradicts the fact that $I(p) \cap I(\bar{p}) = \emptyset$, and the lemma is proved. ///

The converse of the above lemma is not true in general. (For instance, for any predicate symbols p and q, the L-scheme $pq \cup qp$ is semdet, but not syntdet). But in the next lemma we show that for standard L-schemes the converse of the above lemma does hold (the reader may compare this lemma with Lemma 10.12).

Lemma 14.4. Let A be a standard L-scheme. Then the following three statements are equivalent.

(1) A is semdet,

(2) $I_2(A)$ is a partial function †, and

(3) A is syntdet.

Proof

(1) ⇒ (2). By the definition of semdet.

(3) ⇒ (1). by Lemma 14.3.

(2) ⇒ (3). Let us assume that $I_2(A)$ is a partial function. We have to show that A is syntdet. Since A is a standard L-scheme, it is easy to see that it suffices to show, that, for each ϕ in W_S, either $A \cap \phi\Sigma^* = \emptyset$, or $A \cap \phi\Sigma^* = \{\phi\}$, or $A \cap \phi\Sigma^* \subset \phi f\Sigma^*$ for some f in F. So let ϕ be an arbitrary standard word such that $A \cap \phi\Sigma^* \neq \emptyset$. We distinguish the following two cases.

Case 1: $\phi \in A$. We have to show that $A \cap \phi\Sigma^* = \{\phi\}$. Suppose, to the contrary, that there is a word ψ in $(F\cdot T_S)^+$ such that $\phi\psi \in A$. Let us write ϕ as $\phi_1 t$, where $\phi_1 \in (T_S F)^*$ and $t \in T_S$, and ψ as $\psi_1 t'$, where $\psi_1 \in F(T_S F)^*$ and $t' \in T_S$. Then, by Lemma 10.9, $(\phi\psi, t\psi) \in I_o(\phi)$ and $(\phi\psi, t') \in I_o(\phi\psi)$. Hence, since ϕ and $\phi\psi$ are both in A, $(\phi\psi, t\psi)$ and $(\phi\psi, t')$ are both in $I_o(A)$. It follows from Lemma 11.7 and the proof of Theorem 11.12, that, for the argument $\{(\varepsilon, \phi\psi)\}$, the relation $I_2(A)$ has (at least) the values $\{(\phi_1, t\psi)\}$ and $\{(\phi\psi_1, t')\}$. Since these values are

---

† For the definition of I_2, see Definition 11.9.

different, $I_2(A)$ is not a partial function. This is a contradiction.

Case 2: $\phi \notin A$. We have to show that $A \cap \phi\Sigma^* \subset \phi f\Sigma^*$ for some f in F. Suppose, to the contrary, that there are f and g in F, such that $f \neq g$, and that there are ϕ_1, ϕ_2 in $(T_SF)^*$ and t_1, t_2 in T_S such that both $\phi f\phi_1 t_1$ and $\phi g\phi_2 t_2$ are in A. Let $X = \{(\varepsilon, \phi f\phi_1 t_1), (\varepsilon, \phi g\phi_2 t_2)\}$. It is easy to see that, for the argument X, the relation $I_2(\phi f\phi_1 t_1)$ has the value $Y_1 = \{(\phi f\phi_1, t_1)\}$ and the relation $I_2(\phi g\phi_2 t_2)$ has the value $Y_2 = \{(\phi g\phi_2, t_2)\}$. Since both $\phi f\phi_1 t_1$ and $\phi g\phi_2 t_2$ are in A, it follows that, for the argument X, the relation $I_2(A)$ has (at least) the values Y_1 and Y_2. However, since $f \neq g$, Y_1 and Y_2 are different. Hence $I_2(A)$ is not a partial function. This is a contradiction. ///

For later use we state the following corollary to the above lemma.

Lemma 14.5. Let A be a syntdet L-scheme. Then S(A) is syntdet.

Proof. If A is syntdet, then, by Lemma 14.3, A is semdet. Thus, since $S(A) \equiv A$, S(A) is semdet. Hence, by Lemma 14.4, S(A) is syntdet. ///

The main result of this section is a direct consequence of Lemma 14.4.

Theorem 14.6. Let A be an L-scheme. Then the following three statements are equivalent.

(1) A is semantically deterministic,
(2) $I_2(A)$ is a partial function, and
(3) S(A) is syntactically deterministic.

Proof. Note that $S(A) \equiv A$ and apply Lemma 14.4 to S(A). ///

As a corollary, we obtain the following result on program schemes.

Theorem 14.7. Let U be a program scheme. Then the following three statements are equivalent.

(1) U is semantically deterministic,
(2) $I_2(U)$ is a partial function, and
(3) S(L(U)) is syntactically deterministic.

Proof. Note that $L(U) \equiv U$ and apply Theorem 14.6 to L(U). ///

In the sequel, Theorems 14.6 and 14.7 will both be referred to as the determinism theorem. Note that the determinism theorem consists of two results. The first is a "standard form theorem for determinism" (the equivalence of (1) and (3) above), and the second states the existence of an interpretation which is "universal with respect to determinism" (the equivalence of (1) and (2) above).

Example 14.8. Let F = {f} and P = {p}. Consider the L-scheme $A = (pf \cup \bar{p})^* \bar{p}$. Clearly A is not syntdet. But its standard form $S(A) = (pf)^* \bar{p}$ is syntdet, and so, by the determinism theorem, A is semdet. ///

We make the following three comments on the determinism theorem.

Remark 14.9.† In the statement of the determinism theorem, I_2 cannot be replaced by I_0 or I_1 as shown by the following example. Let f and g be different elements of F. Then the L-scheme $f \cup g$ is not semdet. However, it is easy to see that both $I_0(f \cup g)$ and $I_1(f \cup g)$ are partial functions. ///

Remark 14.10. One should note that I_2 is a tτ-interpretation (Lemma 11.10). Hence, in the definition of semantic determinism (Definition 14.1), "pτ" may be replaced by "tτ" (recall Remark 9.3 and Theorem 11.13). ///

Remark 14.11. A theorem analogous to the determinism theorem can easily be proved for generalized shift distributions (section 13). ///

We conclude this section by considering π-interpretations.††

Definition 14.12. A program scheme U is called π-semantically deterministic if, for all pπ-interpretations I, I(U) is a partial function.

---

† For the reader familiar with Engelfriet [1973] we can remark that the determinism theorem is stated wrongly in § G 14 of that paper.

†† See section 12; readers not familiar with that section may skip the rest of this one.

Let us remark first, that the analogue of the determinism theorem for π-semantic determinism does not hold. In particular, if A is a π-semantically deterministic L-scheme, then $S_\pi(A)$ need not be syntdet. (For instance, let $P = \{p,q\}$ and consider the L-scheme $A = p$. Clearly A is π-semantically deterministic and syntdet. But $S_\pi(A) = \{p,pq,p\bar{q}\}$ is not syntdet.) It is an open question whether there exists a better candidate for the π-standard mapping, such that the "π-determinism theorem" can be proved.

We now show that the concepts of π-semantic and semantic determinism coincide.

<u>Lemma 14.13</u>. Let U be a program scheme. Then U is π-semantically deterministic if and only if U is semantically deterministic.

<u>Proof</u>. The only-if part of the proof follows immediately from the definitions. For the if part, let U be an arbitrary semdet program scheme. Let I be an arbitrary $p\pi$-interpretation. We have to show that I(U) is a partial function. Let I' be a $p\tau$-interpretation with the same domain as I, such that, for each σ in Σ, $I(\sigma) \subset I'(\sigma)$. (It is easy to see that such $p\tau$-interpretations exist). Then, for each L-scheme A, $I(A) \subset I'(A)$. Hence $I(U) \subset I'(U)$. Since U is semdet and I' is a $p\tau$-interpretation, I'(U) is a partial function. Thus, since $I(U) \subset I'(U)$, I(U) is also a partial function. ///

Note that, by Lemmas 14.3 and 14.13, each syntdet L-scheme is π-semantically deterministic.

We finally show that the analogue of the "universal" part of the determinism theorem is true for the π-case.

<u>Theorem 14.14</u>. Let A be an L-scheme. Then A is π-semantically deterministic if and only if $I_2^\pi(A)$ is a partial function.

<u>Proof</u>. Let $I_2^\pi(A)$ be a partial function. It is left to the reader to show that $I_2(A) \subset I_2^\pi(A)$. Hence $I_2(A)$ is a partial function. Consequently, by the determinism theorem, A is semdet. Thus, by Lemma 14.13, A is π-semantically deterministic. ///

15. Semantic regularity of program schemes

In section 3 we considered the class of regular schemes (Definition 3.16) †. The class of L-schemes corresponding to these regular schemes is the class of regular languages. One of the nice features of regular languages is their simple structure: it is well known that each regular language can be obtained from simple languages (namely the empty set and all singletons $\{\sigma\}$, where $\sigma \in \Sigma$) by a finite number of applications of simple operations (namely union, product and closure) ††. From this result it easily follows ††† that each regular scheme computes, under any interpretation I, a relation with a very simple structure: it can be obtained from simple relations (namely the empty relation and all basic relations $I(\sigma)$, where $\sigma \in \Sigma$) by applying simple operations (namely union, composition and transitive-reflexive closure) a finite number of times. For this reason it is natural to investigate the following semantic concept of regularity which is applicable to any kind of program scheme: a program scheme will be called "semantically regular" if, under any interpretation, it computes a relation which can be obtained from the basic relations (and the empty relation) by the operations of union, composition and transitive-reflexive closure.

The main results of this section (stated in Theorem 15.9) are the following ††††. Firstly, a program scheme is semantically regular if and only if its L-scheme has a certain syntactic property (its standard form is a regular language). Secondly, their exists an interpretation I which is "universal with respect to semantic regularity".

Given a set X of relations, a relation which can be obtained from the relations in X by the operations of union, composition and transitive-reflexive closure, will be called "regular in X".

---

† Recall that, roughly speaking, regular schemes are the same as non-deterministic Ianov schemes (Theorem 8.14(1)).

†† This result is called the Kleene theorem. See, for instance, Hopcroft and Ullman [1969, Theorem 3.10).

††† By Lemma 2.9.

†††† Note the analogy with the results of the previous section.

Definition 15.1. Let D be an arbitrary set, and X an arbitrary set of relations on D. For a relation on D we define the property of being regular in X recursively as follows.

(1) $\emptyset$ is regular in X.

(2) If f is in X, then f is regular in X.

(3) If f and g are regular in X, then so are $f \cup g$, $f \circ g$ and f^*.

For a given X, the set of all relations regular in X will be denoted by $\mathcal{R}(X)$ [†].

Thus, $\mathcal{R}(X)$ is the smallest set of relations, which contains the empty relation and all elements of X, and is closed under the operations of union, composition and transitive-reflexive closure.

Example 15.2. Let D be the set of all integers, and let $X = \{p,f\}$, where $p = \{(x,x) \mid x>0\}$ and $f = \{(x,y) \mid y=x-1\}$. Then the relation $\{(x,y) \mid x>0 \text{ and } 0 \leq y \leq x\}$ is regular in X, since it is equal to $p \circ f \circ (p \circ f)^* \cup p$. ///

We now define the notion of semantic regularity.

Notation 15.3. For each interpretation I, the set of relations $\{I(\sigma) \mid \sigma \in \Sigma\}$ will be denoted by Σ_I. ///

Definition 15.4. A program scheme U is called semantically regular (abbreviated by semregular) if, for all interpretations I, I(U) is regular in Σ_I.

Note that, for any two program schemes U and V, if $U \equiv V$ and U is semregular, then V is semregular. In particular, for each program scheme U, U is semregular if and only if L(U) is semregular. Therefore, in the general study of semantic regularity, we shall concentrate on L-schemes.

Example 15.5. Let $F = \{f\}$ and $P = \{p\}$. Consider the context-free

---

† In Mazurkiewicz [1972 a, Definition 1], the set $\mathcal{R}(X)$ is called the "closure of X".

L-scheme $A = \{p^n pff^n | n \geq 0\}$. Clearly, $A \equiv pff^*$. It follows from Lemma 2.9 that, for each interpretation I, $I(pff^*) = I(p) \circ I(f) \circ (I(f))^*$. Hence, for each interpretation I, I(A) is regular in Σ_I. Consequently, A is a semregular L-scheme. ///

The next lemma provides a simple and obvious criterion for regularity of a relation.

Lemma 15.6. Let I be an interpretation, and let f be a relation on D_I. Then, f is regular in Σ_I if and only if $f = I(A)$ for some regular language A over Σ.

Proof. This lemma can easily be proved from Lemma 2.9 and the Kleene theorem mentioned before. Obviously the proof will be by induction on the structure of the relation f and the language A respectively. As it is straightforward, we leave most of it to the reader, and we consider the case of closure as an example.

(If): Let A be a language over Σ such that I(A) is regular in Σ_I. Since, by Lemma 2.9, $I(A^*) = (I(A))^*$, it follows from Definition 15.1 that $I(A^*)$ is regular in Σ_I.

(Only if): Let f be a relation on D_I, and let A be a regular language over Σ such that $f = I(A)$. Then, by Lemma 2.9, $f^* = I(A^*)$. And so, f^* is the relation computed by a regular language over Σ. ///

Note that the above lemma can also be expressed in the following way: for each interpretation I, $\mathcal{R}(\Sigma_I) = \{I(U) | U \in NIAN(\Sigma)\}$ †. (To see this, recall from Theorem 8.14 that $NIAN(\Sigma) =_{\ell(eff)} REG(\Sigma)$).

The next corollary is an immediate consequence of Lemma 15.6.

Corollary 15.7. Each regular L-scheme is semregular.

We now state the main result of this section.

---

† This result is proved in Mazurkiewicz [1972 a].

Theorem 15.8. Let A be an arbitrary L-scheme, and let I be an arbitrary universal interpretation †. Then the following three statements are equivalent.

(1) A is semantically regular,

(2) I(A) is regular in Σ_I, and

(3) S(A) is a regular language.

Proof

(1) ⇒ (2). By the definition of semregular.

(3) ⇒ (1). By Corollary 15.7, S(A) is semregular. Consequently, since A ≡ S(A), A is semregular.

(2) ⇒ (3). Suppose that I(A) is regular in Σ_I. By Lemma 15.6, there is a regular language B over Σ, such that I(A) = I(B). Then, by the universality of I, A ≡ B. Hence, by the standard form theorem, S(A) = S(B). It follows from Theorem 16.2 ††, that S(B) is a regular language, and so S(A) is a regular language. ///

As a corollary, we obtain the following result on program schemes.

Theorem 15.9. Let U be a program scheme, and let I be a universal interpretation. Then the following three statements are equivalent.

(1) U is semantically regular,

(2) I(U) is regular in Σ_I, and

(3) S(L(U)) is a regular language.

Proof. Note that L(U) ≡ U and apply Theorem 15.8 to L(U). ///

In the sequel, Theorems 15.8 and 15.9 will both be referred to as the regularity theorem. Note that the regularity theorem consists of

---

† For the definition of universal interpretation, see Definition 11.1.

†† It is rather unusual (except for the description of programming languages) to use results that are stated only later in the text. Nevertheless, we decided to do so in this particular case, because the subject matter of section 16 really belongs to Part III. (Of course no circularity is involved!).

two results. The first is a "standard form theorem for regularity" (the equivalence of (1) and (3) above), and the second states the existence of an interpretation which is "universal with respect to regularity" (the equivalence of (1) and (2) above).

Example 15.10. Let $F = \{f\}$ and $P = \{p\}$. Consider the L-scheme $A = \{(pf)^n\ p(pf)^n\ \bar{p} \mid n \geq 0\}$. Clearly, A is not regular. But its standard form $S(A) = (pfpf)^* pfpf\bar{p}$ is regular, and so, by the regularity theorem, A is semregular. ///

We conclude this section with the following three comments on the regularity theorem.

Remark 15.11. I_2 is a universal tτ-interpretation (Lemma 11.10 and Theorem 11.12). Hence, by the regularity theorem, one may replace in the definition of semantic regularity (Definition 15.4)the word "interpretations" by the word "tτ-interpretations" (cf. Remark 14.10). ///

Remark 15.12. Let us call a program scheme U "π-semantically regular" if, for all π-interpretations I, I(U) is regular in Σ_I. It is left to the reader to show that, by the appropriate changes in the regularity theorem, one obtains a regularity theorem for the π-case. Note that the concepts "π-semantically regular" and "semantically regular" do not coincide. (For instance, let $F = \{f\}$ and $P = \{p,q\}$, and consider the L-scheme $A = \{(prf)^n\ pf(psf)^n\ \bar{p} \mid n \geq 0$ and $r, s \in \{q,\bar{q}\}\}$. It is easy to see that S(A) is regular, while $S_\pi(A)$ is not. Hence, by the regularity theorems, A is semantically regular, but not π-semantically regular).///

Remark 15.13. A theorem analogous to the regularity theorem can easily be proved for regular shift distributions (Definition 13.30). ///

PART III

SOME SPECIFIC PROBLEMS

CONCERNING PROGRAM SCHEMES

Survey of Contents

As a consequence of the results of Parts I and II we can now apply known results from formal language theory to solve a number of specific problems in program scheme theory.

First of all, we show in section 16 that the standard mapping is a (nondeterministic) sequential transduction. This implies that many classes of program schemes are closed under the standard mapping.

In section 17 we investigate decidability of equivalence for various types of program schemes. It is proved that equivalence of regular schemes is decidable, whereas equivalence of context-free schemes is not recursively enumerable. Restricted cases of equivalence are decidable for macro schemes.

In section 18 the class of L-schemes corresponding to Ianov schemes (rsi's) is shown to be the class of all syntactically deterministic regular languages (syntactically deterministic s-languages respectively). We also prove that the class of Ianov schemes is closed under the standard mapping, whereas the class of rsi's is not.

In section 19 we consider the problem of translatability between program schemes. We compare the computing power of several classes of program schemes by (1) investigating decidability of translatability from one class into another, and (2) providing semantic characterizations of translatability from one class into another.

In sections 20 and 21 we augment program schemes with a finite number of variables over a finite domain (the elements of which are called "markers"), and we investigate the computing power of the resulting program schemes. First of all it is shown in section 20 that the L-scheme point of view is also applicable to program schemes with markers (in the sense that for each program scheme with markers there is an equivalent L-scheme). Using this point of view we prove that, for most classes of program schemes considered so far, addition of markers has no effect on their computing power. The only exception is the class of rsi's: addition of markers increases its computing power. Hence the class of rsi's with markers is investigated separately in section 21. It is shown there that the class of L-schemes corresponding to rsi's with markers is the class of all syntactically deterministic dpda languages. It is also shown that the class of rsi's with markers is closed under the standard mapping. These two results enable us to rephrase many known properties of dpda languages as properties of rsi's with markers.

Diagram of Sections

Below we give a rough diagram of the interrelations between the sections of Part III. In this diagram, "x→y" means that some knowledge of section x is required to be able to understand (a part of) section y.

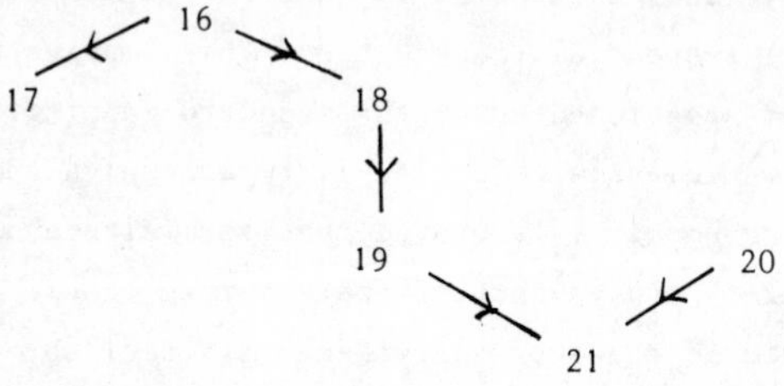

16. Closure under the standard mapping.
17. Decidability of equivalence.
18. An L-scheme characterization of IAN and RSI.
19. Translation of program schemes.
20. Program schemes with markers.
21. Recursive schemes with markers.

Roughly speaking, Part III uses results and definitions from the following sections: sections 2,3,4 and 8 (plus Definition 7.13) of Part I, and sections 9,10,14 and 15 of Part II. Moreover, results and definitions from sections 5,12 and 13 are used, but Part III may be read "selectively" with respect to these sections in the sense that everything referring to them may be skipped by the reader.

Finally we point out that as far as section 20 is concerned sections 2 and 8 are sufficient as prerequisite.

More Terminology

First of all, the terminology and conventions of the introduction to Part II will also be used in this Part. In particular we assume that Σ is a fixed, but arbitrary, alphabet of instruction symbols.

Next we introduce the concept of effective closure.

Definition. Let f be an n-ary operation on L-schemes, and let $\mathcal{L}$ be a pss. We say that the pss $\mathcal{L}$ is effectively closed under f if, for each n-tuple $U_1, U_2, \ldots, U_n$ of program schemes from $\mathcal{L}$, a program scheme U from $\mathcal{L}$ can effectively be found such that $L(U) = f(L(U_1), \ldots, L(U_n))$. In that case, we also say that the class of languages Lang($\mathcal{L}$) is effectively closed under f.

Remark (on closure). In what follows, we shall make free use of the fact that the pss's REG, CFG, MAC and TYPE-0 are effectively closed under sequential transductions, subtraction of and intersection with a regular language, union, substitution, etc. In fact, the classes of regular, context-free, macro and type 0 languages are full abstract families of languages (abbreviated "full AFL's")†, and so these classes are in particular closed under the above operations. ///

Remark (on decidability and enumerability). As already mentioned in section 1.5, the reader is assumed to be familiar with the basic results on decision problems of formal language theory. However, as an aid to the reader, we shall always give the proper references.

Whenever, in the sequel, we shall use a result stating that a particular problem is not recursively enumerable, we shall quote a reference in which the problem is shown to be undecidable. This leaves

---

† For the notion of a full AFL, see Salomaa [1973, Chapter IV]. See Theorem 1.5 in that reference for the fact that the regular, context-free and type 0 languages constitute full AFL's. In Fischer [1968, Corollary 5.9] it is shown that the class of macro languages is a full AFL. For the fact that full AFL's are closed under the above mentioned operations, see Ginsburg, Greibach and Hopcroft [1969].

the reader with the (mostly easy) task of proving that the problem is even not recursively enumerable †. The reason that we are interested in recursive enumerability at all, is the fact that, roughly speaking, a problem is recursively enumerable if and only if there exists an axiomatic system in which each solvable instance of the problem can be proved ††. For instance, we are interested in the fact whether, for a given pss $\mathcal{L}$, there is a complete axionatic system in which equivalence of program schemes from $\mathcal{L}$ can be proved. That is, we are interested in the recursive enumerability of the equivalence relation in $\mathcal{L}$.

We would also like to point out that all decision problems which we prove to be decidable, are in fact uniformly decidable in Σ, in the sense that their decidability does not depend upon specific properties of the alphabet Σ. ///

---

† In fact, the reader will also have to check that the result can always be modified to take care of the fact that the alphabet involved is fixed. (Mostly we shall consider alphabets of size two at least).

†† For an intuitive discussion of this fact, see Hermes [1965, § 2.4].

16. Closure under the standard mapping

In Part II we showed that several semantic properties of program schemes can be expressed as syntactic properties of their standard forms (see the standard form theorem, the determinism theorem and the regularity theorem). Thus, whenever a pss $\mathcal{L}$ † is closed under the standard mapping S ††, we may use syntactic properties of program schemes in $\mathcal{L}$ to obtain some of their semantic properties. In particular, if $\mathcal{L}$ is effectively closed under S, then the decidability of a semantic property in $\mathcal{L}$ can be proved by showing the decidability of the corresponding syntactic property in $\mathcal{L}$.

In this section it will be shown that the mappings S and S_π are sequential transductions (Theorem 16.1). Since many classes of languages are effectively closed under sequential transductions, it follows that many pss's are effectively closed under the standard mappings S and S_π. Thus we obtain, that the pss's REG, CFG, MAC and TYPE-0 ††† are effectively closed under S and S_π (Theorem 16.2). In addition, these pss's are effectively closed under S_H, for any regular shift distribution H (Theorem 16.3).

†††† <u>Theorem 16.1</u>. S and S_π are sequential transductions.

<u>Proof</u>. To realize the mapping S we construct a sequential transducer with accepting states $M = (K,\Sigma,\Sigma,R,k_o,E)$ as follows. $K = P(P \cup \bar{P}) \cup \{\underline{stop}\}$ (where <u>stop</u> is a new symbol), $k_o = \emptyset$ and $E = \{\underline{stop}\}$. For each k in $P(P \cup \bar{p})$, let T_k denote the set

---

† For the notion of a pss, see section 8.

†† Note that a pss $\mathcal{L}$ is closed under S if and only if each program scheme of $\mathcal{L}$ has at least one standard form in $\mathcal{L}$ itself (see Corollary 10.26).

††† Recall that, for instance, REG denotes REG(Σ), where Σ is our fixed alphabet of instruction symbols. For the definitions of REG, CFG, MAC and TYPE-0, see Part I.

†††† The idea expressed in this theorem is originally due to W. Ogden (see Ito [1968,§ III]). Note that, since $S(\varepsilon) \neq \varepsilon$ and $S_\pi(\varepsilon) \neq \varepsilon$, S and S_π cannot be gsm mappings.

$\{t \epsilon T_S |$ for all a in $P \cup \overline{P}$, if $a \epsilon k$, then a $\underline{\underline{in}}$ t$\}$. † The following rules are in R (for each k in $P(P \cup \bar{p})$, t in T_K, a in $P \cup \overline{P}$ and f in F):

$(k,a) \rightarrow (k \cup \{a\}, \varepsilon)$,

$(k,f) \rightarrow (\emptyset, tf)$ and

$(k,\varepsilon) \rightarrow (\underline{stop}, t)$

The straightforward, but tedious, proof of the fact that $\overline{M} = S$, is left to the reader. Here we just indicate the way M operates.

Let $\phi = t_1 f_1 t_2 f_2 \cdots t_k f_k t_{k+1}$ (with $t_1, \ldots, t_{k+1} \in T$ and $f_1, \ldots, f_k \in F$) be an input to M. First M collects all predicate symbols occurring in t_1 into its state. Then, if possible, it prints $t_1' f_1$ for some standard test t_1' in $S(t_1)$ (recall Lemma 10.19(1)). Next it collects all predicate symbols occurring in t_2 into its state and prints an element of $S(t_2) \cdot f_2$, and so forth. Eventually M collects all predicate symbols of t_{k+1} into its state and prints any element of $S(t_{k+1})$. Hence, by Lemma 10.19 (2), M has printed any element of $S(\phi)$. Thus M realizes S.

A similar sequential transducer M_π can be constructed to realize the mapping S_π. In fact, M_π differs from M only in the definition of T_k, where T_S should be replaced by T_S^π. ///

In the next theorem we consider some pss's closed under S and S_π.

Theorem 16.2. The pss's FIN, REG, CFG, MAC and TYPE-0 are effectively closed under S and S_π.

Proof. For FIN, the theorem follows directly from Lemma 10.19. For the other pss's, the theorem follows from Theorem 16.1 and the well known fact that the classes of regular, context-free, macro and type 0 languages are all effectively closed under sequential transductions. †† ///

We now consider closure under the H-standard mapping S_H, where $H = (Q, \emptyset)$ is a generalized shift distribution (Definition 13.12). Obviously, closure of a pss under S_H depends on the nature of the L-scheme Q. In the next theorem we consider the case that Q is a regular L-scheme (recall Definition 13.30 and the remark following it).

---

† Thus T_k consists of exactly those standard tests in which all elements of k occur. (For the definition of $\underline{\underline{in}}$, see 1.2.1).

†† See the Remark on closure in the introduction to this Part.

Theorem 16.3. Let H be a regular shift distribution. Then the pss's FIN, REG, CFG, MAC and TYPE-0 are effectively closed under S_H.

Proof. Let $H = (Q,\emptyset)$, where Q is a regular language over Σ. According to Definition 13.19, we have, for each L-scheme A, $S_H(A) = S(A) - S(\Sigma^*Q\Sigma^*)$. Since $\Sigma^*Q\Sigma^*$ is a regular language, Theorem 16.2 implies that $S(\Sigma^*Q\Sigma^*)$ is a regular language (and a regular grammar generating it can be found effectively from the regular grammar generating Q). The theorem now follows from Theorem 16.2 and the fact that all mentioned pss's are effectively closed under subtraction of a regular language.† ///

Remark 16.4. The closure of the pss's IAN and RSI under the standard mapping will be considered in section 18. ///

---

† See the Remark on closure in the introduction to this Part.

17. Decidability of equivalence

Why should one be concerned with decidability of a given problem ? From a practical point of view, one would like to know whether in principle an algorithm exists to solve the problem. If so, one can try to find the "best" algorithm for the problem; if not, one should change the problem. From a theoretical point of view, decidability or nondecidability of a problem provides some insight into the degree of complexity of the problem. Intuitively, a decidable problem is "easier" than an undecidable one.

In the case of program schemes, decidability questions were first studied in Ianov [1960]. It was proved there that equivalence of Ianov schemes is decidable. Undecidable questions concerning program schemes were first discussed in Ito [1968] and in Luckham, Park and Paterson [1970].

In this section we examine decidability of equivalence of program schemes in various pss's. The essential tools used to obtain a number of results, are the standard form theorem and the "closure theorem" of the previous section (Theorem 16.2). These theorems enable us to apply well known facts from formal language theory to the equivalence problem of program schemes.

First we prove that equivalence of regular schemes is decidable (Theorem 17.1). Then we show that equivalence of context-free schemes is not recursively enumerable (Theorem 17.4). However, nonequivalence of context-free schemes is recursively enumerable (Theorem 17.5). Finally some restricted cases of equivalence are proved to be decidable for context-free schemes and even for macro schemes (Theorem 17.6).

All decidability results of this section also hold in the case of regular shift distributions. In Example 17.2 we point out that regular shift distributions can be used to detect equivalence of program schemes "with variables".

It was proved by Ianov that equivalence of Ianov schemes (with or without shift distributions) is decidable. We now prove a slightly more general result.

Theorem 17.1. Let $\mathcal{L}$ be a pss effectively ℓ-included in REG, and let H be a regular shift distribution. Then the relations $\leq$, $\equiv$, $\leq_{\pi}$, $\equiv_{\pi}$, $\leq_{H}$ and $\equiv_{H}$ are all decidable in $\mathcal{L}$.

Proof. By the definition of effective ℓ-inclusion (Definition 8.11) it suffices to prove the theorem for $\mathcal{L}$ = REG. We first show that $\equiv$ is decidable in REG.

Consider arbitrary regular schemes U and V. By the standard form theorem, $U \equiv V$ if and only if $S(L(U)) = S(L(V))$. But, by Theorem 16.2, REG is effectively closed under S, and so we can effectively find regular grammars U_1 and V_1 generating S(L(U)) and S(L(V)) respectively. Thus we have reduced the question whether $U \equiv V$, to the question whether two regular grammars U_1 and V_1 generate the same language. Since the latter question is well known to be decidable †, the decidability of $\equiv$ is established.

The easy proof of the decidability of $\leq$ is left to the reader. The proofs for the other relations can be obtained likewise from the π-standard form theorem (see section 12), the H-standard form theorem (Theorem 13.24) and Theorems 16.2 and 16.3. ///

Theorem 17.1 is an extension of the original result of Ianov in the following three respects.

(1) It shows that $\equiv$ and $\leq$ are decidable for nondeterministic Ianov schemes. ††

(2) It shows the decidability of equivalence and covering with partial predicates and functions. †††

(3) It takes into consideration regular shift distributions which generalize Rutledge shift distributions.

---

† See Hopcroft and Ullman [1968, Theorem 3.12].

†† The decidability of $\equiv$ for nondeterministic Ianov schemes was shown in Ito [1968, Theorem 5].

††† For deterministic Ianov schemes this result is stated in de Bakker and Scott [1969, p.4] and in Milner [1970, Theorem 6.2].

We now show by way of an example that regular shift distributions can be of help in the automatic detection of equivalence of program schemes "with variables and assignments". (Compare Kaplan [1969]).†

Example 17.2. Let x and y be two new symbols.
Let $\Sigma = \{f_x, f_y, g, p_x, \bar{p}_x, p_y, \bar{p}_y\}$ with $F = \{f_x, f_y, g\}$ and $P = \{p_x, p_y\}$. The symbols f_x, f_y, g, p_x and p_y will also be denoted by x := f(x), y := f(y), y := x, p(x) and p(y) respectively. Intuitively, Ianov schemes over Σ will be thought of as program schemes with two variables x and y, with assignments x := f(x), y := f(y) and y := x, and with tests p(x) and p(y). Formally, we restrict the class of possible interpretations to the "LPP-interpretations" defined as follows ††. An interpretation I will be called an LPP-interpretation if it has the form $I = (D \times D, h)$, where D is a set and h satisfies the following conditions:

(1) $h(g) = \{((d_1,d_2),(d_1,d_1)) \mid d_1,d_2 \in D\}$,

(2) there is a total function $\hat{f}$ from D into D such that
$h(f_x) = \{((d_1,d_2),(\hat{f}(d_1),d_2)) \mid d_1,d_2 \in D\}$ and
$h(f_y) = \{((d_1,d_2),(d_1,\hat{f}(d_2))) \mid d_1,d_2 \in D\}$,

(3) there is a total predicate $\hat{p}$ on D such that
$h(p_x) = \{((d_1,d_2),(d_1,d_2)) \mid d_1,d_2 \in D \text{ and } (d_1,d_1) \in \hat{p}\}$ and
$h(p_y) = \{((d_1,d_2),(d_1,d_2)) \mid d_1,d_2 \in D \text{ and } (d_2,d_2) \in \hat{p}\}$.

Ianov schemes U and V over Σ will be called LPP-equivalent, denoted by $U \equiv_{LPP} V$, if they compute the same function under all LPP-interpretations.

We now observe that, as shown in Luckham, Park and Paterson [1970, Theorem 4.1], LPP-equivalence is undecidable in IAN(Σ). Still, following Kaplan [1969], we may try to find algorithms which, given two arbitrary program schemes, will either tell us that they are equivalent or will halt with no answer at all. In other words, we may try to find decidable relations which are included in the relation $\equiv_{LPP}$ (in the sense that, if $\sim$ is such a relation, then, for Ianov schemes U and V, if $U \sim V$

---

† Readers who did not read section 13, may skip this example.

†† LPP refers to Luckham, Park and Paterson [1970], where program schemes with variables are investigated.

then U $\equiv_{LPP}$ V). Evidently, equivalence is an instance of such a relation (it was proved decidable in Theorem 7.1). To obtain stronger decidable relations included in $\equiv_{LPP}$, we may consider shift distributions.

For instance, the fact that y := f(y) and y := x do not change the value of p(x) can be expressed by the Rutledge shift distribution $(Q_1,\emptyset)$, where

$$Q_1 = p_x(p_y \cup \bar{p}_y)(f_y \cup g)\bar{p}_x(p_y \cup \bar{p}_y) \cup \bar{p}_x(p_y \cup \bar{p}_y)(f_y \cup g)p_x(p_y \cup \bar{p}_y).$$

Similarly, the fact that x := f(x) does not change p(y) is expressed by $(Q_2,\emptyset)$ where

$$Q_2 = (p_x \cup \bar{p}_x)p_y f_x(p_x \cup \bar{p}_x)\bar{p}_y \cup (p_x \cup \bar{p}_x)\bar{p}_y f_x(p_x \cup \bar{p}_x)p_y.$$

Moreover, the fact that, after execution of y:= x, the values of p(x) and p(y) are equal is expressed by the Rutledge shift distribution $(Q_3,\emptyset)$, where $Q_3 = T_S g(p_x\bar{p}_y \cup \bar{p}_x p_y)$. Now let Hm be the Rutledge shift distribution $(Q_1 \cup Q_2 \cup Q_3,\emptyset)$. Since each LPP-interpretation obviously satisfies Hm, it follows that $\equiv_{Hm}$ is included in $\equiv_{LPP}$. Also, by Theorem 17.1, $\equiv_{Hm}$ is decidable. Hence $\equiv_{Hm}$ is indeed a decidable relation included in $\equiv_{LPP}$ (and stronger than $\equiv$). Actually it is easy to show that $\equiv_{Hm}$ is the maximal Rutledge shift distribution equivalence included in $\equiv_{LPP}$: $Q_1 \cup Q_2 \cup Q_3$ is the largest subset of $T_S F T_S$ which is LPP-equivalent to $\emptyset$. We now show that, by allowing arbitrary regular shift distributions H, still stronger relations $\equiv_H$, included in $\equiv_{LPP}$, can be obtained. Consider the fact that, after execution of (y:=x)(x:=f(x))(y:=f(y)), the values of p(x) and p(y) are equal. This can be easily expressed by the regular shift distribution $(Q_4,\emptyset)$ where $Q_4 = gf_x f_y(p_x\bar{p}_y \cup \bar{p}_x p_y)$. (Notice that Q_4 is even finite) Let H_4 be the regular shift distribution $(Q_1 \cup Q_2 \cup Q_3 \cup Q_4,\emptyset)$. Then $\equiv_{H_4}$ is a decidable relation included in $\equiv_{LPP}$, and stronger than $\equiv_{Hm}$.

As another example we consider the regular shift distribution $H = (Q_1 \cup Q_2 \cup Q_5,\emptyset)$, where $Q_5 = g(f_x f_y)^* (p_x\bar{p}_y \cup \bar{p}_x p_y)$. Obviously, $\equiv_H$ is a decidable relation, included in $\equiv_{LPP}$ and stronger than $\equiv_{H_4}$. For instance, the decision method for $\equiv_H$ will detect the H-equivalence of the following schemes U and V.

U = 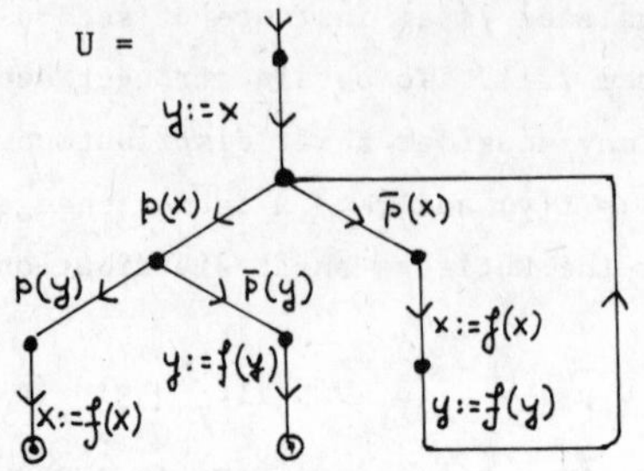

V = 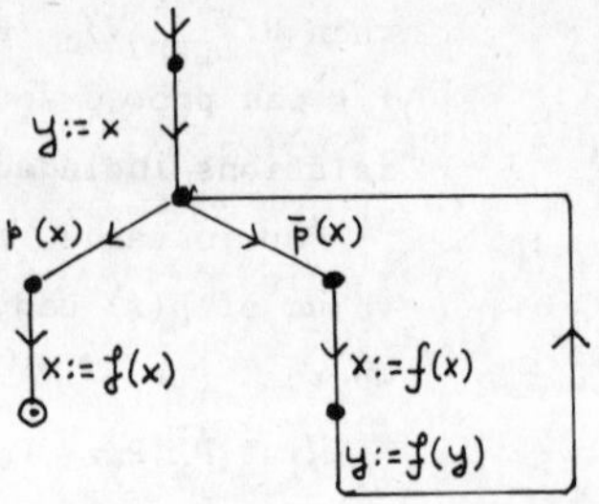

(Let us prove that $U \equiv_H V$. By Lemma 13.7 it suffices to prove that $L(U) \equiv_H L(V)$. Obviously,
$L(U) = g(\bar{p}_x f_x f_y)^* p_x (p_y f_x \cup \bar{p}_y f_y)$ and $L(V) = g(\bar{p}_x f_x f_y)^* p_x f_x$. But, since evidently $g(\bar{p}_x f_x f_y)^* p_x \bar{p}_y \leq_H Q_5$, we have $g(\bar{p}_x f_x f_y)^* p_x \bar{p}_y f_y \equiv_H \emptyset \equiv_H g(\bar{p}_x f_x f_y)^* p_x \bar{p}_y f_x$. Hence

$$\begin{aligned} L(U) &\equiv_H g(\bar{p}_x f_x f_y)^* p_x (p_y f_x \cup \bar{p}_y f_x) \\ &\equiv g(\bar{p}_x f_x f_y)^* p_x f_x \\ &= L(V). \end{aligned}$$

Thus $L(U) \equiv_H L(V)$.)

Finally we note that the generalized shift distribution $(Q,\emptyset)$, where $Q = \{\phi \in \Sigma^* \mid \phi \equiv_{LPP} \emptyset\}$, is maximal with respect to LPP-equivalence. Unfortunately, as can easily be seen, Q is not regular. ///

Before proceeding with the discussion of equivalence in other pss's we state the following useful lemma.

<u>Lemma 17.3</u>. Let Σ_1 and Σ_2 be alphabets such that $\Sigma_1 \subset \Sigma_2$ †, and let A and B be L-schemes over Σ_1. Then, A and B are equivalent in the pss $P(\Sigma_2^*)$ if and only if they are equivalent in the pss $P(\Sigma_1^*)$ ††.

---

† We assume that $F_{\Sigma_1} \subset F_{\Sigma_2}$ and $P_{\Sigma_1} \subset P_{\Sigma_2}$.

†† Note that every concept introduced in Part II (and in particular equivalence) depends on the alphabet Σ of instruction symbols.

Proof. This follows from the obvious fact that, for interpretations I of Σ_2, the relations computed by A and B under I do not depend on the relations $I(\sigma)$ with σ in $\Sigma_2 - \Sigma_1$. ///

In the next theorem we prove a result about equivalence in the pss CFG.†

Theorem 17.4. If $\#(F) \geq 2$, or if $\#(F) = 1$ and $P \neq \emptyset$, then the relations $\leq$, $\equiv$, $\leq_\pi$ and $\equiv_\pi$ are not recursively enumerable in CFG††. In particular, it is not recursively enumerable for U in CFG whether $U \equiv \Sigma^*$ (or $U \equiv_\pi \Sigma^*$ respectively).

If $F = \emptyset$, or if $\#(F) = 1$ and $P = \emptyset$, then the above relations are decidable in CFG.

Proof. Since the proofs for the π-case are similar to those for the τ-case, we only consider the latter.

First, let $\#(F) \geq 2$. Let U be an arbitrary context-free grammar over F. By Theorem 9.6 and Lemma 17.3, $U \equiv F^*$ if and only if $L(U) = F^*$. Also, since $S(F^*)$ and $S(\Sigma^*)$ are both equal to W_S, we have $\Sigma^* \equiv F^*$ (by the standard form theorem). Thus, $U \equiv \Sigma^*$ if and only if $L(U) = F^*$. In this way, the question whether the context-free grammar U over F generates F^* is reduced to the question whether the context-free scheme U over Σ is equivalent to Σ^*. Since the former question is not recursively enumerable†††, it follows that neither is the latter.††††

We next consider the case that $\#(F) = 1$ and $P \neq \emptyset$. By Lemma 17.3 we may assume that $\#(P) = 1$. Let $F = \{f\}$ and $P = \{p\}$. Let c and d be two symbols not in Σ, and let G be an arbitrary context-free grammar over $\{c,d\}$. Let s be the substitution from $\{c,d\}$ into Σ defined by $s(c) = pf$ and $s(d) = \bar{p}f$. Then one can easily verify that $s(L(G)) \equiv \Sigma^*$

---

† Recall from section 8 that CFG $=_{\ell(\mathrm{eff})}$ NRSI. Thus the theorem also holds for NRSI.

†† For gsd's $H = (Q,\emptyset)$, decidability of $\equiv_H$ depends on the nature of Q. For instance, if $Q = \emptyset$, then $\equiv_H = \equiv$, and so $\equiv_H$ is not recursively enumerable; but if $Q = \Sigma^*$ then all program schemes are H-equivalent to $\emptyset$, and so $\equiv_H$ is decidable.

††† See Hopcroft and Ullman [1969, Theorem 14.4]. Recall also the Remark on decidability and enumerability in the introduction to this Part, and note that F contains at least two symbols.

†††† This was proved in Ito [1968, Theorem 6].

if and only if $L(G) = \{c,d\}^*$ (use the standard form theorem). Since the context-free languages are effectively closed under substitution, we can find a context-free scheme U over Σ such that $L(U) = s(L(G))$, and so $U \equiv \Sigma^*$ if and only if $L(G) = \{c,d\}^*$. Hence, as in the previous case, it is not recursively enumerable, for U in CFG, whether $U \equiv \Sigma^*$.

We now turn to the case that $F = \emptyset$. Let U and V be arbitrary context-free schemes over P. By the standard form theorem, $U \equiv V$ if and only if $S(L(U)) = S(L(V))$. By Theorem 16.2 we can find context-free schemes U_1 and V_1 generating $S(L(U))$ and $S(L(V))$ respectively. Thus $U \equiv V$ if and only if $L(U_1) = L(V_1)$. We now observe that, since $F = \emptyset$, both $L(U_1)$ and $L(V_1)$ are contained in the finite set T_S. Thus, by deciding which elements of T_S belong to $L(U_1)$ and $L(V_1)$ †, it can be decided whether $L(U_1) = L(V_1)$. Hence it is decidable whether $U \equiv V$.

Finally we discuss the case that $\#(F) = 1$ and $P = \emptyset$. Let U and V be arbitrary context-free schemes over F. By Theorem 9.6, $U \equiv V$ if and only if $L(U) = L(V)$. Since $L(U)$ and $L(V)$ are context-free languages over a one-letter alphabet, they are actually regular (effectively) ††, and so their equality can be decided. †††

The decidability of $\leq$ in the above two cases is proved similarly. ///

Note that the above theorem means that (for sufficiently large Σ) there is no complete axiomatic system for equivalence in CFG ††††. For nonequivalence the situation is more favourable. Of course, nonequivalence cannot be decidable in CFG, but in the next theorem it is shown that in "most" pss's (and particularly in CFG) nonequivalence is recursively enumerable. For the sake of this theorem let us call a pss $\mathcal{L}$ <u>decidable</u> if, for each program scheme U in $\mathcal{L}$, we can effectively find a decision method for the question of membership in L(U).

---

† Note that context-free languages are decidable, see for instance Hopcroft and Ullman [1969, Theorem 2.2].

†† See Salomaa [1973, Theorem II 7.3].

††† See Hopcroft and Ullman [1969, Theorem 3.12].

†††† See the Remark on decidability and enumerability in the introduction to this Part.

<u>Theorem 17.5</u>. Let $\mathcal{L}$ be a decidable pss, which is effectively closed under S. Let H = (Q,∅) be a gsd such that Q is a decidable language. Then the relations $\not\leq$, $\not\equiv$, $\not\leq_\pi$, $\not\equiv_\pi$, $\not\leq_H$ and $\not\equiv_H$ are recursively enumerable in $\mathcal{L}$.

<u>Proof</u>. Consider arbitrary program schemes U and V from $\mathcal{L}$. By the standard form theorem, U $\not\equiv$ V if and only if S(L(U)) $\neq$ S(L(V)). Since $\mathcal{L}$ is a decidable pss which is effectively closed under S, the languages S(L(U)) and S(L(V)) are decidable (effectively). Hence their nonequality is recursively enumerable.

Similar proofs can easily be given for all other relations. ///

Note that this theorem applies to CFG and MAC. Note also that if the theorem applies to $\mathcal{L}$ and if $\mathcal{L}_1$ is a decidable sub-pss of $\mathcal{L}$, then nonequivalence is recursively enumerable in $\mathcal{L}_1$. Finally note that, as a direct consequence of the above theorem, we obtain that in "most" pss's equivalence is either decidable or not recursively enumerable.

Some restricted cases in which equivalence can be decided in CFG, and even in MAC, are discussed in the following theorem.†

<u>Theorem 17.6</u>. Let $\mathcal{L}$ be a pss effectively ℓ-included in MAC. For arbitrary U in $\mathcal{L}$, U_1 in FIN and U_2 in REG, the following questions are decidable.

(1) U ≡ ∅,

(2) U ≡ U_1,

(3) U ≡ V for some V in FIN, and

(4) U ≤ U_2.

The same questions are decidable for π-equivalence and H-equivalence, where H is a regular shift distribution.

<u>Proof</u>. By the definition of effective ℓ-inclusion, it suffices to prove the theorem for $\mathcal{L}$ = MAC. Let us first consider question (4).

---

† Recall that CFG $\subset_{\ell(\text{eff})}$ MAC and NPP $=_{\ell(\text{eff})}$ MAC (see section 8).

(4). By the standard form theorem, $U \leq U_2$ if and only if $S(L(U)) \subset S(L(U_2))$. By Theorem 16.2, $S(L(U))$ is a macro language and $S(L(U_2))$ is a regular language (both effectively). Since MAC is effectively closed under subtraction of a regular language, and since the emptiness problem is decidable for macro languages †, it is decidable whether $S(L(U)) - S(L(U_2)) = \emptyset$ (in other words whether $S(L(U)) \subset S(L(U_2))$). And so, it is decidable whether $U \leq U_2$.

Obviously, (1) is a particular case of (4). We now prove (2) and (3).

(2). Program schemes U and U_1 are equivalent if and only if they cover each other. The decidability of $U \leq U_1$ follows from (4), and the decidability of $U_1 \leq U$ is proved as follows. By the standard form theorem, $U_1 \leq U$ if and only if $S(L(U_1)) \subset S(L(U))$. Also, by Theorem 16.2, $S(L(U_1))$ is a finite language and $S(L(U))$ is a macro language. Consequently, since macro languages are decidable ††, it is decidable whether each element of the finite set $S(L(U_1))$ belongs to $S(L(U))$.

(3). Evidently, by the standard form theorem, U is equivalent to some V in FIN if and only if $S(L(U))$ is finite. Decidability now follows from the fact that finiteness of macro languages is decidable. †††

Similar proofs can easily be given for the π-case and the H-case. ///

We have shown decidability of equivalence in IAN and REG, and we have shown nonenumerability of equivalence in CFG (and so, trivially, in MAC and TYPE-0). We close this section by stating one of the main open problems in program scheme theory: are the relations $\leq$, $\equiv$, $\leq_\pi$ and $\equiv_\pi$ decidable in RSI ?

---

† This follows from the fact that the class of macro languages equals the class of so called indexed languages of Aho [1968] and the fact that the emptiness problem for indexed languages is decidable. See Fischer [1968, Theorem 5.3 and Corollary 5.4].

†† See Fischer [1968, Corollary 5.7].

††† See Rounds [1970].

18. An L-scheme characterization of IAN and RSI

In section 8 we characterized the classes of L-schemes corresponding to various pss's (see Theorem 8.14 and Corollary 8.15). The most important pss's left for consideration were IAN and RSI. In this section the classes of L-schemes corresponding to these pss's are characterized. It should be clear by now that such characterizations are useful in the investigation of IAN and RSI from the language theoretic point of view.

We first show that Lang(IAN) is the set of all syntdet regular languages (Theorem 18.7) †. It follows from this characterization that IAN is closed under the standard mapping (Theorem 18.11).

Then we show that Lang(RSI) is the set of all syntdet s-languages (Theorem 18.17) ††. From this characterization it follows that RSI is not closed under the standard mapping (Theorem 18.21).

Finally we point out that Lang(RSI) is properly contained in the set of all syntdet context-free languages (Remark 18.24).

To show that Lang(IAN) is identical to the class of syntdet regular languages we first define deterministic regular schemes and prove that the languages they generate are precisely the syntdet regular languages. Then the result follows from the obvious correspondence between deterministic regular schemes and deterministic Ianov schemes.

<u>Definition 18.1.</u> A regular scheme $G = (N,\Sigma,R,Z)$ will be called <u>deterministic</u> if, for every nonterminal S, either $R(S) = \emptyset$ †††, or $R(S) = \{S \to \varepsilon\}$, or $R(S) = \{S \to \sigma T\}$ for certain σ in Σ and T in N, or $R(S) = \{S \to pT_1, S \to \bar{p}T_2\}$ for certain p in P and T_1,T_2 in N.

---

† For the definition of "syntdet", see Definition 7.13. For the importance of the concept, see section 14.

†† For the definition of s-language, see 1.4.1.4. The relevance of s-languages to RSI is discussed in Zeiger [1969, § 8], Ashcroft, Manna and Pnueli [1973, § 6] and Paterson [1972, section 3].

††† Recall from 1.4.1.2 that R(S) denotes the set of all rules with left hand side S.

<u>Example 18.2</u>. Let $F = \{f\}$ and $P = \{p\}$. Consider the regular scheme $G = (\{S,T_1,T_2\},\Sigma,R,S)$, where $R = \{S \to pT_1,\ S \to \bar{p}T_2,\ T_1 \to fS,\ T_2 \to \varepsilon\}$. Obviously, G is deterministic. ///

We first show that each deterministic regular scheme generates a syntdet language.

<u>Lemma 18.3</u>. Let G be a deterministic regular scheme. Then L(G) is syntdet.

<u>Proof</u>. Let $G = (N,\Sigma,R,Z)$ be a deterministic regular scheme, and let ϕ be an arbitrary word over Σ. If there is no nonterminal S such that $Z \overset{*}{\Rightarrow} \phi S$, then $L(G) \cap \phi\Sigma^* = \emptyset$. Otherwise, it easily follows from the determinism of G that there is a unique nonterminal S such that $Z \overset{*}{\Rightarrow} \phi S$. Depending on the form of R(S) we show that $L(G) \cap \phi\Sigma^*$ satisfies the requirements of syntactic determinism as follows. If $R(S) = \emptyset$, then $L(G) \cap \phi\Sigma^* = \emptyset$. If $R(S) = \{S \to \varepsilon\}$, then $L(G) \cap \phi\Sigma^* = \{\phi\}$. If $R(S) = \{S \to \sigma T\}$, then $L(G) \cap \phi\Sigma^* \subset \phi\sigma\Sigma^*$. Finally, if $R(S) = \{S \to pT_1,\ S \to \bar{p}T_2\}$, then $L(G) \cap \phi\Sigma^* \subset \phi(p \cup \bar{p})\Sigma^*$. Thus L(G) is syntdet. ///

<u>Example 18.4</u>. Let G be the deterministic regular grammar of Example 18.2. It is easy to see that $L(G) = (pf)^*\bar{p}$. It was shown in Example 7.14 that L(G) is syntdet. ///

We next show that each syntdet regular language can be generated by a deterministic regular scheme, and we also prove that it is decidable, for an arbitrary regular scheme, whether it generates a syntdet language.

<u>Lemma 18.5</u>. There is an algorithm which, for an arbitrary regular scheme G, determines whether L(G) is syntdet or not, and, if so, constructs a deterministic regular scheme G_1 such that $L(G_1) = L(G)$.

<u>Proof</u>. We first decide whether $L(G) = \emptyset$. If L(G) is empty, then it is syntdet. Let $G_1 = (\{Z\},\Sigma,\{Z \to \sigma Z\},Z)$, where σ is an arbitrary element of Σ. Then G_1 is obviously a deterministic regular grammar such that

$L(G_1) = L(G)$.

If $L(G) \neq \emptyset$, then we can effectively find a regular grammar $G_1 = (N,\Sigma,R,Z)$, generating the same language, with the following properties.[†]

(1) Each rule of G_1 is of one of the forms $S \to \sigma T$ or $S \to \varepsilon$ (with S,T in N and σ in Σ).

(2) If $S \to \sigma T_1$ and $S \to \sigma T_2$ are rules of G_1 (with S,T_1,T_2 in N and σ in Σ), then $T_1 = T_2$.

(3) G is reduced.

We now claim that $L(G_1)$ is syntdet if and only if G_1 is deterministic (and from this claim the lemma follows). The if part of the claim was proved in Lemma 18.3. To prove the only-if part, suppose that $L(G_1)$ is syntdet and let S be an arbitrary nonterminal of G_1. We have to show that $R(S)$ has one of the forms displayed in Definition 18.1. We distinguish the following two cases.

Case 1: $S \to \varepsilon$ belongs to $R(S)$. It has to be shown that $R(S) = \{S \to \varepsilon\}$. Assume, to the contrary, that the rule $S \to \sigma T$ is in $R(S)$ for certain σ in Σ and T in N. Since G_1 is reduced, there are words ϕ and ψ in Σ^* such that $Z \overset{*}{\Rightarrow} \phi S$ and $T \overset{*}{\Rightarrow} \psi$. Consequently, $L(G_1) \cap \phi\Sigma^*$ contains both ϕ and $\phi\sigma\psi$. This contradicts the syntactic determinism of $L(G_1)$. Hence $R(S) = \{S \to \varepsilon\}$.

Case 2: $S \to \varepsilon$ does not belong to $R(S)$. It has to be shown that $R(S)$ is of one of the forms $\{S \to \sigma T\}$ or $\{S \to pT_1,\ S \to \bar{p}T_2\}$. Since the proof is similar to the one of case 1, it is left to the reader. ///

The characterization of Lang(IAN) is stated in the next theorem.

Notation 18.6. We shall denote by SyntdetREG(Σ), or simply SyntdetREG, the sub-pss of REG consisting of all regular schemes over Σ which generate a syntdet L-scheme.[††] ///

---

† For the first two properties, see Salomaa [1973, the proof of Theorem II 6.1]. These properties actually express that G_1, viewed as a finite automaton, is a deterministic finite automaton. For the third property, see 1.4.1.2.

†† For the notion of sub-pss, recall Definition 8.3 and Remark 8.4. Note that, by Lemma 18.5, SyntdetREG is a decidable sub-pss of REG.

† Theorem 18.7. IAN $=_{\ell(\text{eff})}$ SyntdetREG.

Proof

To show that IAN $\subset_{\ell(\text{eff})}$ SyntdetREG, let U be an arbitrary Ianov scheme. Consider the regular grammar G_U, generating L(U), defined in Definition 3.9. It easily follows from Definition 3.13 that G_U is a deterministic regular grammar. Hence, by Lemma 18.3, G_U belongs to SyntdetREG.

To show that SyntdetREG $\subset_{\ell(\text{eff})}$ IAN, let $G = (N,\Sigma,R,Z)$ be a regular scheme such that L(G) is syntdet. By Lemma 18.5 we may assume that G is deterministic. Let U be the nondeterministic Ianov scheme $(\Sigma,N_1,n^o,E,A,e,\ell)$, where $N_1 = N$, $n^o = Z$, $E = \{S\in N \mid R(S)=\{S \to \varepsilon\}\}$, and A, e and ℓ are such that if $S \to \sigma T$ is a rule in R, then there is an arc leading from S to T labelled by σ ††. It easily follows from the determinism of G that U is actually an element of IAN. Moreover, it is evident that L(U) = L(G). Hence SyntdetREG $\subset_{\ell(\text{eff})}$ IAN. ///

Example 18.8. Let G be the regular grammar of Example 18.2. It can easily be verified that the Ianov scheme corresponding to G according to the proof of Theorem 18.7 is the one of Example 3.8. ///

Another way of formulating the above theorem (without mentioning its effectiveness) is the following. †††

Corollary 18.9. Lang(IAN(Σ)) is the set of all syntactically deterministic regular languages over Σ.

Notice that it follows from Theorem 18.7 that IAN and SyntdetREG

---

† A related result is proved in Dubinsky [1973, § 10].

†† The same construction was used to prove Theorem 8.14(1).

††† Cf. Corollary 8.15.

have "the same computing power" (recall Remark 8.10).

As another consequence of Theorem 18.7 we prove the following elementary property of Ianov schemes.†

Corollary 18.10. Each Ianov scheme is semantically deterministic.††

Proof. Immediate from Theorem 18.7 and Lemma 14.3. ///

The characterization of IAN in Theorem 18.7 also enables us to prove that IAN is effectively closed under the standard mapping (cf. section 16). Thus, for each Ianov scheme U we can find a Ianov scheme V such that V is a standard form of U.†††

Theorem 18.11. The pss IAN is effectively closed under S. Also, if H is a regular shift distribution, then IAN is effectively closed under S_H.

Proof. By Theorem 18.7 it suffices to show that the pss SyntdetREG is effectively closed under S and S_H. Moreover, since, by Theorems 16.2 and 16.3, REG is effectively closed under S and S_H, it suffices to show that the class of syntdet L-schemes is closed under S and S_H. So let A be an arbitrary syntdet L-scheme. By Lemma 14.5, S(A) is syntdet. Now observe that $S_H(A)$ is a subset of S(A) (recall Definition 13.19). It is easy to see that every subset of a syntdet L-scheme is syntdet itself. Hence $S_H(A)$ is syntdet. ///

Notice that IAN is not closed under S_π. For instance, if P = {p,q}, then $S_\pi(p) = \{p, pq, p\bar{q}\}$. Obviously, by Theorem 18.7, p belongs to Lang(IAN), while $\{p, pq, p\bar{q}\}$ does not.

---

† This property was mentioned in a remark following Definition 3.13; recall Lemma 14.13.

†† For the notion of semantic determinism, see section 14.

††† For the notion of standard form, recall Definition 10.5 and Corollary 10.26.

We now turn to the pss RSI. To show that Lang(RSI) is the set of all syntdet s-languages, we first define deterministic s-grammars and prove that the languages they generate are precisely the syntdet s-languages. Then we show that deterministic s-grammars and rsi's correspond to each other.

Definition 18.12. An s-grammar $G = (N,\Sigma,R,Z)$ will be called deterministic if either
(1) $G = (\{Z\},\Sigma,\{Z \to \varepsilon\},Z)$ †, or
(2) for each nonterminal S, R(S) has one of the forms $\{S \to \sigma\alpha\}$ or $\{S \to p\alpha, S \to \bar{p}\beta\}$ with σ in Σ, p in P and α,β in N^*.

Example 18.13. Let $F = \{f,g\}$ and $P = \{p,q\}$. Consider the s-grammar $G = (\{S,T,A,B\},\Sigma,R,S)$, where $R = \{S \to pB, S \to \bar{p}TS, T \to qAS, T \to \bar{q}B, A \to f, B \to g\}$. Obviously, G is deterministic. ///

The next lemma shows that deterministic s-grammars generate syntdet languages.

Lemma 18.14. Let G be a deterministic s-grammar. Then L(G) is syntdet.

Proof. Let $G = (N,\Sigma,R,Z)$ be a deterministic s-grammar. If G satisfies (1) of Definition 18.12, then $L(G) = \varepsilon$, and so L(G) is syntdet. Now suppose that G satisfies (2) of Definition 18.12. To show that L(G) is syntdet, consider an arbitrary word ϕ such that $L(G) \cap \phi\Sigma^* \neq \emptyset$. It easily follows from the fact that G is an s-grammar, that there is a unique α in N^* such that $Z \overset{*}{\Rightarrow} \phi\alpha$. Thus, if $\alpha = \varepsilon$, then $L(G) \cap \phi\Sigma^* = \{\phi\}$. If $\alpha \neq \varepsilon$, then $\alpha = S\alpha_1$ for certain S in N and α_1 in N^*. So, if $R(S) = \{S \to \sigma\beta\}$ with σ in Σ and β in N^*, then $L(G) \cap \phi\Sigma^* \subset \phi\sigma\Sigma^*$. Finally, if $R(S) = \{S \to p\beta, S \to \bar{p}\gamma\}$ with p in P and β,γ in N^*, then $L(G) \cap \phi\Sigma^* \subset \phi(p \cup \bar{p})\Sigma^*$. Hence L(G) is syntdet. ///

---

† Recall from 1.4.1.4 that this is an s-grammar.

We now prove that each syntdet s-language can be generated by a deterministic s-grammar. We also prove that it is decidable for an s-grammar whether it generates a syntdet language.

Lemma 18.15. There is an algorithm which, for an arbitrary s-grammar G, determines whether L(G) is syntdet or not, and, if so, constructs a deterministic s-grammar G_1 such that $L(G_1) = L(G)$.

Proof. We first decide whether $L(G) = \emptyset$ †. If L(G) is empty, then it is syntdet. Let $G_1 = (\{Z\},\Sigma,\{Z \to \sigma Z\},Z)$, where σ is an arbitrary element of Σ. Obviously, G_1 satisfies the requirements.

If $L(G) \neq \emptyset$, then we can effectively find a reduced s-grammar G_1 generating the same language. We now claim that $L(G_1)$ is syntdet if and only if G_1 is a deterministic s-grammar (and this proves the lemma). The proof of this claim, which is similar to the one in Lemma 18.5, is left to the reader. ///

The characterization of Lang(RSI) is stated in the next theorem.

Notation 18.16. We shall denote by SyntdetSCFG(Σ), or simply SyntdetSCFG, the sub-pss of CFG consisting of all s-grammars over Σ which generate a syntdet language. †† ///

Theorem 18.17. RSI $=_{\ell(\text{eff})}$ SyntdetSCFG.

Proof

We first show that SyntdetSCFG $\subset_{\ell(\text{eff})}$ RSI. Let $G = (N,\Sigma,R,Z)$ be an arbitrary s-grammar generating a syntdet language. By Lemma 18.15, we may assume that G is deterministic. First suppose that $G = (\{Z\},\Sigma,\{Z \to \varepsilon\},Z)$. Let U be the rsi $(\Sigma,\mathfrak{F},Z,b)$, where $\mathfrak{F} = \{Z\}$ and b(Z)

---

† It is well known that the emptiness problem for context-free languages is decidable, see Hopcroft and Ullman [1969, Theorem 4.1].

†† Note that, by Lemma 18.15, SyntdetSCFG is a decidable sub-pss of CFG.

is the Ianov scheme $(\Sigma,\{n^o\},n^o,\{n^o\},\emptyset,\emptyset,\emptyset)$. Obviously, $L(U) = L(G) = \varepsilon$. Next suppose that G satisfies requirement (2) of Definition 18.12. Let U be the rsi $(\Sigma,\mathcal{F},Z_1,b)$, where $\mathcal{F} = N$, $Z_1 = Z$ and, for every S in $\mathcal{F}$,

if $R(S) = \{S \to \sigma\alpha\}$, then b(S) is a Ianov scheme such that $L(b(S)) = \{\sigma\alpha\}$, and

if $R(S) = \{S \to p\alpha,\ S \to \bar{p}\beta\}$, then b(S) is a Ianov scheme such that $L(b(S)) = \{p\alpha, \bar{p}\beta\}$.†

The existence of the above mentioned Ianov schemes easily follows from Theorem 18.7. It is easy to see that $L(U) = L(G)$. Hence SyntdetSCFG $\subset_{\ell(\text{eff})}$ RSI.

We now show that RSI $\subset_{\ell(\text{eff})}$ SyntdetSCFG. Let U be an arbitrary rsi. We shall show that we can find a deterministic s-grammar G such that $L(G) = L(U)$ (from this and Lemma 18.14 the ℓ-inclusion follows). Consider the context-free grammar $G_U = (N,\Sigma,R,Z)$, generating L(U), defined in Definition 4.8. It easily follows from Definition 4.13 that G_U satisfies the following condition (*).

(*) For every S in N,
either $R(S) = \emptyset$,
or $R(S) = \{S \to \varepsilon\}$,
or $R(S) = \{S \to \sigma T\}$ for certain σ in Σ and T in N,
or $R(S) = \{S \to pT_1,\ S \to \bar{p}T_2\}$ for certain p in P and T_1,T_2 in N,
or $R(S) = \{S \to T_1T_2\}$ for certain T_1,T_2 in N.

We first decide whether $L(G_U) = \emptyset$. If so, then $(\{Z\},\Sigma,\{Z \to \sigma Z\},Z)$ is a deterministic s-grammar generating L(U) (where σ is an arbitrary element of Σ). If $L(G_U) \neq \emptyset$, then we can find a reduced context-free grammar G_1 such that $L(G_1) = L(U)$. Moreover, G_1 still satisfies (*). We now decide whether $L(G_1) = \varepsilon$. If so, then $(\{Z\},\Sigma,\{Z \to \varepsilon\},Z)$ is a deterministic s-grammar generating L(U). If $L(G_1) \neq \varepsilon$, then it is easy to see from (*) that ε is not an element of $L(G_1)$. Then we can find a reduced context-free grammar $G_2 = (N,\Sigma,R,Z)$ without ε-rules, such that $L(G_2) = L(U)$. If we use the usual algorithm to obtain G_2 from G_1 ††, then it easily follows that G_2 satisfies the following condition (**).

---

† The same construction is used in the proof of Theorem 8.14(2).

†† See, for instance, Hopcroft and Ullman [1969, Theorem 4.2].

(**) For every S in N,

either $R(S) = \{S \to \sigma\alpha\}$ for certain σ in Σ and α in N^*,

or $R(S) = \{S \to p\alpha,\ S \to \bar{p}\beta\}$ for certain p in P and α,β in N^*,

or $R(S) = \{S \to T\alpha\}$ for certain T in N and α in N^*.

Next we remove the third kind of R(S) from G_2 as follows. Let us write, for arbitrary S and T in N, $S < T$ if $R(S) = \{S \to T\alpha\}$ for some α in N^*. Since G_2 is reduced, there can be no chain $S_1 < S_2 < \dots < S_n$ with $S_1 = S_n$ ($S_i \in N$ for $1 \le i \le n, n \ge 2$). We now construct a new grammar as follows.

Let S and T be nonterminals such that $S < T$.† Thus $R(S) = \{S \to T\alpha\}$ for some α in N^*. Let $R(T) = \{T \to \beta_1, \dots, T \to \beta_k\}$, where $k = 1$ or $k = 2$, and $\beta_1, \dots, \beta_k \in (N \cup \Sigma)^*$. Replace the rule $S \to T\alpha$ by all rules $S \to \beta_1\alpha, \dots, S \to \beta_k\alpha$.

The resulting grammar still generates L(U) and still satisfies (**). Moreover, it has the same nonterminals as the old grammar, and the same <-relations hold between these nonterminals, except for the relation $S < T$ which was removed by the above process. Thus, by repeating the process until it cannot be applied any more, we obtain a context-free grammar $G = (N,\Sigma,R,Z)$ generating L(U), such that G satisfies (**) and such that there are no nonterminals S and T with $S < T$. Hence, for every S in N, either $R(S) = \{S \to \sigma\alpha\}$ for some σ in Σ and α in N^*, or $R(S) = \{S \to p\alpha,\ S \to \bar{p}\beta\}$ for some p in P and α,β in N^*. Obviously G is a deterministic s-grammar, and the theorem is proved. ///

<u>Example 18.18</u>. Let $F = \{f,g\}$ and $P = \{p,q\}$. Consider the rsi U of Example 4.3. Let us construct a deterministic s-grammar generating L(U). The grammar G_U was given in Example 4.9. We first obtain a reduced context-free grammar G_2 without ε-rules, by substituting ε for each nonterminal S with $R(S) = \{S \to \varepsilon\}$ in all the rules of G_U. The rules of G_2 are $n_1 \to pn_2$, $n_1 \to \bar{p}n_3$, $n_2 \to g$, $n_3 \to n_5n_1$, $n_5 \to qn_6$, $n_5 \to \bar{q}n_9$, $n_6 \to fn_7$, $n_7 \to n_1$ and $n_9 \to g$. We now see that $n_3 < n_5$ and $n_7 < n_1$ (using the terminology of the proof of the previous theorem). After applying the procedure from the proof of Theorem 18.17 two times, and reducing the resulting grammar, we obtain the following deterministic s-grammar G, generating L(U). $G = (N,\Sigma,R,Z)$, where $N = \{n_1,n_2,n_3,n_6,n_7,n_9\}$, $Z = n_1$ and R consists of the rules $n_1 \to pn_2$, $n_1 \to \bar{p}n_3$, $n_2 \to g$, $n_3 \to qn_6n_1$, $n_3 \to \bar{q}n_9n_1$, $n_6 \to fn_7$, $n_7 \to pn_2$, $n_7 \to \bar{p}n_3$ and $n_9 \to g$.

A deterministic s-grammar with a smaller set of rules, generating

---

† We also assume that T is maximal (for no T' in N $T < T'$).

the same language, was given in Example 18.13. The rules of this grammar were read off the pictures in Example 4.3. ///

Another way of formulating the above result (without mentioning its effectiveness) is as follows. †

<u>Corollary 18.19</u>. Lang(RSI(Σ)) is the set of all syntactically deterministic s-languages over Σ.

Notice that it follows from Theorem 18.17 that RSI and SyntdetSCFG have "the same computing power" (recall Remark 8.10).

We now prove the following elementary property of rsi's. ††

<u>Corollary 18.20</u>. Each rsi is semantically deterministic.

<u>Proof</u>. Immediate from Theorem 18.17 and Lemma 14.3. ///

The characterization of RSI in Theorem 18.17 enables us to show that RSI is <u>not</u> closed under the standard mapping (cf. Section 16). Thus, there exists an rsi U such that no rsi V is a standard form of U. †††

<u>Theorem 18.21</u>. Let F and P be nonempty. Then RSI is not closed under S.

<u>Proof</u>. Let f be in F and p in P. Consider the rsi U = $(\Sigma,\mathcal{F},Z,b)$, where $\mathcal{F} = \{Z\}$ and

---

† Cf. Corollary 8.15 and Corollary 18.9.

†† This property was mentioned in a remark following Definition 4.13; recall Lemma 14.13.

††† The rsi U without standard form in RSI, given in the proof of the following theorem, is adapted from an example in Ashcroft, Manna and Pnueli [1973, Theorem 2].

b(Z) =

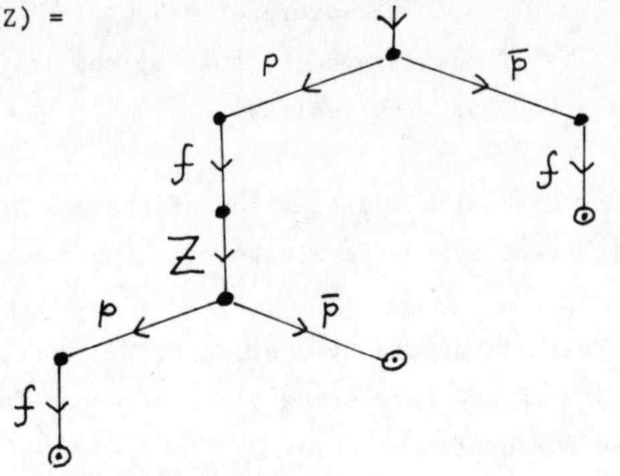

Obviously L(U) is generated by the context-free grammar with rules $Z \to \bar{p}f$, $Z \to pfZ\bar{p}$ and $Z \to pfZpf$. It easily follows that $L(U) = \bigcup_{n\geq 0} (pf)^n\ \bar{p}f(\bar{p} \cup pf)^n$.

We shall prove that S(L(U)) is not an s-language. Hence, by Theorem 18.17, there is no rsi generating S(L(U)). Consequently, RSI is not closed under S.

For ease of exposition we assume that $F = \{f\}$ and $P = \{p\}$. The similar proof for the general case is left to the reader.

Suppose, to the contrary, that there is an s-grammar $G = (N,\Sigma,R,Z)$ such that $L(G) = S(L(U))$. Consider the languages $A_1 = (pf)^*\bar{p}f\bar{p}$ and $A_2 = \{(pf)^n\ \bar{p}f(pf)^n\ p \mid n\geq 0\}$. Obviously, both A_1 and A_2 are contained in S(L(U)), and so, in L(G). Now consider, for each $n \geq 0$, the word $(pf)^n\ \bar{p}f$. Since G is an s-grammar, there is a unique α_n in N^* such that $Z \stackrel{*}{\Rightarrow} (pf)^n\ \bar{p}f\alpha_n$. Also, since both A_1 and A_2 are contained in L(G), $\alpha_n \stackrel{*}{\Rightarrow} \bar{p}$ and $\alpha_n \stackrel{*}{\Rightarrow} (pf)^n p$. From the fact that $\alpha_n \stackrel{*}{\Rightarrow} \bar{p}$ it follows that, for all n, α_n is a single nonterminal. Consequently there are k and m with $0 \leq k < m$ such that $\alpha_k = \alpha_m$. Then

$Z \stackrel{*}{\Rightarrow} (pf)^k\ \bar{p}f\alpha_k = (pf)^k\ \bar{p}f\alpha_m \stackrel{*}{\Rightarrow} (pf)^k\ \bar{p}f(pf)^m p$. But clearly, since $k < m$, $(pf)^k\ \bar{p}f(pf)^m p$ does not belong to S(L(U)). This is a contradiction. Hence S(L(U)) is not an s-language. ///

<u>Remark 18.22</u>. If F is empty, then RSI is effectively closed under S (Proof: each subset of T_S corresponds to an element of SyntdetSCFG). If P is empty, then RSI is also effectively closed under S (Proof: in this case S is the identity). ///

Theorem 18.21 is in a sense disappointing. In fact, since equality

of s-languages is decidable †, the closure of RSI under S would have yielded the decidability of equivalence in RSI (by the standard form theorem). But we have to live with reality!

We conclude this section with a discussion of the pss of all context-free schemes which generate syntdet context-free languages.

Notation 18.23. We shall denote by SyntdetCFG(Σ), or simply SyntdetCFG, the sub-pss of CFG consisting of all context-free schemes over Σ which generate a syntdet L-scheme. ///

Remark 18.24. Since RSI was obtained by imposing certain obvious "deterministic restrictions" on the elements of NRSI (Definition 4.13), one might expect that Lang(RSI) consists precisely of all syntactically deterministic elements of Lang(NRSI), that is, of all syntactically deterministic context-free languages. In other words, one might expect that RSI $=_{\ell}$ SyntdetCFG. However, although Theorem 18.17 implies that RSI $\subset_{\ell}$ SyntdetCFG, it follows from Theorem 18.21 that they are not ℓ-equal. (Proof. By Theorem 16.2 and Lemma 14.5, SyntdetCFG is closed under S. But, by Theorem 18.21, RSI is not closed under S. Therefore RSI and SyntdetCFG are not ℓ-equal. Actually, if U is the rsi of the proof of Theorem 18.21, then S(L(U)) is an element of Lang(SyntdetCFG), but, as shown in that proof, not of Lang(RSI)). Then one might expect that for each element of SyntdetCFG there exists an equivalent program scheme in RSI. However, even this is not true (see Theorem 19.25). ///

---

† Korenjak and Hopcroft [1966].

19. Translation of program schemes

A program scheme U is said to be translatable into a pss $\mathcal{L}$ if $\mathcal{L}$ contains a program scheme equivalent to U. Given two pss's $\mathcal{L}_1$ and $\mathcal{L}_2$, we can ask the following basic questions about translatability from $\mathcal{L}_1$ into $\mathcal{L}_2$.

(1) Do there exist program schemes in $\mathcal{L}_1$ which cannot be translated into $\mathcal{L}_2$? And, if so,

(2) is it decidable (or recursively enumerable) for an arbitrary program scheme in $\mathcal{L}_1$ whether it is translatable into $\mathcal{L}_2$? and

(3) is it possible to characterize those program schemes in $\mathcal{L}_1$ which are translatable into $\mathcal{L}_2$?

The answers to these questions provide us with some insight into the difference in "computing power" between $\mathcal{L}_1$ and $\mathcal{L}_2$. † Translatability (from flow charts to recursive equations and vice versa) was first discussed in McCarthy [1962, § 9]. Other papers on translatability include Paterson and Hewitt [1970], Strong [1971 b], Garland and Luckham [1973], and Chandra and Manna [1973].

In this section we shall be concerned with translatability into the pss's IAN, REG, RSI, CFG and SyntdetCFG ††. As can easily be seen, these pss's are related as follows:

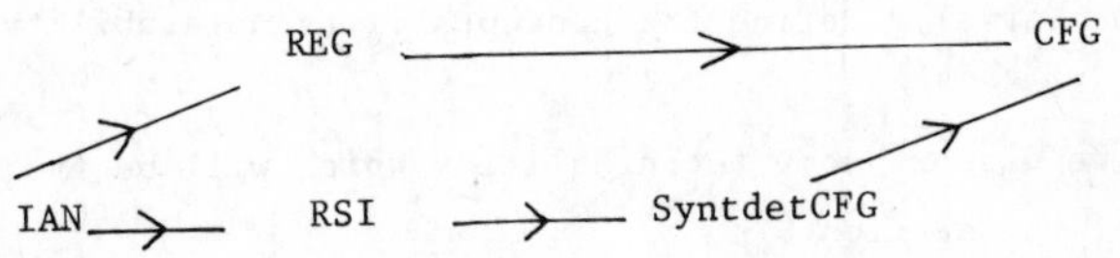

where " $\longrightarrow$ " means "effectively ℓ-included, but not ℓ-equal". †††
Questions (1), (2) and (3) above will be answered for these pss's as follows.

---

† Indeed, the above three questions might be conceived as being part of a definition of program scheme theory.

†† For SyntdetCFG, see Notation 18.23.

††† The proof of this is left to the reader. (Recall the end of section 8, and section 18, in particular Remark 18.24).

(1) The above diagram is also valid if "$\mathcal{L}_1 \rightarrow \mathcal{L}_2$" is interpreted to mean, firstly, that each program scheme of $\mathcal{L}_1$ is translatable into $\mathcal{L}_2$, and secondly, that there exist program schemes in $\mathcal{L}_2$ which are not translatable into $\mathcal{L}_1$ (in other words, that $\mathcal{L}_1$ has "less computing power" than $\mathcal{L}_2$).

(2) Translatability from REG and RSI into IAN is decidable (the latter fact will be proved in section 21). It is an open problem whether translatability from CFG and SyntdetCFG into RSI is decidable. In the remaining cases, it will be shown that translatability is not recursively enumerable.

(3) One should observe that, for a program scheme U, the property of being translatable into a particular pss $\mathcal{L}$ is a mixture of a syntactic and a semantic condition. In fact, by definition, U is translatable into $\mathcal{L}$ if there is a program scheme V with a certain syntactic structure (namely, V is in $\mathcal{L}$), such that V is semantically related to U (namely, V is equivalent to U).

For the above pss's $\mathcal{L}$, except for RSI, translatability into $\mathcal{L}$ will be characterized as a fully semantic property of program schemes. Such a characterization can be viewed as a semantic description of the computing power of $\mathcal{L}$. †

This section is organized as follows.

Firstly, we formally define the concepts of translatability and computing power.

Secondly, we discuss some technicalities which will be frequently used in the rest of the section.

Next we discuss translatability into REG. In answer to question (3) above, it is shown that translatability into REG is the same as semantic regularity †† (Theorem 19.9). In Theorem 19.12 it is proved that translatability from CFG into REG is not recursively enumerable.

---

† Note that, by the various theorems in Part II, these characterizations are equivalent to fully syntactic ones.

†† For the notion of semantic regularity, see section 15.

Then translatability into IAN is discussed. In answer to question (3) above, it is shown that a program scheme is translatable into IAN if and only if it is both semantically regular and semantically deterministic † (Theorem 19.13). This implies that REG and IAN have the same "deterministic computing power" (Theorem 19.14). It also implies that RSI and IAN have the same "regular computing power" (Theorem 19.17). Translatability from REG into IAN is decidable (Theorem 19.16), but from CFG (and SyntdetCFG) into IAN it is not recursively enumerable (Theorem 19.19).

Then we introduce the notion of a semantically equational program scheme (Definition 19.22), and show that such program schemes are precisely those which are translatable into CFG (Theorem 19.24). Next we prove that RSI has less computing power than SyntdetCFG (Theorem 19.25). Surprisingly, this means that CFG has more "deterministic computing power" than RSI (Corollary 19.26).

Finally we investigate the pss SyntdetCFG. In answer to question (3) above, it can easily be shown that a program scheme is translatable into SyntdetCFG if and only if it is both semantically equational and semantically deterministic. Translatability from CFG into SyntdetCFG is not recursively enumerable (Theorem 19.30). Moreover, it is not recursively enumerable whether a context-free scheme belongs to SyntdetCFG (Theorem 19.31). We conclude the section by proving that equivalence is not recursively enumerable in SyntdetCFG (Theorem 19.32).

Translatability is defined as follows.

Definition 19.1. Let $\mathcal{L}$ be a pss, and U a program scheme. U is translatable into $\mathcal{L}$ if there is a program scheme V in $\mathcal{L}$ such that $V \equiv U$ ††.

Example 19.2. Let F = {f} and P = {p}. Consider the context-free L-scheme $\{(\bar{p}f)^n pp^n \mid n \geq 0\}$. Since this L-scheme is equivalent to the

† For the notion of semantic determinism, see section 14.

†† Note that we only discuss "τ-translatability", which is the same as "tτ-translatability" (recall Theorem 11.13).

L-scheme $(\bar{p}f)^*p$, it is translatable into IAN. ///

Intuitively, the following (apparently weaker) notion of translatability is more obvious. Let us say that U is weakly translatable into $\mathcal{L}$ if $\mathcal{L}$ can compute all relations which U computes (formally: for each interpretation I there exists a program scheme V in $\mathcal{L}$ such that I(V) = I(U)). Obviously, if a program scheme is translatable into $\mathcal{L}$, then it is weakly translatable into $\mathcal{L}$. To see the converse, let U be weakly translatable into $\mathcal{L}$. Then, in particular, there is V in $\mathcal{L}$ such that $I_o(V) = I_o(U)$ †. By the universality of I_o it follows that $V \equiv U$. Hence U is translatable into $\mathcal{L}$.

Next we define the notion of computing power of a pss.

<u>Definition 19.3</u>. Let $\mathcal{L}_1$ and $\mathcal{L}_2$ be pss's. We write $\mathcal{L}_1 \leq \mathcal{L}_2$ if each program scheme of $\mathcal{L}_1$ is translatable into $\mathcal{L}_2$. We say that $\mathcal{L}_1$ and $\mathcal{L}_2$ have <u>the same computing power</u>, denoted by $\mathcal{L}_1 \equiv \mathcal{L}_2$, if $\mathcal{L}_1 \leq \mathcal{L}_2$ and $\mathcal{L}_2 \leq \mathcal{L}_1$. We say that $\mathcal{L}_1$ has <u>less computing power</u> than $\mathcal{L}_2$, denoted by $\mathcal{L}_1 < \mathcal{L}_2$, if $\mathcal{L}_1 \leq \mathcal{L}_2$ and $\mathcal{L}_1 \not\equiv \mathcal{L}_2$.

<u>Example 19.4</u>. It is easy to see that if $\mathcal{L}_1 \subset_\ell \mathcal{L}_2$, then $\mathcal{L}_1 \leq \mathcal{L}_2$ (recall Remark 8.10). Thus, if $\mathcal{L}_1 =_\ell \mathcal{L}_2$, then $\mathcal{L}_1 \equiv \mathcal{L}_2$. For examples of ℓ-equal pss's, see section 8. ///

Note that, if $\mathcal{L}_1 \equiv \mathcal{L}_2$, then a program scheme is translatable into $\mathcal{L}_1$ if and only if it is translatable into $\mathcal{L}_2$. For instance, by the above example, translatability into REG is the same as translatability into NIAN.

Before proceeding to the investigation of translatability we first make some technical observations which will be needed later on (Remark 19.5 - Lemma 19.8).

<u>Remark 19.5</u>. In the sequel we shall assume that F and P are nonempty.

---

† For I_o, see Definition 10.7 and Theorem 11.3.

For, if P is empty then the topic of translatability is a traditional one in formal language theory (recall Theorem 9.6), and if F is empty then most of our problems become trivial.

Moreover, we shall often assume that #(F) ≥ 2 and #(P) ≥ 2. In fact, all results of this section are true under the condition that F and P are nonempty, but the proofs are easier to read if it is assumed that both F and P contain at least two elements. ///

In order to simplify a number of arguments the following lemma is useful as a supplement to Lemma 17.3.

<u>Lemma 19.6</u>. Let $\mathcal{L}$ stand for IAN, REG, RSI, CFG or SyntdetCFG. Let Σ_1 and Σ_2 be alphabets such that $\Sigma_1 \subset \Sigma_2$, and let U be a program scheme over Σ_1. Then U is translatable into $\mathcal{L}(\Sigma_2)$ if and only if U is translatable into $\mathcal{L}(\Sigma_1)$.

<u>Proof</u>. The if part is immediate from Lemma 17.3.

The only-if part is proved as follows. Suppose that U is translatable into $\mathcal{L}(\Sigma_2)$. Thus there is a program scheme V_2 in $\mathcal{L}(\Sigma_2)$ such that $U \equiv V_2$ (with respect to Σ_2). Now, since U is a program scheme over Σ_1, it follows that, if I and I' are two interpretations which agree on Σ_1, then $I(U) = I'(U)$. Therefore the same holds for V_2. Let s be the substitution from Σ_2 into Σ_1 defined as follows: for every positive predicate symbol p in $\Sigma_2 - \Sigma_1$, $s(p) = \varepsilon$ and $s(\bar{p}) = \emptyset$; for every function symbol f in $\Sigma_2 - \Sigma_1$, $s(f) = \varepsilon$; for every σ in Σ_1, $s(\sigma) = \sigma$. Then $L(V_2) \equiv s(L(V_2))$ with respect to Σ_2 (Proof: Let A denote $L(V_2)$. Let I be an arbitrary interpretation of Σ_2. Then, by Lemma 2.12, $I(s(A)) = I_s(A)$, where I_s is the interpretation of Σ_2 such that, for all σ in Σ_2, $I_s(\sigma) = I(s(\sigma))$. Since I_s and I agree on Σ_1, $I_s(A) = I(A)$, and so $I(s(A)) = I(A)$. Consequently, $s(A) \equiv A$ with respect to Σ_2). Hence, by Lemma 17.3, $U \equiv s(L(V_2))$ with respect to Σ_1. We now claim that we can (effectively) find a program scheme V_1 in $\mathcal{L}(\Sigma_1)$ such that $L(V_1) = s(L(V_2))$. (Then $U \equiv V_1$, and so U is translatable into $\mathcal{L}(\Sigma_1)$, and the theorem is proved). Since the classes of regular and context-free languages are effectively closed under substitution, the claim holds for REG and CFG. Moreover, it is easy to see that the class of syntdet languages is closed under the substitution s. Hence the claim also holds for $\mathcal{L}$ = IAN (recall from section 18 that IAN $=_{\ell(\mathrm{eff})}$ SyntdetREG) and for $\mathcal{L}$ = SyntdetCFG. It is left to the reader to prove that the claim holds for RSI. ///

Note that the lemma holds effectively, in the sense that, for a program scheme U over Σ_1, if we have a program scheme V_2 over Σ_2 such that $U \equiv V_2$, then we can effectively find a program scheme V_1 over Σ_1 such that $U \equiv V_1$.

The following substitution will be used to relate arbitrary languages with program schemes.

Notation 19.7. Let $P = \{p,q\}$ and $F = \{f,g\}$. Let \$ be a new symbol. We shall use v to denote the substitution from $F \cup \{\$\}$ into Σ which is defined by $v(f) = pqf$, $v(g) = p\bar{q}g$ and $v(\$) = \bar{p}q$. ///

Some useful properties of v are summarized in the following lemma.

Lemma 19.8. Let $P = \{p,q\}$ and $F = \{f,g\}$. Let A be a subset of F^*. Then the following statements are true.

(1) $v(A\$)$ is a standard L-scheme over Σ.

(2) $v(A\$)$ is syntactically deterministic.

(3) For every $B \subset F^*$, $v(A\$) \subset v(B\$)$ if and only if $A \subset B$.

(4) $v(A\$)$ is regular if and only if A is regular, and $v(A\$)$ is context-free if and only if A is context-free (both effectively).

(5) $v(A\$)$ is a dpda language † if and only if A is a dpda language (effectively).

Proof. Statements (1) and (2) are obvious. For statements (3) and (4), observe that $A = e(v(A\$))$, where e is the substitution which erases all predicate symbols (that is, for a in $P \cup \bar{P}$, $e(a) = \varepsilon$, and $e(f) = f$ and $e(g) = g$). Notice also that the classes of regular and context-free

---

† For the notion of a dpda language, see 1.4.2.4.

languages are effectively closed under substitution.

We now prove statement (5). It should be obvious that v is a deterministic gsm mapping †. Also, as the reader may easily verify, the inverse gsm mapping v^{-1} is also a deterministic gsm mapping. Moreover, $(v^{-1})^{-1} = v$. Hence both v and v^{-1} are inverse deterministic gsm mappings. Since the class of dpda languages is effectively closed under such mappings ††, and since $v^{-1}(v(A\$)) = A\$$, it follows that v(A \$) is a dpda language if and only if A\$ is one. Statement (5) now follows from the fact that A\$ is a dpda language if and only if A is one†††.

///

We now proceed to the investigation of translatability into REG. In the next theorem we characterize those program schemes which are translatable into REG.

Theorem 19.9. Let U be an arbitrary program scheme. Then U is translatable into REG if and only if U is semantically regular.

Proof. (Only if): Suppose that U is translatable into REG. Thus $U \equiv V$ for some V in REG. It follows from Corollary 15.7 that V is semregular. Hence U is semregular.

(If): Suppose that U is semregular. Then, by the regularity theorem ††††, S(L(U)) is regular. But $U \equiv S(L(U))$, and so U is translatable into REG. ///

The above theorem can be viewed as a semantic description of the computing power of the pss REG. In fact it says that the computing power of REG is the same as that of the pss of all semantically regular L-schemes.

---

† For the notion of a gsm mapping, in particular the notation v^{-1}, see 1.4.2.2.

†† See Hopcroft and Ullman [1969, Theorem 12.3].

††† See Ginsburg and Greibach [1966, Corollary 1 of Theorem 3.4].

†††† Theorem 15.9.

Example 19.10. Let F = {f} and P = {p}. The context-free L-scheme $\{p^n pff^n \mid n \geq 0\}$ is translatable into REG (see Example 15.5). ///

It is now easy to find examples of program schemes which are not translatable into REG.

Corollary 19.11. REG < CFG.

Proof. Let f be in F and p in P (recall Remark 19.5). Consider a context-free scheme U such that $L(U) = \{(\bar{p}f)^n pf^n \mid n \geq 0\}$. Obviously S(L(U)) is not regular (otherwise the language $\{p\} \cup \bigcup_{n\geq 1} (\bar{p}f)^n pf(pf \cup \bar{p}f)^{n-1} (p \cup \bar{p})$, which is obtained from S(L(U)) by erasing all predicate symbols other than p and $\bar{p}$, would be regular). Hence, by Theorem 19.9 and the regularity theorem, U is not translatable into REG. ///

In the next theorem we use Theorem 19.9 to show that translatability from CFG into REG is not recursively enumerable.

Theorem 19.12. It is not recursively enumerable whether an arbitrary context-free scheme is translatable into REG.

Proof. Let us first note that it easily follows from Remark 19.5 and Lemma 19.6 that it suffices to prove the theorem for $\#(F) = \#(P) = 2$. So let F = {f,g} and P = {p,q}. We shall prove that the question whether an arbitrary context-free grammar, over an alphabet with two symbols, generates a regular language, can be reduced to the question whether a context-free scheme is translatable into REG. Since the former question is not recursively enumerable †, the theorem follows.

Let G be an arbitrary context-free grammar over F. Let us denote L(G) by A. By Lemma 19.8(4) we can find a context-free scheme U such that L(U) = v(A \$). Also by Lemma 19.8(4), L(G) is regular if and only if L(U) is regular. Moreover, since L(U) is standard, it follows from Theorem 19.9 and the regularity theorem that U is translatable into REG if and only if

---

† See Hopcroft and Ullman [1969, Theorem 14.6].

L(U) is regular. Consequently, L(G) is regular if and only if U is translatable into REG. Thus, recursive enumerability of the question of translatability of context-free schemes into REG would imply recursive enumerability of the question of regularity of context-free languages. ///

We shall now examine translatability into the pss IAN. The next theorem describes those program schemes that are translatable into IAN.

Theorem 19.13. Let U be an arbitrary program scheme. Then U is translatable into IAN if and only if U is both semantically regular and semantically deterministic.

Proof. Recall from the previous section that IAN $=_\ell$ SyntdetREG (Theorem 18.7). The only-if part of the theorem is an immediate consequence of this fact, Corollary 15.7 and Lemma 14.3. The if part is proved as follows. Let U be a program scheme which is semregular and semdet. From the regularity theorem and the determinism theorem † it follows that S(L(U)) is regular and syntdet. Hence, by the above ℓ-equality, S(L(U)) corresponds to a Ianov scheme. Therefore, since U ≡ S(L(U)), U is translatable into IAN. ///

As an immediate consequence of this theorem we obtain a semantic characterization of translatability from REG into IAN.

Theorem 19.14. Let U be an arbitrary regular scheme. Then U is translatable into IAN if and only if U is semantically deterministic.

Proof. Immediate from Theorem 19.13 and the fact that regular schemes are semregular. ///

This theorem expresses the obvious fact that NIAN and IAN have the

---

† Theorem 14.7.

same "deterministic computing power": each nondeterministic Ianov scheme which computes a partial function under all pτ-interpretations is equivalent to a deterministic Ianov scheme.

Evidently there exist regular schemes which are not translatable into IAN.

Corollary 19.15. IAN < REG.

Proof. By Lemma 19.6 it suffices to consider the case that F and P are singletons. So let F = {f} and P = {p}. Consider a regular scheme U such that $L(U) = (pf)^*p$. Since U is standard, it follows from Theorem 19.14 and the determinism theorem that U is translatable into IAN if and only if L(U) is syntdet. Obviously, this is not the case, and so the corollary holds. ///

The next theorem shows that translatability from REG into IAN is decidable.

Theorem 19.16. It is decidable whether an arbitrary regular scheme is translatable into IAN, and, if so, an equivalent Ianov scheme can effectively be found.

Proof. Let U be an arbitrary regular scheme.By Theorem 19.14 and the determinism theorem, U is translatable into IAN if and only if S(L(U)) is syntdet. Since REG is effectively closed under S (Theorem 16.2), we can find a regular scheme which generates S(L(U)). Hence, by Lemma 18.5, we can decide whether S(L(U)) is syntdet or not. If S(L(U)) is syntdet, then Theorem 18.7 implies that we can find a Ianov scheme which generates S(L(U)). Thus, since U ≡ S(L(U)), U is equivalent to this Ianov scheme. ///

We now consider translatability into IAN from the pss's RSI and SyntdetCFG.

Theorem 19.17. Let U be an element of RSI or SyntdetCFG. Then U is translatable into IAN if and only if U is semantically regular.

Proof. Immediate from Theorem 19.13 and the fact that rsi's and syntdet L-schemes are semdet (Collary 18.20 and Lemma 14.3 respectively). ///

Corollary 19.18. IAN < RSI.

Proof. Let $f \in F$ and $p \in P$, and consider an rsi U such that $L(U) = \{(\bar{p}f)^n pf^n \mid n \geq 0\}$. To see that U is not equivalent to any Ianov scheme, one can apply the proof of Corollary 19.11. ///

It will be proved in section 21 that translatability from RSI into IAN is decidable †. We now prove that neither translatability from SyntdetCFG into IAN nor translatability from CFG into IAN is recursively enumerable.

Theorem 19.19. It is not recursively enumerable whether an arbitrary context-free scheme (or element of SyntdetCFG, respectively) is translatable into IAN.

Proof. It is easy to adapt the proof of Theorem 19.12 into a proof of this theorem. (Note in particular, that by Lemma 19.8, the language L(U) in the proof of Theorem 19.12 is syntdet.) ///

Note that, by Theorems 19.9 and 19.17, a program scheme from RSI or SyntdetCFG is translatable into REG if and only if it is translatable into IAN.

We now turn to translatability into the pss CFG. To obtain a semantic characterization of translatability into CFG we introduce for arbitrary program schemes the property of being "semantically equational". Informally, we say that a program scheme is semantically equational if, under every interpretation, it computes a relation which is definable by a system of equations, using the operations of composition and finite union, a finite number of unknowns, and constant relations (the empty

---

† Theorem 21.18.

relation and all relations $I(\sigma)$ with $\sigma \in \Sigma$).[†] But one can easily prove that a relation is definable by such a system of equations if and only if it can be computed by a context-free L-scheme[††], and this explains the way the following definitions are given.

Definition 19.20. Let I be an interpretation, and let f be a relation on D_I. We say that f is equational in Σ_I if $f = I(A)$ for some context-free language A over Σ.[†††]

Example 19.21. Let $F = \{f,g\}$ and $P = \{p\}$. Let I be the interpretation such that D_I is the set of all nonnegative integers, $I(f) = \{(x,y) | x \geq 1$ and $y = x - 1\}$, $I(g) = \{(x,y) | y = x + 2\}$, $I(p) = \{(0,0)\}$ and $I(\bar{p}) = \{(x,x) | x > 0\}$. Then the relation $w = \{(x,y) | y = 2x\}$ is equational in Σ_I. In fact, $w = I(A)$ where A is the context-free language $\{(\bar{p}f)^n pg^n | n \geq 0\}$. Observe that w is the solution of the equation $w = I(\bar{p}) \circ I(f) \circ w \circ I(g) \cup I(p)$. ///

Definition 19.22. A program scheme U is called semantically equational if, for all interpretations I, I(U) is equational in Σ_I.

Example 19.23. Let $F = \{f\}$ and $P = \{p\}$. Consider the L-scheme $A = \{p^n (pf)^n \bar{p}f^n | n \geq 1\}$. Obviously A is equivalent to the context-free L-scheme $\{(pf)^n \bar{p}f^n | n \geq 1\}$. Hence A is a semantically equational L-scheme. ///

In the next theorem (the easy proof of which is left to the reader) we characterize translatability into CFG and we state some results analogous to those concerning semantic regularity (recall Theorem 15.9).

---

† For systems of equations in arbitrary algebras, see Mezei and Wright [1967]. For systems of equations in cslm's, see Blikle [1973, § 8].

†† This follows from the well known fact that each context-free language can be defined by a system of equations, using the operations of product and finite union, a finite number of unknowns, and constant languages (the empty language and the languages $\{\sigma\}$ with $\sigma \in \Sigma$). See Ginsburg [1966, section 1.2].

††† Compare this definition with Lemma 15.6. Recall that $\Sigma_I = \{I(\sigma) | \sigma \in \Sigma\}$ (Notation 15.3).

Theorem 19.24. Let U be a program scheme. Let I be a universal interpretation. Then the following four statements are equivalent.

(1) U is translatable into CFG,

(2) U is semantically equational,

(3) I(U) is equational in Σ_I, and

(4) S(L(U)) is context-free.

Note that this result implies that CFG < NPP (see section 5). To see this, let F = {f,g} and P = {p}, and recall from Example 5.13 that there is a (deterministic) npp U such that $L(U) = \{(pf)^n \bar{p} g^n f^n | n \geq 0\}$. Obviously S(L(U)) is not context-free, and so, by the above theorem, U is not translatable into CFG.

As far as translatability into RSI is concerned one would expect a result saying that each semantically deterministic context-free scheme is translatable into RSI †. In fact, since RSI was obtained from NRSI by imposing obvious deterministic restrictions on the control structure of the nrsi's, one would expect RSI and CFG to have the same "deterministic computing power" ††. Actually, as shown in the next theorem, CFG has more deterministic computing power than RSI. As a consequence we are unable to give a "nice" semantic characterization of translatability into RSI.

Theorem 19.25. RSI < SyntdetCFG.

Proof. The proof of this theorem is based on the fact that RSI is ℓ-equal to SyntdetSCFG (Theorem 18.17). It is similar to (but more complicated than) the proof of Theorem 18.21 (both proofs essentially go back to the fact that the language $\{a^n b | n \geq 1\} \cup \{a^n c^n | n \geq 1\}$ is not an s-language).

By Remark 19.5 and Lemma 19.6 it suffices to prove the theorem for

---

† Cf. Theorem 19.14.

†† See also Remark 18.24.

$\#(F) = \#(P) = 1$. So let $F = \{f\}$ and $P = \{p\}$. Consider the nrsi $U = (\Sigma, \mathcal{F}, Z_0, b)$, where $\mathcal{F} = \{Z_0, Z_1, Z_2\}$ and the bodies of Z_0, Z_1 and Z_2 are shown below.

$b(Z_o) =$

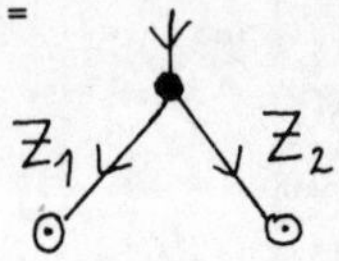

$b(Z_1) =$

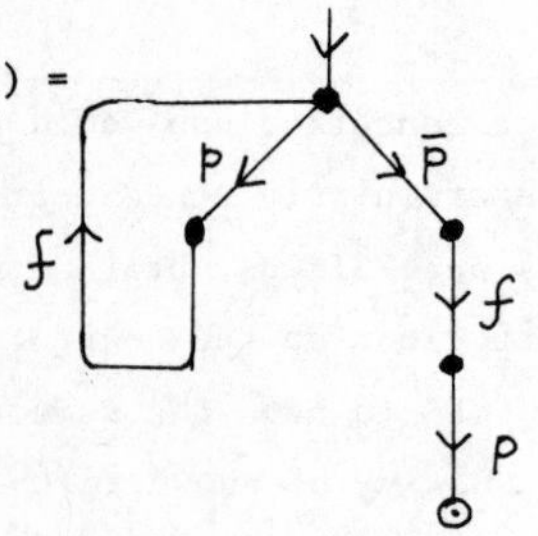

$b(Z_2) =$

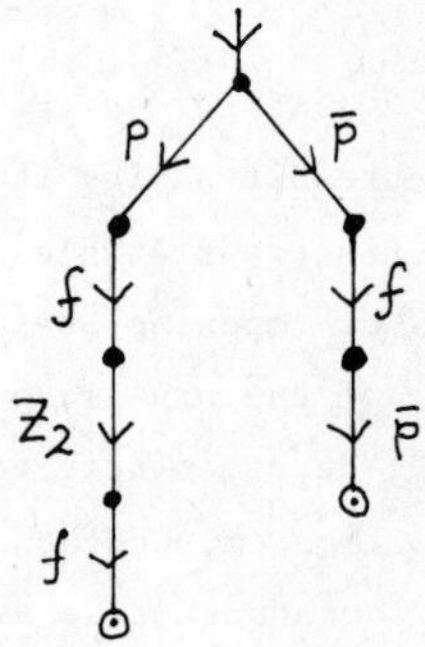

We shall denote $L(U)$ by A. It is easy to see that $A = \bigcup_{n\geq 0} (pf)^n \bar{p}f(p \cup \bar{p}f^n)$. Clearly, A is syntactically deterministic. Thus, since NRSI $=_\ell$ CFG, A corresponds to an element of SyntdetCFG. In what follows we shall prove that there is no s-grammar G such that $L(G)$ is syntdet and $S(L(G)) = S(A)$. Then, by the standard form theorem and the fact that RSI is ℓ-equal to SyntdetSCFG, A is not translatable into RSI, and the theorem is proved.

Assume to the contrary, that $G = (N,\Sigma,R,Z)$ is an s-grammar such that $L(G)$ is syntdet and $S(L(G)) = S(A)$. It is easy to see that $S(A) = \{\bar{p}fp, \bar{p}f\bar{p}\} \cup \bigcup_{n\geq 1} (pf)^n \bar{p}f(p \cup \bar{p}f(pf \cup \bar{p}f)^{n-1}(p \cup \bar{p}))$. Consider, for all $n \geq 1$, the words

(1) $(pf)^n \bar{p}fp$ and (2) $(pf)^n \bar{p}f\bar{p}f(pf)^{n-1}p$.

Obviously all these words belong to $S(A)$, and so to $S(L(G))$. It follows from Lemma 10.19 that, corresponding to the above words, there exist words in $L(G)$ of the following form: †

---

† Note that, for t in T and a in $P \cup \bar{P}$, t <u>in</u> a if and only if $t \in a^*$.

(1) $t_{n,1}ft_{n,2}f \cdots t_{n,n}ft_{n,n+1}ft_{n,n+2}$

such that $t_{n,1}, t_{n,2}, \ldots, t_{n,n} \in p^*$, $t_{n,n+1} \in \bar{p}^*$ and $t_{n,n+2} \in p^*$,

and

(2) $t'_{n,1}ft'_{n,2}f \cdots t'_{n,n}ft'_{n,n+1}fu_{n,1}fu_{n,2}f \cdots u_{n,n}fu_{n,n+1}$

such that $t'_{n,1}, t'_{n,2}, \ldots, t'_{n,n} \in p^*$, $t'_{n,n+1} \in \bar{p}^*$,

$u_{n,1} \in \bar{p}^*$ and $u_{n,2}, \ldots, u_{n,n+1} \in p^*$.

From the fact that L(G) is syntactically deterministic and the fact that, for each i in $\{1,2,\ldots,n+1\}$, $t_{n,i}$ and $t'_{n,i}$ both belong to the same a^* for some a in $\{p,\bar{p}\}$, it easily follows that, for all i in $\{1,2,\ldots,n+1\}$, $t_{n,i} = t'_{n,i}$. Consequently, since G is an s-grammar, there exists for each $n \geq 1$, a (unique) word α_n in N^* such that

(i) $Z \stackrel{*}{\Rightarrow} t_{n,1}ft_{n,2}f \cdots t_{n,n}ft_{n,n+1}f\alpha_n$,

(ii) $\alpha_n \stackrel{*}{\Rightarrow} t_{n,n+2}$ and

(iii) $\alpha_n \stackrel{*}{\Rightarrow} u_{n,1}fu_{n,2}f \cdots u_{n,n}fu_{n,n+1}$.

We shall now show that, for at least one n, α_n can be divided into two parts such that we can make a new derivation from α_n in which derivation (ii) is used for the left part of α_n and derivation (iii) for the right part of α_n. The result ϕ of derivation (i) together with this new derivation will be such that $S(\phi)$ contains a word not in S(A), contradicting the fact that S(L(G)) = S(A).

To obtain such a word ϕ we need to be sure that both the left and the right part of α_n generate at least one symbol f in derivation (iii). We now show that such an α_n can be found. Assume, to the contrary, that, for each $n \geq 1$, a single nonterminal T_n in α_n generates all symbols f in derivation (iii). Thus α_n can be written as $\alpha_n = \beta_n T_n \gamma_n$ (where $\beta_n, \gamma_n \in N^*$), such that $\beta_n \stackrel{*}{\Rightarrow} u^{\ell}_{n,1}$, $T_n \stackrel{*}{\Rightarrow} u^r_{n,1}fu_{n,2}f \cdots u_{n,n}fu^{\ell}_{n,n+1}$ and $\gamma_n \stackrel{*}{\Rightarrow} u^r_{n,n+1}$ with $u_{n,1} = u^{\ell}_{n,1}u^r_{n,1}$ and $u_{n,n+1} = u^{\ell}_{n,n+1}u^r_{n,n+1}$.†
Obviously, there are integers k and m such that $1 \leq k < m$ and $T_k = T_m$. But then, using derivation (i) for n = k,

---

† Note that $u^{\ell}_{n,1}$ denotes some left part of $u_{n,1}$, not the ℓth power of $u_{n,1}$.

$Z \stackrel{*}{\Rightarrow} t_{k,1}ft_{k,2}f \cdots t_{k,k}ft_{k,k+1}f\alpha_k$

$= t_{k,1}ft_{k,2}f \cdots t_{k,k}ft_{k,k+1}f\beta_k T_m \gamma_k$

$\stackrel{*}{\Rightarrow} t_{k,1}ft_{k,2}f \cdots t_{k,k}ft_{k,k+1}fu^{\ell}_{k,1}u^{r}_{m,1}fu_{m,2}f \cdots u_{m,m}fu^{\ell}_{m,m+1}u^{r}_{k,k+1}$.

Denote this last word by ψ. Now, since both $u^{\ell}_{k,1}$ and $u^{r}_{m,1}$ are in $\bar{p}^*$, and both $u^{\ell}_{m,m+1}$ and $u^{r}_{k,k+1}$ are in p^*, it easily follows that the word $(pf)^k\bar{p}f\bar{p}f(pf)^{m-1}p$ is an element of $S(\psi)$, and, so, of $S(A)$. Since $m \neq k$, this is a contradiction. This proves that there is an integer n such that no single nonterminal of α_n generates all symbols f in derivation (iii).

Hence α_n has the form $\beta_n\gamma_n$ (where $\beta_n, \gamma_n \in N^*$) such that both β_n and γ_n generate at least one symbol f in derivation (iii). Consequently, from this derivation, we can find derivations $\beta_n \stackrel{*}{\Rightarrow} u_{n,1}f \cdots u_{n,m-1}fu^{\ell}_{n,m}$ and $\gamma_n \stackrel{*}{\Rightarrow} u^{r}_{n,m}fu_{n,m+1} \cdots fu_{n,n+1}$, where m is an integer such that $2 \leq m \leq n$, and $u^{\ell}_{n,m}$ and $u^{r}_{n,m}$ are strings such that $u_{n,m} = u^{\ell}_{n,m}u^{r}_{n,m}$. Let us now consider derivation (ii): $\beta_n\gamma_n \stackrel{*}{\Rightarrow} t_{n,n+2}$. Suppose that $\beta_n \stackrel{*}{\Rightarrow} t^{\ell}_{n,n+2}$ and $\gamma_n \stackrel{*}{\Rightarrow} t^{r}_{n,n+2}$, where $t_{n,n+2} = t^{\ell}_{n,n+2}t^{r}_{n,n+2}$. But then, using derivation (i),

$Z \stackrel{*}{\Rightarrow} t_{n,1}ft_{n,2}f \cdots t_{n,n+1}f\beta_n\gamma_n$

$\stackrel{*}{\Rightarrow} t_{n,1}ft_{n,2}f \cdots t_{n,n+1}ft^{\ell}_{n,n+2}u^{r}_{n,m}fu_{n,m+1} \cdots fu_{n,n+1}$.

Let us denote this last word by ϕ. Now, $t^{\ell}_{n,n+2}$ is in p^* and, since $m \geq 2$, $u^{r}_{n,m}$ is also in p^*. Hence, as can easily be seen, the word $(pf)^n\bar{p}f(pf)^{n-m+1}p$ is in $S(\phi)$, and so, in $S(A)$. But, since $m \leq n$, $n-m+1 \geq 1$. Thus this word cannot be in $S(A)$. Hence we have a contradiction, and the theorem is proved. ///

It is an immediate consequence of this theorem that the analogue of Theorem 19.14 does not hold for recursive schemes.

<u>Corollary 19.26</u>. There exists a semantically deterministic context-free scheme which is not translatable into RSI.

<u>Proof</u>. Immediate from Theorem 19.25 and Lemma 14.3. ///

Finally we investigate the pss SyntdetCFG .

It is left to the reader to show that a program scheme is translatable into SyntdetCFG if and only if it is both semantically equational and semantically deterministic. Consequently, a context-free scheme is translatable into SyntdetCFG if and only if it is semantically deterministic. It easily follows that SyntdetCFG < CFG (see the proof of Corollary 19.15).

We shall now prove that it is not recursively enumerable whether a context-free scheme is semantically deterministic (that is, translatable into SyntdetCFG). Also, we show that it is not recursively enumerable whether a context-free scheme generates a syntdet language. To do this we need the following concept.

Definition 19.27. A language A over an alphabet Δ is prefix-free if, for every word ϕ in A, $A \cap \phi\Delta^* = \{\phi\}$.

Note that each syntdet language is prefix-free.

In the next lemma we show that prefix-freedom is not recursively enumerable for context-free languages.

Lemma 19.28. It is not recursively enumerable whether an arbitrary context-free grammar generates a prefix-free language.†

Proof. Consider two arbitrary context-free languages A_1 and A_2. Let A be the context-free language $A_1\$ \cup A_2\$\$$, where \$ is a new symbol. Evidently, A is prefix-free if and only if $A_1 \cap A_2 = \emptyset$. Since it is not recursively enumerable whether the intersection of two arbitrary context-free languages is empty ††, the lemma follows. ///

We now prove a lemma from which the previously mentioned results about SyntdetCFG will follow.

Lemma 19.29. It is not recursively enumerable for an arbitrary context-free scheme U whether S(L(U)) is syntdet.

---

† For dpda languages prefix-freedom is decidable (Geller and Harrison [1973, Theorem 3.2]).

†† Hopcroft and Ullman [1969, Theorem 14.3].

Proof. Let F = {f,g} and P = {p,q}. Consider an arbitrary context-free language A over F, and let $A_1 = v(A) \cdot p(q \cup \bar{q})$, where v is the substitution defined in Notation 19.7. Obviously A_1 is a standard context-free language, and so, $S(A_1) = A_1$. We leave it to the reader to show that A_1 is syntdet if and only if A is prefix-free. The lemma now follows from Lemma 19.28.† ///

The next theorem shows that translatability from CFG into SyntdetCFG is not recursively enumerable.

Theorem 19.30. It is not recursively enumerable whether an arbitrary context-free scheme is semantically deterministic.

Proof. Immediate from Lemma 19.29 and the determinism theorem. ///

Another consequence of Lemma 19.29 is that syntactic determinism is not recursively enumerable for context-free languages.

Theorem 19.31. It is not recursively enumerable whether an arbitrary context-free scheme generates a syntactically deterministic L-scheme.

Proof. Immediate from Lemma 19.29 and the fact that CFG is effectively closed under S (Theorem 16.2). ///

Thus, by this theorem, SyntdetCFG is an undecidable sub-pss of CFG. It is an open question whether there exists a decidable sub-pss of CFG with the same computing power as SyntdetCFG (in other words, with the same computing power as the pss of all semantically deterministic context-free schemes).

We conclude this section by showing that equivalence is not recursively

---

† It is also left to the reader to show that Lemma 19.28 also holds with a fixed alphabet of two symbols.

enumerable in SyntdetCFG.[†]

Theorem 19.32. The equivalence relation is not recursively enumerable in SyntdetCFG.

Proof. Let F = {f,g} and P = {p,q} (recall Remark 19.5 and Lemma 19.6). Consider arbitrary context-free languages A and B over F. We shall prove that the question whether A and B are equal is reducible to the question whether two syntdet context-free L-schemes are equivalent. Since the former question is not recursively enumerable[††], this proves the theorem. Let $A_1 = v(A\,\$)$ and $B_1 = v(B\,\$)$, where v is the substitution defined in Notation 19.7. By Lemma 19.8, A_1 and B_1 belong to SyntdetCFG. By the same lemma A_1 and B_1 are standard. Hence, by the standard form theorem, $A_1 \equiv B_1$ if and only if $A_1 = B_1$. Again by Lemma 19.8, $A_1 = B_1$ if and only if $A = B$. Consequently, $A_1 \equiv B_1$ if and only if $A = B$. ///

Note that, in the same way, it can be shown that the relations $\leq$, $\equiv_\pi$ and $\leq_\pi$ are not recursively enumerable in SyntdetCFG.

Remark 19.33. The reader may easily see that all "positive" results of this section also hold for the case of regular shift distributions. ///

---

† This result strengthens Theorem 17.4.

†† Hopcroft and Ullman [1969, Corollary 14.1].

20. Program schemes with markers

A natural way to extend the computing flexibility of a program scheme is to provide it, in addition to its usual features, with a finite number of variables. We shall consider the case that these variables take on values in a finite set, the elements of which are called markers†. To operate on its variables the program scheme has at its disposal assignment statements to set a variable to a certain value (e.g. v := k, where v is a variable and k one of its values), and test statements to examine the value of a variable (e.g. v = k and v ≠ k, where v is a variable and k a marker). The addition of markers to program schemes was studied, for example, in †† Böhm and Jacopini [1966], Ashcroft and Manna [1971], Bruno and Steiglitz [1972] and Constable and Gries [1972].

In this section we first define the general notion of a program scheme with markers (Definition 20.5), and the relation computed by it under an arbitrary interpretation (Definition 20.9).

Then we show that with each program scheme with markers we may associate, in a natural manner, a language (Definition 20.15), which, as an L-scheme, is equivalent to that program scheme (Theorem 20.19). This result shows that also program schemes with markers can be investigated from the L-scheme point of view.

Next we show that, for most of the pss's considered so far, addition of markers does not increase their computing power (Theorems 20.22 and 2o.24). The computing power of the pss RSI is increased by the addition

---

† A variable which has only a finite number of values is sometimes called a flag (see Bruno and Steiglitz [1972, § 4]). If the number of its values is two, then it is called a boolean variable. It should be clear to the reader that a program scheme with an arbitrary number of flags can easily be translated into one with one flag only.

†† Very often, in the literature, program schemes with just boolean variables are considered, but it is easy to see that every program scheme with markers can be translated into a program scheme with boolean variables.

of markers (Theorem 20.25), but not beyond that of NRSI (Theorem 20.26). The pss of rsi's with markers will be considered more closely in the next section.

Before proceeding to formal definitions we first consider two informal examples in which we discuss the effect of adding markers to program schemes on the computing power of some specific pss's.

Example 20.1. The addition of markers to Ianov schemes has been studied by various authors in connection with the problem of translating a Ianov scheme into a "while program scheme"†. As an example, consider the following Ianov scheme U (where F = {f} and P = {p}).

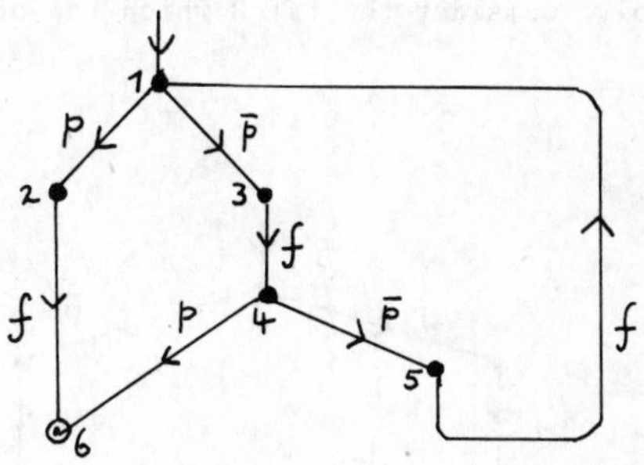

It is easy to see that U is equivalent to the following while program scheme which uses one variable v to hold the markers 1,2,...,6. (We use "(" and ")" rather than "begin" and "end").

```
v := 1;
while v ≠ 6 do
          if v = 1 then (if p then v := 2 else v := 3)
   else   if v = 2 then (f; v := 6)
   else   if v = 3 then (f; v := 4)
   else   if v = 4 then (if p then v := 6 else v := 5)
   else   if v = 5 then (f; v := 1)
```

---

† As the notion of a while program scheme should be intuitively clear, and as it is used in this example only, we shall not bother the reader with its formal definition.

In this way (that is, by using the nodes of the Ianov scheme as markers) every Ianov scheme can be translated into a while program scheme with markers †. But it can be proved ††, that there exists a Ianov scheme which is not equivalent to any while program scheme without markers. Thus the use of markers increases the computing power of while program schemes. On the other hand it has been shown that every Ianov scheme with markers is equivalent to one without markers †††. Hence the use of markers does not increase the computing power of Ianov schemes. Note that it follows from this result (and the obvious fact that every while program scheme is equivalent to a Ianov scheme) that the computing power of the pss of while program schemes with markers is the same as that of the pss of Ianov schemes. ///

<u>Example 20.2.</u> Let f be a function symbol and p a positive predicate symbol. Consider the rsi U which has one procedure symbol S with body

b(S) =

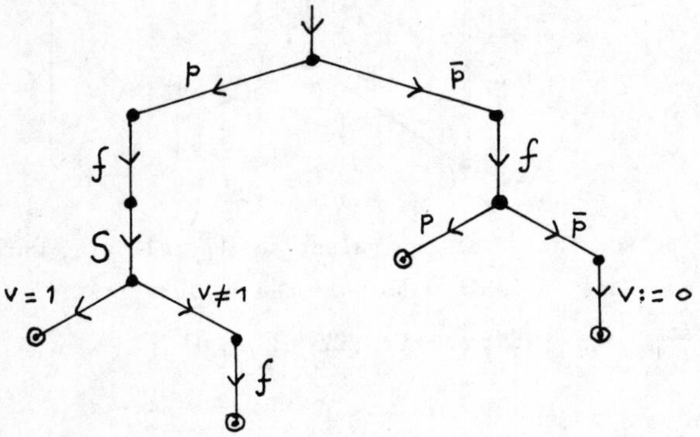

---

† See Böhm and Jacopini [1966] and Cooper [1967].

†† See Knuth and Floyd [1971] and Ashcroft and Manna [1971].
In fact, it can be shown that the above Ianov scheme U is not equivalent to any while program scheme without markers.

††† Bruno and Steiglitz [1972, § 4].

U makes use of a variable v which may have the values 1 and 0 (thus v is a boolean variable). It is assumed that the initial value of v is always 1.

Let us consider the execution of U under some interpretation I of $\{f,p,\bar{p}\}$. Denote the predicate $(I(p),I(\bar{p}))$ by p_I and the relation I(f) by f_I. First U applies f_I while p_I is true, say n times. Then U applies f_I once more and sets v to the value of the predicate p_I (in the sense that, if p_I is false, then v is set to 0, and otherwise the value of v remains 1). In the case that v is 0, U applies n times the relation f_I (each time checking whether v is still 0) and halts. In the case that v is 1, U checks n times whether v is still 1 and halts.

From the above description of the execution of U under an arbitrary interpretation it easily follows that U is equivalent to the L-scheme $\bigcup_{n\geq 0} (pf)^n \bar{p}f(p \cup \bar{p}f^n)$. Since it was shown in the proof of Theorem 19.25 that this L-scheme is not equivalent to any rsi, we can conclude that the use of markers increases the computing power of rsi's.

In fact our investigation of program schemes with markers originated from an effort to define a "natural" pss with the same "deterministic computing power" as CFG (recall the remark preceding Theorem 19.25 and the remark following Theorem 19.31). It will be shown in the next section that we failed in this respect: the pss of rsi's with markers has still less computing power than SyntdetCFG. ///

We now proceed to the formal definitions.

In what follows we shall restrict attention to program schemes with markers which use one variable only †. In such a program scheme the instruction symbols are taken from both the set of instruction symbols Σ and the set of symbols denoting assignments to and tests on its variable. This combined set of instruction symbols is defined in the next definition.

<u>Definition 20.3.</u> Let K be a finite set. Then the alphabet Σ_K is defined as follows. ††

For every k in K, let a_k, e_k and $\bar{e}_k$ be new symbols. The alphabets $F\cup\{a_k \mid k\in K\}$, $P\cup\{e_k \mid k\in K\}$ and $\bar{P}\cup\{\bar{e}_k \mid k\in K\}$ will be denoted by F_K, P_K and $\bar{P}_K$ respectively.

Σ_K is defined to be the alphabet $F_K \cup P_K \cup \bar{P}_K$, such that the

---

† Obviously this is not an essential restriction.

†† Recall that Σ denotes our fixed alphabet of instruction symbols.

elements of F_K are its function symbols, those of P_K its positive predicate symbols and those of $\overline{P}_K$ its negative predicate symbols.

This definition should be interpreted as follows. K is a set of markers to be used as values of the variable v in a program scheme with markers (recall that we shall only deal with program schemes with one additional variable). For each k in K, a_k stands for v := k ("assign k to v"), e_k stands for v = k and $\bar{e}_k$ for $v \neq k$ ("is the value of v equal to k ?").

Example 20.4. Let F = {f}, P = {p} and K = {1,2}. Then $F_K = \{f,a_1,a_2\}$, $P_K = \{p,e_1,e_2\}$ and $\overline{P}_K = \{\bar{p},\bar{e}_1,\bar{e}_2\}$. And so $\Sigma_K = \{f,a_1,a_2,p,\bar{p},e_1,\bar{e}_1,e_2\bar{e}_2\}$. ///

We now define program schemes with markers.

Definition 20.5. Let, for every alphabet Δ, $\mathcal{L}(\Delta)$ be a pss over Δ †. An $\mathcal{L}$ program scheme with markers (over Σ) is a 4-tuple $U_1 = (\Sigma, K, k_o, U)$, where

(1) K is a finite nonempty set (of markers),

(2) k_o is a distinguished element of K (the initial marker), and

(3) U is a program scheme from $\mathcal{L}(\Sigma_K)$.

Terminology 20.6. To simplify terminology we shall, in the sequel, use phrases like Ianov schemes with markers, context-free schemes with markers, L-schemes with markers, etc., in the obvious sense. ///

Here are some examples of program schemes with markers.

---

† Roughly speaking, we have here a mapping $\mathcal{L}$ which to an arbitrary alphabet Δ assigns a pss over Δ. (In this sense we can talk about "$\mathcal{L}$ program schemes with markers"). However, to avoid cumbersome set-theoretical details needed for defining $\mathcal{L}$ formally, we have decided on the given terminology and notation (which should not lead to confusion).

Example 20.7. Let $F = \{f,g,k\}$ and $P = \{p,q\}$.

(1) Let $K = \{0,1\}$, and let U be the following Ianov scheme over Σ_K:

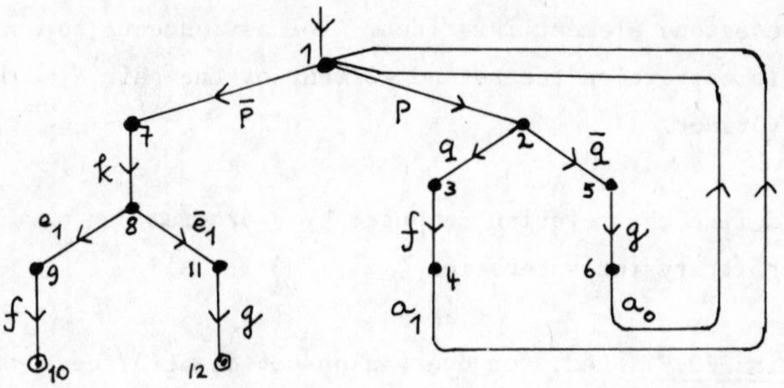

Then $(\Sigma,K,1,U)$ is a Ianov scheme with markers (over Σ).

(2) The 4-tuple $A_1 = (\Sigma,K,k_o,A)$, where $K = \{0,1\}$, $k_o = 1$ and $A = (pqfa_1 \cup p\bar{q}ga_0)^*\bar{p}k(e_1f \cup \bar{e}_1g)$, is an L-scheme with markers. Note that $A = L(U)$, where U is defined as in (1).

(3) Let $K = \{0,1\}$, $k_o = 1$ and let G be the context free scheme (N,Σ_K,R,Z) such that $N = \{S,T\}$, $Z = S$ and R consists of the rules $S \to \bar{p}$, $S \to pfST$, $T \to e_1ga_0$ and $T \to \bar{e}_1fa_1$. Then (Σ,K,k_o,G) is a context-free scheme with markers. ///

To define the relation computed by a program scheme with markers under an arbitrary interpretation, we have to extend the given interpretation (of Σ) to an interpretation of Σ_K, where K is the set of markers used by the program scheme. We do this as follows.

Definition 20.8. Let $I = (D,h)$ be a general interpretation of Σ †, and let K be a finite set. Then the general interpretation $I_K = (D_K,h_K)$ is defined as follows.

(1) $D_K = D \times K$.

(2) For each σ in Σ,

$h_K(\sigma) = \{((x,k),(y,k)) \mid (x,y) \in h(\sigma) \text{ and } k \in K\}$.

(3) For each k in K,

$h_K(a_k) = \{((x,k'),(x,k)) \mid x \in D \text{ and } k' \in K\}$,

$h_K(e_k) = \{((x,k),(x,k)) \mid x \in D\}$, and

$h_K(\bar{e}_k) = \{((x,k'),(x,k')) \mid x \in D, k' \in K \text{ and } k' \neq k\}$.

---

† For the notion of "general interpretation", recall Definition 2.1.

In words, an element of D_K is a pair consisting of an element of the original domain D followed by a marker which is the value of the variable used by a program scheme with markers. The interpreted instruction symbols from Σ operate on the first element of such a pair, leaving the second element invariant. The assignments to and tests on the variable operate on the second element of the pair, leaving the first element invariant.

We now define the relation computed by a program scheme with markers under an arbitrary interpretation.

<u>Definition 20.9</u>. Let, for every alphabet Δ, $\mathcal{L}(\Delta)$ be a pss over Δ. For an $\mathcal{L}$ program scheme with markers $U_1 = (\Sigma,K,k_o,U)$ and a general interpretation I of Σ, we define $I(U_1)$, the <u>relation computed by U_1 under I</u>, to be

$\{(x,y)\in D_I \times D_I \mid ((x,k_o),(y,k))\in I_K(U)$ for some k in K$\}$. †

Thus the relation computed by U_1 is obtained from the relation computed by U by considering inputs with the initial marker only, and then disregarding the markers in the input and output.

<u>Example 20.10</u>. Consider the Ianov scheme with markers $U_1 = (\Sigma,K,k_o,U)$ from Example 20.7(1). Let I be the interpretation of Σ, such that D_I is the set of all integers,

$h(f) = \{(x,y) \mid y=x-1\}$, $h(g) = \{(x,y) \mid y=x-3\}$, $h(k) = id_{D_I}$,

$h(p) = \{(x,x) \mid x>0\}$, $h(\bar{p}) = \{(x,x) \mid x\leq 0\}$,

$h(q) = \{(x,x) \mid x$ is even$\}$ and $h(\bar{q}) = \{(x,x) \mid x$ is odd$\}$.

For the argument (4,1) $I_K(U)$ has the value (-3,0). (The corresponding execution of U under I_K, recall Definition 3.5, is $(1,(4,1)) \vdash (2,(4,1)) \vdash (3,(4,1)) \vdash (4,(3,1)) \vdash (1,(3,1)) \vdash (2,(3,1)) \vdash (5,(3,1)) \vdash (6,(0,1)) \vdash (1,(0,0)) \vdash (7,(0,0)) \vdash (8,(0,0)) \vdash (11,(0,0)) \vdash (12,(-3,0))$).

---

† Note that U is an element of the pss $\mathcal{L}(\Sigma_K)$. Therefore, by the definition of a pss, $I_K(U)$ is a well defined relation on D_K.

Consequently, for the argument 4, $I(U_1)$ has the value -3. ///

We now show how to associate with each program scheme with markers an equivalent L-scheme "without markers" (meaning that the L-scheme is again over the alphabet Σ). In fact this L-scheme consists of the sequences of instruction symbols from Σ obtained by following all those paths through the program scheme, which are "correct" according to the assignments to and tests on the variable of the program scheme. Thus we first define the set of all "correct" sequences of instruction symbols from Σ_K (where K is the set of markers); then we define the substitution from Σ_K into Σ which erases all symbols in $\Sigma_K - \Sigma$, and finally we define the L-scheme corresponding to a program scheme with markers (Definition 20.15).

Definition 20.11. Let K be a finite set and k_o an element of K. For all k_1, k_2 in K, we recursively define a language $C(k_1,k_2)$ over Σ_K as follows.

(1) For every k in K, ε is in $C(k,k)$.

(2) For all k_1,k_2 in K, if ϕ is in $C(k_1,k_2)$, then

(2.1) for all σ in Σ, $\phi\sigma$ is in $C(k_1,k_2)$,

(2.2) for all k in K, ϕa_k is in $C(k_1,k)$,

(2.3) ϕe_{k_2} is in $C(k_1,k_2)$, and

(2.4) for all k in K, if $k \neq k_2$, then $\phi\bar{e}_k$ is in $C(k_1,k_2)$.

Furthermore we define the language of all correct words over Σ_K, denoted by $C_{k_o,K}$, to be $\bigcup_{k\in K} C(k_o,k)$.

Whenever the element k_o is understood (in most cases k_o is the "initial marker"), we shall write C_K rather than $C_{k_o,K}$.

Intuitively, for a set K of markers and for k_1,k_2 in K, $C(k_1,k_2)$ consists of all words over Σ_K which can be "executed" on a variable v, such that the initial value k_1 of v is transformed into the final value k_2 of v (where it is understood that, during this "execution", symbols from Σ are ignored).

Example 20.12. Let $F = \{f,g\}$, $P = \{p,q\}$, $K = \{1,2\}$ and $k_o = 1$. Then $\bar{e}_2 f p a_2 g e_2$ belongs to $C(1,2)$ and $f e_1 e_1 a_1 p \bar{p} a_2 a_1$ belongs to $C(1,1)$. To see this, note that, intuitively, execution of ($v \neq 2$; $v:=2$; $v=2$) **and** ($v=1$; $v=1$; $v:=1$; $v:=2$; $v:=1$) transforms the initial value 1 of the variable v into the final values 2 and 1 respectively (where execution of a test means checking its truth). Thus both these words belong to C_K. Words not in C_K are, for instance, ge_2 and $a_2e_2q\bar{e}_2$. ///

It is easy to transform the clauses of Definition 20.11 into a regular grammar generating the set of all correct words over Σ_K. Hence the following lemma holds.

Lemma 20.13. Let K be a finite set and k_o an element of K. Then $C_{k_o,K}$ is a regular language.

Next we define the substitution which erases all symbols not in Σ.

Definition 20.14. Let K be a finite set. The substitution s_K from Σ_K into Σ is defined as follows.

(1) For every σ in Σ, $s_K(\sigma) = \sigma$.

(2) For every k in K, $s_K(a_k) = s_K(e_k) = s_K(\bar{e}_k) = \varepsilon$.

We can now define the L-scheme corresponding to a program scheme with markers.

Definition 20.15. Let, for every alphabet Δ, $\mathcal{L}(\Delta)$ be a pss over Δ. Let $U_1 = (\Sigma,K,k_o,U)$ be an $\mathcal{L}$ program scheme with markers. We define $L(U_1)$, the L-scheme corresponding to U_1, to be the language $s_K(L(U) \cap C_K)$ over Σ. †

Example 20.16.

(1) Consider the Ianov scheme with markers $U_1 = (\{f,g,k,p,\bar{p},q,\bar{q}\},\{0,1\},1,U)$ from Example 20.7(1). It is easy to see that $L(U) \cap C_K = (pqfa_1 \cup p\bar{q}ga_o)^*(pqfa_1\bar{p}ke_1f \cup p\bar{q}ga_o\bar{p}k\bar{e}_1g) \cup \bar{p}ke_1f$.

---

† Note that U is an element of the pss $\mathcal{L}(\Sigma_K)$. Therefore, by the definition of a pss, L(U) is a well defined language over Σ_K. Recall that C_K is the language $C_{k_o,K}$ defined in Definition 20.11.

Hence $L(U_1) = (pqf \cup p\bar{q}g)^*(pqf\bar{p}kf \cup p\bar{q}g\bar{p}kg) \cup \bar{p}kf$.

(2) Consider the L-scheme with markers $A_1 = (\Sigma, K, k_0, A)$ from Example 20.7(2). Since A is an L-scheme, $L(A) = A$, and so $L(A_1) = s_K(A \cap C_K)$. Hence $L(A_1) = L(U_1)$, where U_1 is the Ianov scheme with markers from Example 20.7(1).

(3) Consider the context free scheme G_1 from Example 20.7(3). It can easily be verified that

$L(G_1) = \{(pf)^{2n}\ \bar{p}(gf)^n | n \geq 0\} \cup \{(pf)^{2n+1}\ \bar{p}(gf)^n g | n \geq 0\}$. ///

In Theorem 20.19 we shall prove that the class of $\mathcal{L}$ program schemes with markers is a pss over Σ (in other words, for any program scheme U_1 with markers and any general interpretation I, $I(L(U_1)) = I(U_1)$). To do this we shall prove that the class of all L-schemes with markers constitutes a pss (Lemma 20.18). Let us first compare (for a given set K of markers) the relation computed by a word ϕ over Σ_K with the relation computed by $s_K(\phi)$.

<u>Lemma 20.17</u>. Let K be a finite set, let I be a general interpretation of Σ, and let ϕ be a word over Σ_K. Then, for all k_1, k_2 in K and (x,y) in D_I, $((x,k_1),(y,k_2)) \in I_K(\phi)$ if and only if $(x,y) \in I(s_K(\phi))$ and $\phi \in C(k_1,k_2)$.

<u>Proof</u>. The proof of the if part of the statement is easy. It can be done by induction on the definition of $C(k_1,k_2)$ (Definition 20.11). As a sample we consider here one case leaving all other cases to the reader.

Let $\phi = \psi\bar{e}_k$ for some ψ in $C(k_1,k_2)$ and some k in K such that $k \neq k_2$. Suppose that $(x,y) \in I(s_K(\phi))$. Since $s_K(\phi) = s_K(\psi\bar{e}_k) = s_K(\psi)$, $(x,y) \in I(s_K(\psi))$. Hence, by the induction hypothesis, $((x, k_1),(y,k_2)) \in I_K(\psi)$. Also, since $k \neq k_2$, $((y,k_2),(y,k_2)) \in I_K(\bar{e}_k)$. Consequently, $((x,k_1),(y,k_2)) \in I_K(\psi\bar{e}_k) = I_K(\phi)$.

The proof of the only-if part of the statement can easily be given by induction on the length of ϕ. It is left to the reader. ///

We now prove that the class of L-schemes with markers is a pss.

<u>Lemma 20.18</u>. Let A_1 be an L-scheme with markers, and let I be a general interpretation of Σ. Then $I(L(A_1)) = I(A_1)$.

Proof. Let $A_1 = (\Sigma, K, k_o, A)$. Since A is an L-scheme, $L(A) = A$, and so $L(A_1) = s_K(A \cap C_K)$. Let x and y be arbitrary elements of D_I. Then

$$(x,y) \in I(A_1)$$
$$\Leftrightarrow \quad ((x,k_o),(y,k)) \in I_K(A) \text{ for some k in K} \qquad \text{(by Definition 20.9)}$$
$$\Leftrightarrow \quad ((x,k_o),(y,k)) \in I_K(\phi) \text{ for some } \phi \text{ in A and k in K}$$
$$\Leftrightarrow \quad (x,y) \in I(s_K(\phi)) \text{ and } \phi \in C(k_o,k) \text{ for some } \phi \text{ in A and k in K} \qquad \text{(by Lemma 20.17)}$$
$$\Leftrightarrow \quad (x,y) \in I(s_K(\phi)) \text{ and } \phi \in C_K \text{ for some } \phi \text{ in A} \qquad \text{(by Definition 20.11)}$$
$$\Leftrightarrow \quad (x,y) \in I(\psi) \text{ for some } \psi \text{ in } s_K(A \cap C_K)$$
$$\Leftrightarrow \quad (x,y) \in I(s_K(A \cap C_K))$$
$$\Leftrightarrow \quad (x,y) \in I(L(A_1)) \qquad \text{(by Definition 20.15).}$$

///

We now show that every program scheme with markers is equivalent to the L-scheme corresponding to it.

Theorem 20.19. Let, for every alphabet Δ, $\mathcal{L}(\Delta)$ be a pss over Δ. For any $\mathcal{L}$ program scheme U_1 with markers and any general interpretation I of Σ, we have $I(L(U_1)) = I(U_1)$.

Proof. Let $U_1 = (\Sigma, K, k_o, U)$. Since U is a program scheme from $\mathcal{L}(\Sigma_K)$ and I_K is a general interpretation of Σ_K, it follows from the definition of a pss, that $I_K(U) = I_K(L(U))$. Let us now denote $L(U)$ by A, and let $A_1 = (\Sigma, K, k_o, A)$. (Obviously A_1 is an L-scheme with markers). Since $I_K(U) = I_K(A)$, it easily follows from Definition 20.9 that $I(U_1) = I(A_1)$. Also, by Lemma 20.18, $I(A_1) = I(L(A_1))$. But, by Definition 20.15, $L(A_1) = s_K(L(A) \cap C_K) = s_K(A \cap C_K) = s_K(L(U) \cap C_K) = L(U_1)$. Consequently $I(U_1) = I(A_1) = I(L(A_1)) = I(L(U_1))$, and the theorem is proved. ///

Notation 20.20. Let, for every alphabet Δ, $\mathcal{L}(\Delta)$ denote a pss over Δ. Then we shall denote by $\mathcal{L}^m(\Sigma)$, or simply $\mathcal{L}^m$, the pss of all $\mathcal{L}$ program schemes with markers. More precisely, $\mathcal{L}^m = (\Sigma, \theta, L)$ †, where θ is the

---

† Recall Notation 8.2(1).

class of $\mathcal{L}$ program schemes with markers (over Σ), and L is the mapping from θ into $P(\Sigma^*)$ defined as in Definition 20.15.

For instance, IAN^m denotes the pss of all Ianov schemes with markers (over Σ), and similarly for all other pss's discussed so far. ///

In the next lemma some obvious relationships between pss's with and without markers are considered.

Lemma 20.21. Let, for every alphabet Δ, $\mathcal{L}_1(\Delta)$ and $\mathcal{L}_2(\Delta)$ be pss's over Δ. Then the following two statements hold.

(1) $\mathcal{L}_1(\Sigma) \subset_{\ell(eff)} \mathcal{L}_1^m(\Sigma)$.

(2) If, for every alphabet Δ, $\mathcal{L}_1(\Delta) \subset_{\ell(eff)} \mathcal{L}_2(\Delta)$, then $\mathcal{L}_1^m(\Sigma) \subset_{\ell(eff)} \mathcal{L}_2^m(\Sigma)$.

Proof. (1) Consider an arbitrary program scheme U in $\mathcal{L}_1(\Sigma)$. Let U_1 be the $\mathcal{L}$ program scheme with markers $(\Sigma,\{k_o\},k_o,U)$ †. By Definition 20.15, $L(U_1) = s_K(L(U) \cap C_K)$, but, since L(U) is a language over Σ, it easily follows that $s_K(L(U) \cap C_K) = L(U)$. Hence $L(U_1) = L(U)$ and the statement is proved.

(2) Let $U_1 = (\Sigma,K,k_o,U)$ be an arbitrary $\mathcal{L}_1$ program scheme with markers. Thus U is a program scheme from $\mathcal{L}_1(\Sigma_K)$. Since, by assumption, $\mathcal{L}_1(\Sigma_K) \subset_{\ell(eff)} \mathcal{L}_2(\Sigma_K)$, we can effectively find a program scheme V from $\mathcal{L}_2(\Sigma_K)$ such that $L(V) = L(U)$. Let $V_1 = (\Sigma,K,k_o,V)$ be the corresponding $\mathcal{L}_2$ program scheme with markers. Then $L(V_1) = s_K(L(V) \cap C_K) = s_K(L(U) \cap C_K) = L(U_1)$, and the statement is proved. ///

In the rest of this section we shall compare $\mathcal{L}$ and $\mathcal{L}^m$ for specific pss's $\mathcal{L}$. The first result concerns some of the "nondeterministic pss's" discussed previously.

---

† Note that, strictly speaking, we assume that, if U is in $\mathcal{L}(\Sigma)$, then U is also in $\mathcal{L}(\Sigma_K)$ (and has the same L-scheme in both pss's). It is left to the reader to verify that this assumption holds whenever Lemma 20.21(1) is applied.

Theorem 20.22. $REG^m =_{\ell(eff)} REG$, $CFG^m =_{\ell(eff)} CFG$ and $MAC^m =_{\ell(eff)} MAC$.

Proof. We shall prove the theorem for CFG, and leave the analogous proofs for REG and MAC to the reader.

By Lemma 20.21(1), $CFG \subset_{\ell(eff)} CFG^m$. To prove the converse, let $U_1 = (\Sigma,K,k_o,U)$ be an arbitrary context-free scheme with markers. Then $L(U_1) = s_K(L(U) \cap C_K)$, where $L(U)$ is a context-free language over Σ_K and, by Lemma 20.13, C_K is a regular language over Σ_K. Since the class of context-free languages is effectively closed under intersection with a regular language and under substitution, we can find a context-free scheme V such that $L(V) = L(U_1)$. This proves that $CFG^m \subset_{\ell(eff)} CFG$. ///

Thus the addition of markers to the pss's REG, CFG and MAC does not give an increase in their computing power †. The next lemma will be used to prove a similar result for the "deterministic pss's" IAN and SyntdetCFG.

Lemma 20.23. Let K be a finite set. If A is a syntdet L-scheme over Σ_K, then $s_K(A \cap C_K)$ is syntdet.

Proof. A formal proof of this lemma is left to the reader. Informally the truth of this lemma can be understood as follows.

Let us recall from section 7 (Definition 7.4 and the remark following Definition 7.13) that an L-scheme is syntdet if and only if it corresponds to a generalized deterministic Ianov scheme, which has the form of a tree. Consequently there is a generalized Ianov scheme U (in the form of a tree) such that $L(U) = A$. We shall now show how to transform U into a generalized deterministic Ianov scheme U_2 such that $L(U_2) = s_K(L(U) \cap C_K)$, and then the lemma is proved.

Intersection of $L(U)$ with C_K corresponds to the deletion of certain parts of U. Namely, if the configuration

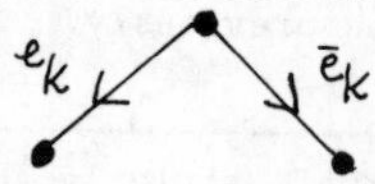

occurs in U (for some k in K), then one of these arcs, with the entire subtree beneath

---

† Recall that, if $\mathcal{L}_1 =_\ell \mathcal{L}_2$, then $\mathcal{L}_1 \equiv \mathcal{L}_2$ (Example 19.4).

it, should be deleted. (Note that all paths through one of the arcs give rise to words in C_K, while all paths through the other arc give rise to words not in C_K). Obviously it is also possible that both arcs have to be deleted; this is the case when both of them belong to a subtree of another arc which should be deleted (the previous remark only holds for configurations which can be "reached by a word from C_K").

The generalized Ianov scheme U_1, with $L(U_1) = L(U) \cap C_K$, resulting from these deletions, is obviously still deterministic.

We now delete each arc of the form $1 \bullet\!\xrightarrow{\sigma}\!\bullet 2$ with σ in $\Sigma_K - \Sigma$, and identify nodes 1 and 2. Since in U_1 all branching nodes are of the form 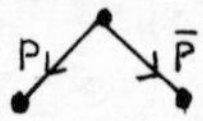 with p in P, it is easy to see that the resulting

generalized Ianov scheme U_2 with $L(U_2) = s_K(L(U_1))$ is still deterministic. Hence $L(U_2) = s_K(A \cap C_K)$ is syntdet.

The following example illustrates the above process for a finite L-scheme. Let $F = \{f,g\}$, $P = \{p\}$, $K = \{1,2\}$ and $A = a_2(e_1f \cup \bar{e}_1f(pa_1 \cup \bar{p}a_1(e_1g \cup \bar{e}_1)))$. Then U =

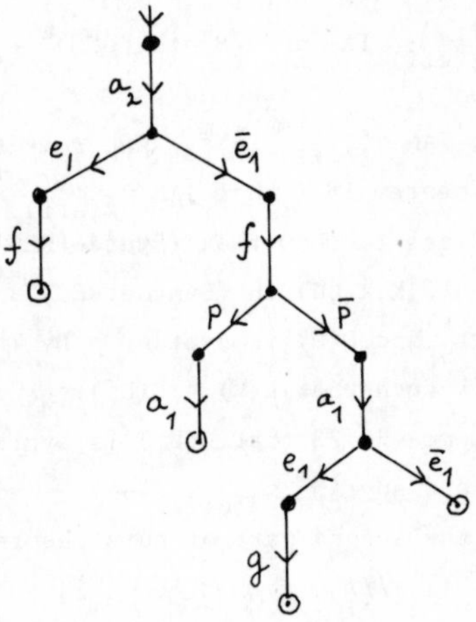

$U_1 =$

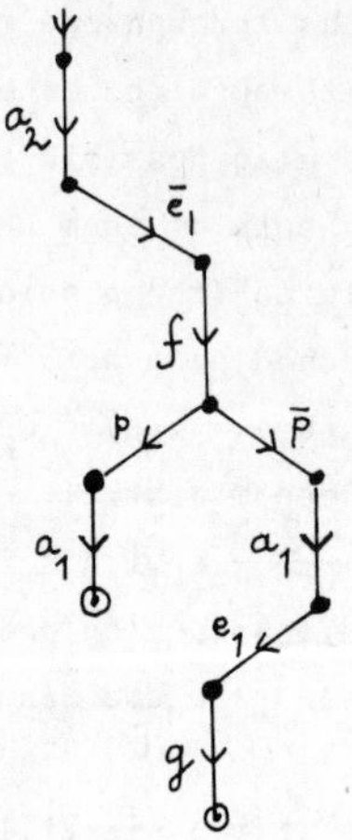

and $U_2 =$

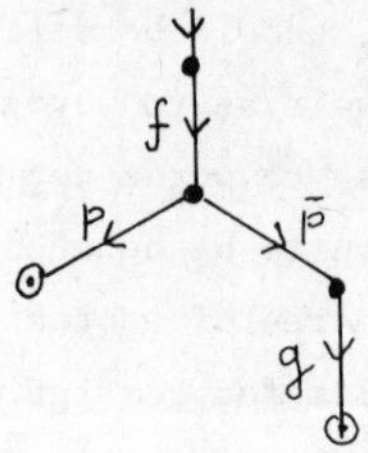

///

In the next theorem it is proved that the use of markers does not increase the computing power of IAN and SyntdetCFG. †

<u>Theorem 20.24</u>. $\text{IAN}^m =_{\ell(\text{eff})} \text{IAN}$ and $(\text{SyntdetCFG})^m =_{\ell(\text{eff})} \text{SyntdetCFG}$.

<u>Proof</u>. By Lemma 20.21(1), $\text{IAN} \subset_{\ell(\text{eff})} \text{IAN}^m$. We prove that $\text{IAN}^m \subset_{\ell(\text{eff})} \text{IAN}$ as follows. Recall from Theorem 18.7 that $\text{IAN} =_{\ell(\text{eff})} \text{SyntdetREG}$. Thus, by Lemma 20.21(2), it suffices to show that $(\text{SyntdetREG})^m \subset_{\ell(\text{eff})} \text{SyntdetREG}$. Consider an arbitrary $U_1 = (\Sigma,K,k_o,U)$ in $(\text{SyntdetREG})^m$. So U_1 is a regular scheme with markers, and L(U) is syntdet. By Theorem 20.22 we can find a regular scheme V such that $L(V) = L(U_1)$. Since L(U) is syntdet, it follows from Lemma 20.23 that $L(U_1)$ is syntdet. Hence V is an element of SyntdetREG, and so $\text{IAN}^m \subset_{\ell(\text{eff})} \text{IAN}$.

The analogous proof of the second part of this theorem is left to the reader. ///

It has already been mentioned in Example 20.2 that the computing power of RSI is increased by the addition of markers. We now state this as a theorem.

---

† For a direct proof of $\text{IAN}^m =_{\ell(\text{eff})} \text{IAN}$, see Bruno and Steiglitz [1972, Theorem 3].

For SyntdetCFG, see Notation 18.23.

Theorem 20.25. RSI < RSI^m.

Proof. By Lemma 20.21(1), RSI $\subset_{\ell(eff)}$ RSI^m, and so RSI ≤ RSI^m. We now show that RSI has less computing power than RSI^m. Let f be in F and p in P (recall Remark 19.5). Consider the rsi with markers $U_1 = (\Sigma,\{0,1\},1,U)$, where U is the rsi $(\Sigma_K,\{S\},S,b)$ such that the body of S is the one given in Example 20.2 (in this example, v := 0 should be replaced by a_o, v = 1 by e_1 and v ≠ 1 by $\bar{e}_1$). It is easy to see that $L(U) = \bigcup_{n\geq 0} (pf)^n \bar{p}f(p \cup \bar{p}a_o)(e_1 \cup \bar{e}_1 f)^n$, and that $L(U) \cap C_K = \bigcup_{n\geq 0} (pf)^n \bar{p}f(pe_1^n \cup \bar{p}a_o(\bar{e}_1 f)^n)$. Hence $L(U_1) = s_K(L(U) \cap C_K) = \bigcup_{n\geq 0} (pf)^n \bar{p}f(p \cup \bar{p}f^n)$. Since it has been shown in the proof of Theorem 19.25 that $L(U_1)$ is not translatable into RSI, the theorem is proved. ///

Although RSI^m has more computing power than RSI, it is still within the computing power of NRSI, as the next theorem shows.

Theorem 20.26. $RSI^m \subset_{\ell(eff)}$ SyntdetCFG.

Proof. Since, for every alphabet Δ, RSI(Δ) $\subset_{\ell(eff)}$ SyntdetCFG(Δ), it follows from Lemma 20.21(2) that $RSI^m \subset_{\ell(eff)} (\text{SyntdetCFG})^m$. Hence by Theorem 20.24, the theorem holds. ///

It will be shown in the next section that RSI^m < SyntdetCFG.

21. Recursive schemes with markers

In this section we shall discuss some results concerning the pss RSI^m of all rsi's with markers.

We first introduce a special type of dpda (Definition 21.2), which accepts precisely the class of languages corresponding to rsi's with markers (Theorem 21.5).

Then we prove that RSI^m is effectively closed under the standard mapping (Theorem 21.8), and we characterize RSI^m by proving that $Lang(RSI^m)$ is the set of all syntactically deterministic dpda languages † (Theorem 21.11).

From the latter two results many properties of RSI^m follow. With respect to equivalence we prove the following. It is decidable for an arbitrary rsi with markers and an arbitrary Ianov scheme whether they are equivalent (Theorem 21.15). The relation $\leq$ is not recursively enumerable in RSI^m (Theorem 21.16). The question whether two rsi's with markers are equivalent is equivalent to the question whether two dpda's accept the same language (Theorem 21.17). With respect to translatability we prove the following. Translatability from RSI^m into IAN is decidable (Theorem 21.18). RSI^m has less computing power than SyntdetCFG (Theorem 21.20). Translatability from CFG (and SyntdetCFG) into RSI^m is not recursively enumerable (Theorem 21.22). Finally we prove that if translatability from CFG into RSI would be decidable (and this is an open problem), then the translation could not be effective (for a more precise statement see Theorem 21.23).

The section is concluded by an appendix in which part of a formal proof of Theorem 21.11 is given.

As we saw in Theorem 18.17, the pss RSI is strongly related to the class of s-languages. Since the s-languages are those context-free languages which can be accepted by a one-state dpda by empty store ††, it should be evident that the addition of markers to rsi's will result in

---

† For the term "dpda language", see 1.4.2.4.

†† Korenjak and Hopcroft [1966, Theorem 1].

languages acceptable by a dpda with an arbitrary number of states. (Note that both markers and states are a formalization of the concept of a "finite memory"). In other words, a strong relationship between the pss RSI^m and the class of dpda languages is to be expected. We start the discussion of this relationship by proving that a rather direct correspondence exists between rsi's with markers and a special type of dpda which we now define.†

Notation 21.1. Let $M = (K,\Sigma,\Gamma,R,k_o,Z,E)$ be a dpda. For k in K and S in Γ, we shall denote by $R(k,S)$ the set of all rules of M with left hand side (k,σ,S) for some σ in $\Sigma \cup \varepsilon$. Formally,
$R(k,S) = R \cap (\{k\} \times (\Sigma \cup \varepsilon) \times \{S\} \times \Gamma \times K \times \Gamma^*)$. ///

Definition 21.2. Let $M = (K,\Sigma,\Gamma,R,k_o,Z)$ be a dpda accepting by empty store. We shall say that M is a special dpda if, for every state k and every pushdown symbol S,

either $R(k,S) = \emptyset$,

or $R(k,S) = \{(k,\sigma,S) \to (k',\alpha)\}$ for certain σ in $\Sigma \cup \varepsilon$, k' in K and α in Γ^*,

or $R(k,S) = \{(k,p,S) \to (k_1,\alpha_1), (k,\bar{p},S) \to (k_2,\alpha_2)$ for certain p in P, k_1,k_2 in K and α_1,α_2 in Γ^*.

Intuitively, a dpda is special if it can be viewed as a deterministic program scheme.††

Notation 21.3. We shall denote by SpecialDPDAε the pss of all special dpda's with input alphabet Σ. (More precisely, SpecialDPDAε = (Σ,θ,L), where θ is the class of all special dpda's with input alphabet Σ, and, for every M in θ, L(M) is the language accepted by empty store as defined in 1.4.2.3). ///

---

† For terminology concerning pda's, see 1.4.2.3 and 1.4.2.4. In what follows we shall mostly discuss dpda's accepting by empty store.

†† Compare Definitions 18.1. and 18.12. It would have been natural (but confusing) to use the term deterministic dpda rather than the term special dpda.

<u>Example 21.4</u>. Let $F = \{f,g\}$ and $P = \{p\}$. Consider the pda $M = (\{1,0\},\Sigma,\Gamma,R,1,S)$, where $\Gamma = \{S,T,\bar{f},\bar{g},A_1,A_o\}$ and R consists of the following rules:

$$
\begin{array}{lll}
(1,p,S) \to (1,\bar{f}ST) & \to\ , & (0,p,S) \to (1,\bar{f}ST)\ , \\
(1,\bar{p},S) \to (1,\varepsilon) & \to\ , & (0,\bar{p},S) \to (0,\varepsilon)\ , \\
(1,\varepsilon,T) \to (1,\bar{g}A_o) & \to\ , & (0,\varepsilon,T) \to (0,\bar{f}A_1)\ , \\
(1,f,\bar{f}) \to (1,\varepsilon) & \to\ , & (0,f,\bar{f}) \to (0,\varepsilon)\ , \\
(1,g,\bar{g}) \to (1,\varepsilon) & \to\ , & (0,g,\bar{g}) \to (0,\varepsilon)\ , \\
(1,\varepsilon,A_1) \to (1,\varepsilon) & \to\ , & (0,\varepsilon,A_1) \to (1,\varepsilon)\ , \\
(1,\varepsilon,A_o) \to (0,\varepsilon) & \to\ , & (0,\varepsilon,A_o) \to (0,\varepsilon)\ .
\end{array}
$$

Obviously M is a special dpda. ///

The class of languages accepted by special dpda's is identical to the class of L-schemes corresponding to rsi's with markers. This is proved in the next theorem.

<u>Theorem 21.5</u>. $RSI^m =_{\ell(eff)} \text{SpecialDPDA}\varepsilon$.

<u>Proof</u>. By Theorem 18.17 and Lemma 20.21(2), $RSI^m =_{\ell(eff)} (\text{SyntdetSCFG})^m$. Thus it suffices to prove that $(\text{SyntdetSCFG})^m =_{\ell(eff)} \text{SpecialDPDA}\varepsilon$.

We first show that $(\text{SyntdetSCFG})^m \subset_{\ell(eff)} \text{SpecialDPDA}\varepsilon$. Let $U_1 = (\Sigma,K,k_o,U)$ be an arbitrary element of $(\text{SyntdetSCFG})^m$. Thus U is an s-grammar over Σ_K such that L(U) is syntdet. By Lemma 18.15 we may assume that U is a deterministic s-grammar (recall Definition 18.12). Let $U = (N,\Sigma_K,R,Z)$. If $N = \{Z\}$ and $R = \{Z \to \varepsilon\}$, then $L(U_1) = L(U) = \varepsilon$, and so there is a special dpda M such that $L(M) = L(U_1)$, namely $M = (\{k_o\},\Sigma,\{Z\},\{(k_o,\varepsilon,Z) \to (k_o,\varepsilon)\},k_o,Z)$. Otherwise, by Definition 18.12, U has the property that, for each nonterminal S

(*) either $R(S) = \{S \to \sigma\alpha\}$ for some σ in Σ_K and α in N^*,
or $R(S) = \{S \to u\alpha,\ S \to \bar{u}\beta\}$ for some u in P_K and α,β in N^*.

We now construct a special dpda M such that $L(M) = L(U_1)$. Let $M = (K,\Sigma,N,R',k_o,Z)$ †, where R' consists of the following rules. For S in N, σ in Σ, α in N^* and k in K,

---

† Note that K and k_o are taken from U_1, and N and Z from U.

(1) if $S \to \sigma\alpha$ is in R, then, for every k_1 in K, $(k_1,\sigma,S) \to (k_1,\alpha)$ is in R',

(2) if $S \to a_k\alpha$ is in R, then, for every k_1 in K, $(k_1,\varepsilon,S) \to (k,\alpha)$ is in R',

(3) if $S \to e_k\alpha$ is in R, then $(k,\varepsilon,S) \to (k,\alpha)$ is in R', and

(4) if $S \to \bar{e}_k\alpha$ is in R, then, for every k_1 in K such that $k_1 \neq k$, $(k_1,\varepsilon,S) \to (k_1,\alpha)$ is in R'.

It easily follows from (*) that M is a special dpda. Also, by a straightforward induction argument, it can easily be proved that, for all k_1,k_2 in K, ϕ in Σ^* and α in N^*,

(**) $(k_1,\phi,\alpha) \overset{*}{\underset{M}{\vdash}} (k_2,\varepsilon,\varepsilon)$ if and only if there exists ψ in Σ_K^* such that $\alpha \overset{*}{\underset{U}{\Rightarrow}} \psi$, $\psi \in C(k_1,k_2)$ and $s_K(\psi) = \phi$.

Hence, for every ϕ in Σ^*,

$\phi \in L(M)$

$\Leftrightarrow (k_o,\phi,Z) \overset{*}{\underset{M}{\vdash}} (k,\varepsilon,\varepsilon)$ for some k in K

$\Leftrightarrow$ there exists ψ in Σ_K^* such that $Z \overset{*}{\underset{U}{\Rightarrow}} \psi$, $\psi \in C(k_o,k)$ for some k in K, and $s_K(\psi) = \phi$

$\Leftrightarrow s_K(\psi) = \phi$ for some ψ in $L(U) \cap C_K$

$\Leftrightarrow \phi \in s_K(L(U) \cap C_K)$

$\Leftrightarrow \phi \in L(U_1)$.

Consequently $L(M) = L(U_1)$, and we have proved that $(\text{SyntdetSCFG})^m \subset_{\ell(\text{eff})} \text{SpecialDPDA}\varepsilon$.

Next we show that $\text{SpecialDPDA}\varepsilon \subset_{\ell(\text{eff})} (\text{SyntdetSCFG})^m$. Let $M = (K,\Sigma,\Gamma,R,k_o,Z)$ be an arbitrary special dpda. We shall construct a context-free scheme U_1 with markers such that $L(U_1) = L(M)$. Although the corresponding context-free scheme will not be an s-grammar, it will follow from the specialty of M that it can be transformed into a deterministic s-grammar generating the same language (and this proves the above ℓ-inclusion).

Let $U_1 = (\Sigma,K,k_o,U)$ where U is the context-free scheme (Γ,Σ_K,R',Z) †, of which the rules are obtained as follows. First we order the elements of K in some arbitrary manner, e.g. $k_o,k_1,\ldots,k_n$, where $\#(K) = n + 1$ for

---

† Note that K, k_o, Γ and Z are taken from M. Note also that we have assumed that $\Gamma \cap \Sigma_K = \emptyset$ (obviously this may be assumed).

some $n \geq 0$. Then we define for each k in K the test t_k in $(P_K \cup \overline{P}_K)^*$ by $t_k = \overline{e}_{k_o} \overline{e}_{k_1} \cdots \overline{e}_{k_{m-1}} e_{k_m}$, where $k = k_m$ for some m in $\{0,1,\ldots,n\}$.†

Finally, we define R' to consist of all rules of the form $S \to t_{k_1} \sigma a_{k_2} \alpha$ such that the rule $(k_1,\sigma,S) \to (k_2,\alpha)$ is in R, where $k_1,k_2 \in K$, $\sigma \in \Sigma \cup \varepsilon$, $S \in \Gamma$ and $\alpha \in \Gamma^*$.

It is easy to prove that the above statement (**) also holds in this case. Thus, repeating the arguments following statement (**), we have that $L(U_1) = L(M)$. It is left to the reader to verify that the so constructed context-free grammar U can easily be transformed into a deterministic s-grammar V such that $L(V) = L(U)$. Hence, if $V_1 = (\Sigma,K,k_o,V)$, then $L(V_1) = L(M)$, and so SpecialDPDA$\varepsilon \subset_{\ell(\mathrm{eff})}$ (SyntdetSCFG)^m. ///

Example 21.6. Let $F = \{f,g\}$ and $P = \{p\}$. Consider the following element U_1 of (SyntdetSCFG)^m. $U_1 = (\Sigma,K,k_o,U)$, where $K = \{1,0\}$, $k_o = 1$ and $U = (N,\Sigma_K,R,Z)$, where $N = \{S,T,\overline{f},\overline{g},A_1,A_o\}$, $Z = S$ and R consists of the rules $S \to \overline{p}$, $S \to pfST$, $T \to e_1 gA_o$, $T \to \overline{e}_1 \overline{f} A_1$, $\overline{f} \to f$, $\overline{g} \to g$, $A_1 \to a_1$ and $A_o \to a_o$. It is easy to check that the special dpda M corresponding to U_1 according to the first half of the proof of Theorem 21.5 is the one given in Example 21.4. ///

Example 21.7. Let $F = \{f,g,h\}$ and $P = \{p\}$. Consider the following special dpda M. $M = (\{1,2,3\},\Sigma,\{S,\overline{f},T\},R,1,S)$, where R consists of the following rules: for every k in $\{1,2,3\}$, $(k,p,S) \to (k,\overline{f}ST)$, $(k,\overline{p},S) \to (k,\varepsilon)$ and $(k,f,\overline{f}) \to (k,\varepsilon)$; and $(1,f,T) \to (2,\varepsilon)$, $(2,g,T) \to (3,\varepsilon)$ and $(3,h,T) \to (1,\varepsilon)$. The context-free scheme U_1 with markers corresponding to M according to the second half of the proof of Theorem 21.5 has the following rules: for every k in $\{1,2,3\}$, $S \to t_k pa_k \overline{f}ST$, $S \to t_k \overline{p} a_k$ and $\overline{f} \to t_k fa_k$; and $T \to t_1 fa_2$, $T \to t_2 ga_3$ and $T \to t_3 ha_1$ (where, for instance, $t_1 = e_1$, $t_2 = \overline{e}_1 e_2$ and $t_3 = \overline{e}_1 \overline{e}_2 e_3$). ///

Theorem 21.5 enables us to prove that RSI^m is effectively closed under the standard mapping††. Thus for each rsi U with markers we can

---

† Obviously, for m = n, it would suffice to define $t_{k_n} = \overline{e}_{k_o} \overline{e}_{k_1} \cdots \overline{e}_{k_{n-1}}$.

†† This result should be contrasted with Theorem 18.21.

find an rsi V with markers such that V is a standard form of U.

<u>Theorem 21.8.</u> RSI^m is effectively closed under S.

<u>Proof.</u> By Theorem 21.5 it suffices to prove that SpecialDPDAε is effectively closed under S. To prove this, consider an arbitrary special dpda $M = (K,\Sigma,\Gamma,R,k_o,Z)$. We shall construct a pda M_1 such that $L(M_1) = S(L(M))$. Although M_1 will not be a special dpda, it will follow from the specialty of M that M_1 can be transformed into a special dpda accepting the same language (and this proves the theorem).

Let $M_1 = (K_1,\Sigma,\Gamma,R_1,k_o,Z)$, where $K_1 = (K\times T_S) \cup \{k_o\}$ † and R_1 is constructed as follows ††.

(1) All rules of the form $(k_o,t,Z) \rightarrow ((k_o,t),Z)$ with t in T_S are in R_1.

(2) For all k_1,k_2 in K, T in Γ, α in Γ^*, f in F and a in $P \cup \bar{P}$,

(2.1) if $(k_1,\varepsilon,T) \rightarrow (k_2,\alpha)$ is in R, then, for every t in T_S, $((k_1,t),\varepsilon,T) \rightarrow ((k_2,t),\alpha)$ is in R_1,

(2.2) if $(k_1,f,T) \rightarrow (k_2,\alpha)$ is in R, then, for all t and t' in T_S, $((k_1,t),ft',T) \rightarrow ((k_2,t'),\alpha)$ is in R_1, and

(2.3) if $(k_1,a,T) \rightarrow (k_2,\alpha)$ is in R, then, for every t in T_S such that a <u>in</u> t, $((k_1,t),\varepsilon,T) \rightarrow ((k_2,t),\alpha)$ is in R_1 †††.

By a straightforward induction argument it can be shown that, for all k_1,k_2 in K, t_1,t_2 in T_S, φ in Σ^* and α in Γ^*,

$((k_1,t_1),\phi,\alpha) \overset{*}{\underset{M_1}{\vdash}} ((k_2,t_2),\varepsilon,\varepsilon)$ if and only if there is a word ψ in Σ^* such that $(k_1,\psi,\alpha) \overset{*}{\underset{M}{\vdash}} (k_2,\varepsilon,\varepsilon)$ and $t_1\phi \in S(\psi) \cap (T_SF)^*t_2$.

This implies that $L(M_1) = S(L(M))$. The easy proofs of these statements are left to the reader.

It is also left to the reader to verify that, by an easy construction, M_1 can be transformed into a special dpda accepting the same language. ///

Note that, by the above theorem, each rsi can be brought into standard form by the use of markers (formally: for every U in RSI we can find a V in RSI^m such that $L(V) = S(L(U))$.

---

† Recall that T_S is the set of standard tests (section 10).

†† Note that a pda, as defined in 1.4.2.3, may read a word of input symbols in one step of its computation.

††† For the definition of "<u>in</u>", see 1.2.1.

In the following remark we discuss the "naturalness" of RSI^m as opposed to RSI.

Remark 21.9. If we assume that closure under S is a rather natural requirement on a pss (and we consider this to be the case), then we can now conclude that RSI^m is "more natural" than RSI. †

Another reason to call RSI^m "more natural" than RSI is the following. Intuitively, the use of recursion is equivalent to the use of a pushdown store. Thus, when providing Ianov schemes with the ability to operate on a pushdown store of markers, we might expect to obtain a pss equivalent to RSI. Actually, it is easy to see that the so obtained pss is ℓ-equal to RSI^m. In fact, roughly speaking, a special dpda corresponds to a Ianov scheme with pushdown store (interpret the states of the dpda as nodes of the Ianov scheme, and the rules of the dpda as labelled arcs of the Ianov scheme), and so the above mentioned ℓ-equality can easily be obtained by a modification of the proof of Theorem 21.5. ///

We now characterize RSI^m by proving that Lang(RSI^m) is the set of all syntdet dpda languages ††.

††† Notation 21.10. We shall denote by SyntdetDPDA the pss of all dpda's with input alphabet Σ, accepting a syntdet language by final state. (More precisely, SyntdetDPDA = (Σ,θ,L_f), where θ is the set of all dpda's with input alphabet Σ, and, for every M in θ, $L_f(M)$ is the language accepted by final state as defined in 1.4.2.3). ///

Theorem 21.11. $RSI^m =_{\ell(\mathrm{eff})}$ SyntdetDPDA.

---

† Note the similar situation when comparing the pss of while program schemes with markers to the pss of while program schemes (cf. Example 20.1). Since the pss of while program schemes with markers is ℓ-equal to IAN, it is closed under S. However, it is easy to prove that the pss of while program schemes is not closed under S (for instance, the while program scheme while p do (f; if p then f) has no standard form in the pss of while program schemes).

†† Compare this result with those of section 18.

††† See the remark in the Appendix to this section for the fact that it is decidable whether a dpda accepts a syntdet language by final state.

Proof

Firstly we prove that $RSI^m \subset_{\ell(eff)}$ SyntdetDPDA. Let U be an arbitrary rsi with markers. By Theorem 18.17 and Lemma 20.23, L(U) is syntdet. Thus it suffices to find a dpda accepting L(U) by final state. Now, by Theorem 21.5, we can effectively find a dpda which accepts L(U) by empty store. But, by a well known construction †, this dpda can effectively be transformed into a dpda accepting the same language by final state. This proves the above ℓ-inclusion.

Secondly we prove that SyntdetDPDA $\subset_{\ell(eff)} RSI^m$. Observe that each syntdet language accepted by a dpda by final state can also be accepted by a dpda by empty store (Proof. Note that every syntdet language is prefix-free; recall Definition 19.27. Thus, if M is a dpda accepting a given syntdet language by final state, then, for any given input word, M enters a final state at most once. Hence, by changing M in such a way that it empties its pushdown store whenever it reaches a final state ††, it will accept the given language by empty store). Consequently, by Theorem 21.5, it now suffices to prove the following statement: for each dpda accepting a syntdet language by empty store we can effectively find a special dpda accepting the same language. A formal proof of this statement will be given in the appendix to this section. Here we informally sketch the idea behind the proof.

Let $M = (K,\Sigma,\Gamma,R,k_o,Z)$ be a dpda such that L(M) is a syntdet language. Suppose that M is not a special dpda. Then there are two different rules of the form $(k,\sigma_1,S) \rightarrow (k_1,\alpha_1)$ and $(k,\sigma_2,S) \rightarrow (k_2,\alpha_2)$ (with k,k_1,k_2 in K, σ_1,σ_2 in Σ, S in Γ and α_1,α_2 in Γ^*), such that, for all p in P, $\{\sigma_1,\sigma_2\} \neq \{p,\bar{p}\}$. We now show that in any situation at most one of these two rules is useful (in the sense that application of the rule leads to acceptance). Consider, for some ϕ in Σ^* and α in Γ^*, a computation $(k_o,\phi,Z) \overset{*}{\underset{M}{\vdash}} (k,\varepsilon,S\alpha)$. Then, since L(M) is syntdet, the words ψ such that the computation $(k_o,\phi\psi,Z) \overset{*}{\underset{M}{\vdash}} (k,\psi,S\alpha)$ leads to acceptance (in other words, such that $\phi\psi \in L(M)$), either all start with the same symbol, or all start with a symbol from $\{p,\bar{p}\}$ for some p in P. Consequently, when the machine reaches a configuration in state k and with S on top of the pushdown store, application of (at most) one of the above two rules can ever lead to

---

† See, for instance, the proof of the only-if part of Theorem 5.1 in Hopcroft and Ullman [1969].

†† See the proof of the if part of Theorem 5.1 in Hopcroft and Ullman [1969].

acceptance (which one, may of course depend on ϕ and α). In the appendix it will be shown that we can store extra information in the pushdown stack in such a way that from this information we can extract the knowledge which of the two rules is useful. Thus, obviously, (at least) one of the two corresponding rules $(k,\sigma_1,(S,\gamma)) \to (k_1,\alpha_1)$ and $(k,\sigma_2,(S,\gamma)) \to (k_2,\alpha_2)$, where γ is the extra information, can be deleted from the set of rules of M without changing the accepted language. It easily follows that, by deleting all these "useless" rules, a special dpda accepting the same language is obtained. ///

Another way of formulating the above result (without mentioning its effectiveness) is the following†.

Corollary 21.12. $Lang(RSI^m(\Sigma))$ is the set of all syntactically deterministic dpda languages over Σ.

For the sake of completeness we mention the following corollary to Theorems 21.8 and 21.11.

Corollary 21.13. Let H be a regular shift distribution. Then RSI^m is effectively closed under S_H.

Proof. Since the class of dpda languages is effectively closed under subtraction of a regular language††, the corollary follows directly from Theorems 21.8 and 21.11. ///

Having proved the main properties of RSI^m in Theorems 21.8 and 21.11, we shall now examine RSI^m with regard to decidability of equivalence (cf. section 17) and to translatability (cf. section 19). First we make the following technical remark.

Remark 21.14. In what follows we shall often assume that $\#(F) = \#(P) = 2$. This assumption is based on Remark 19.5, Lemma 17.3 and Lemma 19.6. It is left to the reader to show that Lemma 19.6 also holds for $\mathcal{L} = RSI^m$. ///

---

† Cf. Corollaries 18.9 and 18.19.

†† Hopcroft and Ullman [1969, Theorem 12.2].

We now turn to equivalence and covering of rsi's with markers. A positive result is stated in the next theorem.

Theorem 21.15. It is decidable for an arbitrary rsi U with markers and an arbitrary Ianov scheme V whether $U \equiv V$.

Proof. By the standard form theorem, $U \equiv V$ if and only if $S(L(U)) = S(L(V))$. Since, by Theorems 21.8 and 21.11, $S(L(U))$ is a dpda language, and since, by Theorem 16.2, $S(L(V))$ is a regular language (both effectively), the theorem follows from the fact that it is decidable whether a dpda language and a regular language are the same†. ///

Note that, in particular, the above theorem holds for rsi's without markers.

The next result is a negative one.

Theorem 21.16. The relation $\leq$ is not recursively enumerable in RSI^m.

Proof. The theorem will be proved by using the well known result that inclusion of dpda languages is not recursively enumerable.††

By Remark 21.14 we may assume that $\#(F) = \#(P) = 2$. So let $F = \{f,g\}$ and $P = \{p,q\}$. Consider two arbitrary dpda languages A and B over F. By Lemma 19.8, $v(A\$)$ and $v(B\$)$ are syntdet dpda languages. Thus, by Theorem 21.11, we can find U and V in RSI^m such that $L(U) = v(A\$)$ and $L(V) = v(B\$)$. Since, by Lemma 19.8, $L(U)$ and $L(V)$ are standard languages, it follows from the standard form theorem that $U \leq V$ if and only if $L(U) \subset L(V)$. Hence, by Lemma 19.8(3), $U \leq V$ if and only if $A \subset B$. Consequently, recursive enumerability of the relation $\leq$ in RSI^m would contradict the result mentioned at the beginning of this proof. ///

Finally we point out the relevance of dpda's to the decidability of

---

† Hopcroft and Ullman [1969, section 14.6].

†† Hopcroft and Ullman [1969, Theorem 14.11].

equivalence in RSI^m.

Theorem 21.17. The relation of equivalence is decidable in RSI^m if and only if it is decidable whether two arbitrary dpda's accept the same language by final state.

Proof

(Only if). We only consider the case that $\#(F) = \#(P) = 2$. A similar proof for an arbitrary alphabet is left to the reader. So let $F = \{f,g\}$ and $P = \{p,q\}$, and assume that equivalence is decidable in RSI^m. Consider two arbitrary dpda languages A and B over F. By Lemma 19.8 and Theorem 21.11, we can find U and V in RSI^m such that $L(U) = v(A\$)$ and $L(V) = v(B\$)$. Also, by Lemma 19.8 and the standard form theorem, $U \equiv V$ if and only if $A = B$. Hence equality of A and B is decidable.

(If). Assume that equality of dpda languages is decidable. Then the decidability of equivalence in RSI^m easily follows from the standard form theorem and Theorems 21.8 and 21.11. ///

It is an open question whether equality of dpda languages can be decided. †

In the rest of this section we shall be concerned with translatability. First we consider translatability from RSI^m into IAN.

Theorem 21.18. It is decidable whether an arbitrary rsi with markers is translatable into IAN, and, if so, an equivalent Ianov scheme can effectively be found.

Proof. Let U be an arbitrary element of RSI^m. It follows from Theorem 21.11 and Lemma 14.3, that U is semantically deterministic. Consequently, by Theorem 19.13 and the regularity theorem, U is translatable into IAN if and only if $S(L(U))$ is a regular language. We know from Theorems 21.8 and 21.11 that $S(L(U))$ is a dpda language. Hence, since regularity of dpda languages is decidable ††, it can be decided whether U is translatable

† See Hopcroft and Ullman [1969, section 14.6].

†† Stearns [1967].

into IAN. Now suppose that U is translatable into IAN, that is, S(L(U)) is regular. It is known † that, if a dpda language is regular, then a regular grammar generating it can effectively be found. Thus, by Theorem 18.7, we can effectively find a Ianov scheme V such that $L(V) = S(L(U))$, and so $V \equiv U$. ///

Note that, in particular, the above theorem holds for rsi's without markers.

We now discuss translatability into RSI^m. In the next lemma we give a syntactical characterization of those program schemes which are translatable into RSI^m.

Lemma 21.19. Let U be an arbitrary program scheme. Then U is translatable into RSI^m if and only if S(L(U)) is a syntdet dpda language.

Proof. Immediate from the standard form theorem and Theorems 21.8 and 21.11. ///

It is now easy to see that there exist context-free schemes (generating a syntdet language) which are not translatable into RSI^m (cf. Theorem 19.25).

Theorem 21.20. RSI^m < SyntdetCFG.

Proof. By Theorem 20.26, $RSI^m \leq$ SyntdetCFG. We shall prove that RSI^m has less computing power than SyntdetCFG by exhibiting an element of SyntdetCFG which is not translatable into RSI^m. By Remark 21.14, it suffices to do this for $\#(F) = \#(P) = 2$. So let $F = \{f,g\}$ and $P = \{p,q\}$. Consider the context-free language $A = \{\phi\psi \mid \phi,\psi \in F^*, \psi$ is the reverse of $\phi\}$. By Lemma 19.8 there is an element U of SyntdetCFG such that $L(U) = v(A\$)$. We now prove that U is not translatable into RSI^m. By Lemma 19.8 and

---

† Stearns [1967].

Lemma 21.19, U is translatable into RSI^m if and only if L(U) is a dpda language. Consequently, by Lemma 19.8(5), U is translatable into RSI^m if and only if A is a dpda language. Since A is not a dpda language †, U is not translatable into RSI^m. ///

Thus RSI < RSI^m < SyntdetCFG (recall Theorem 20.25). This shows that, although RSI^m has more ("deterministic") computing power than RSI, it has still less "deterministic computing power" than CFG. This is expressed in the following corollary (cf. Corollary 19.26).

Corollary 21.21. There exists a semantically deterministic context-free scheme which is not translatable into RSI^m.

Proof. Immediate from Theorem 21.20 and Lemma 14.3. ///

Since SyntdetDPDA looks like the largest pss ℓ-included in CFG such that its program schemes can be "executed in a deterministic way", it is unlikely (by Corollary 21.21 and Theorem 21.11) that a decidable "deterministic" sub-pss of CFG can be found with the same "deterministic computing power" as CFG (that is, with the same computing power as SyntdetCFG).††

We now show that neither translatability from CFG into RSI^m nor translatability from SyntdetCFG into RSI^m is recursively enumerable.

Theorem 21.22. It is not recursively enumerable whether an arbitrary context-free scheme (or element of SyntdetCFG, respectively) is translatable into RSI^m.

Proof. We shall prove that the question whether an arbitrary context-free grammar generates a dpda language can be reduced to the question

---

† Ginsburg and Greibach [1966, Corollary 1 of Theorem 3.5].

†† Recall the discussion in Example 20.2 and the remark following Theorem 19.31.

whether a context-free scheme (generating a syntdet language) is translatable into RSI^m. Since the former question is not recursively enumerable †, the theorem follows.

By Remark 21.14 we may assume that #(F) = #(P) = 2. So let F = {f,g} and P = {p,q}. Let G be an arbitrary context-free grammar over F, and let A denote L(G). By Lemma 19.8 we can find a program scheme U from SyntdetCFG such that L(U) = v(A$). Also, by Lemma 21.19 and Lemma 19.8, U is translatable into RSI^m if and only if A is a dpda language. Thus G generates a dpda language if and only if U is translatable into RSI^m, and this proves the theorem. ///

We conclude this section with a result on translatability from CFG into RSI, which is obtained as a corollary to Theorem 21.18.

Theorem 21.23. There is no algorithm which, for an arbitrary context-free scheme U, halts and constructs an equivalent rsi if U is translatable into RSI, and halts with the answer "no" if U is not translatable into RSI.

Proof. Assuming the existence of such an algorithm we shall prove that translatability from CFG into IAN is decidable. Since this contradicts Theorem 19.19, the result follows.

Let U be an arbitrary context-free scheme. To decide whether U is translatable into IAN, apply the algorithm (whose existence is assumed) to U. If the answer is "no", then U is not translatable into IAN. Otherwise an equivalent rsi is obtained. Using Theorem 21.18, we can decide whether this rsi, and so U, is translatable into IAN. ///

Note that this theorem also holds for translatability from SyntdetCFG into RSI.

It is an open question whether translatability from CFG into RSI is decidable. However, if that were the case, then this would be rather useless, in the sense that (by Theorem 21.23) there would be no algorithm which for every context-free scheme translatable into RSI would find an

---

† Ginsburg and Greibach [1966, Theorem 5.2].

equivalent rsi.

Appendix

In this appendix we shall prove the following statement: for each dpda accepting a syntdet language by empty store we can effectively find a special dpda accepting the same language.

We shall first prove a result which is essentially a special case of the construction of a "predicting machine": † every dpda M can be transformed into a dpda N accepting the same language, such that N stores some extra information in its pushdown store, as informally explained in the proof of Theorem 21.11.

Lemma. Let $M = (K,\Sigma,\Gamma,R,k_o,Z)$ be a dpda. Then we can find a dpda $N = (K,\overline{\Gamma},\overline{R},k_o,\overline{Z})$ such that $L(N) = L(M)$ and the following requirements are satisfied.

(1) $\overline{\Gamma} = \Gamma \times C \times C$, where C is the set of all mappings from $K \times (\Sigma \cup \varepsilon)$ into $\{0,1\}$.

(2) For every ϕ,ϕ_1 in Σ^* and every $\bar{\alpha}$ in $\overline{\Gamma}^*$, if $(k_o,\phi,\overline{Z}) \overset{*}{\underset{N}{\vdash}} (k_1,\phi_1,\bar{\alpha})$, then $(k_o,\phi,Z) \overset{*}{\underset{M}{\vdash}} (k_1,\phi_1,\alpha)$, where α is the result of substituting S for (S,f,g) everywhere in $\bar{\alpha}$ (for every S in Γ and f,g in C).

(3) For every ϕ,ϕ_1 in Σ^*, every $\bar{\alpha}$ in $\overline{\Gamma}^*$ and every $\overline{S} = (S,f,g)$ in $\overline{\Gamma}$ (where $S \in \Gamma$ and $f,g \in C$), if $(k_o,\phi,\overline{Z}) \overset{*}{\underset{N}{\vdash}} (k_1,\phi_1,\overline{S}\bar{\alpha})$, then, for every k in K and σ in Σ, the following holds (where α is the same as in (2)):

(3.1) $f(k,\sigma) = 1$ if and only if there is a word ψ in Σ^* such that $(k,\sigma\psi,S\alpha) \overset{*}{\underset{M}{\vdash}} (k',\varepsilon,\varepsilon)$ for some k' in K.

(3.2) $f(k,\varepsilon) = 1$ if and only if $(k,\varepsilon,S\alpha) \overset{*}{\underset{M}{\vdash}} (k,\varepsilon,\varepsilon)$ for some k' in K.

(3.3) $g(k,\sigma) = 1$ if and only if there is a word ψ in Σ^* such that $(k,\sigma\psi,\alpha) \overset{*}{\underset{M}{\vdash}} (k',\varepsilon,\varepsilon)$ for some k' in K.

(3.4) $g(k,\varepsilon) = 1$ if and only if $(k,\varepsilon,\alpha) \overset{*}{\underset{M}{\vdash}} (k',\varepsilon,\varepsilon)$ for some k' in K.

---

† Hopcroft and Ullman [1969, Lemma 12.2].

Proof. Firstly, $\overline{Z}$ is defined to be (Z,f,g), where, for every k in K and σ in Σ,

$f(k,\sigma) = 1$ if and only if there is a word ψ in Σ^* such that $(k,\sigma\psi,Z) \vdash_M^* (k',\varepsilon,\varepsilon)$ for some k' in K,

$f(k,\varepsilon) = 1$ if and only if $(k,\varepsilon,Z) \vdash_M^* (k',\varepsilon,\varepsilon)$ for some k' in K,

$g(k,\sigma) = 0$ and $g(k,\varepsilon) = 1$.

Note that, for every k in K, the language $A_k = \{\phi\in\Sigma^* \mid (k,\phi,Z) \vdash_M^* (k',\varepsilon,\varepsilon)$ for some k' in $K\}$ is context-free. Hence $f(k,\sigma) = 1$ if and only if $A_k \cap \sigma\Sigma^* \neq \emptyset$, and $f(k,\varepsilon) = 1$ if and only if $\varepsilon \in A_k$. Consequently, f can be effectively determined.

Secondly we construct the set $\overline{R}$ of rules of N as follows.

(1) If $(k_1,\sigma_1,S) \to (k_2,\varepsilon)$ is in R (with k_1,k_2 in K, σ_1 in $\Sigma \cup \varepsilon$ and S in Γ), then, for every f and g in C, the rule $(k_1,\sigma_1,(S,f,g)) \to (k_2,\varepsilon)$ is in $\overline{R}$.

(2) If $(k_1,\sigma_1,S) \to (k_2,S_1S_2\cdots S_n)$ is in R (with $n\geq 1$, k_1,k_2 in K, σ_1 in $\Sigma \cup \varepsilon$, S in Γ and $S_1,\ldots,S_n$ in Γ), then, for every f and g in C, the rule $(k_1,\sigma_1,(S,f,g)) \to (k_2,\overline{S}_1\overline{S}_2\cdots\overline{S}_n)$ is in $\overline{R}$, where, for i in $\{1,2,\ldots,n\}$, $\overline{S}_i = (S,f_i,g_i)$ and f_i,g_i are defined as follows.

(2.1) $g_n = g$ and, for every i in $\{2,\ldots,n\}$, $g_{i-1} = f_i$.

(2.2) For every i in $\{1,2,\ldots,n\}$, f_i is defined in terms of g_i by the following requirements.

(2.2.1) For k in K and σ in Σ, $f_i(k,\sigma) = 1$ if and only if either there exists k' in K such that $(k,\varepsilon,S_i) \vdash_M^* (k',\varepsilon,\varepsilon)$ and $g_i(k',\sigma) = 1$, or there exist ψ in Σ^* and k' in K such that $(k,\sigma\psi,S_i) \vdash_M^* (k',\varepsilon,\varepsilon)$ and $g_i(k',\sigma') = 1$ for some σ' in $\Sigma \cup \varepsilon$.

(2.2.2) For k in K, $f_i(k,\varepsilon) = 1$ if and only if there exists k' in K such that $(k,\varepsilon,S_i) \vdash_M^* (k',\varepsilon,\varepsilon)$ and $g_i(k',\varepsilon) = 1$.

It is left to the reader to verify that f_i can effectively be determined from g_i.

The so constructed dpda N satisfies all conditions mentioned in the lemma. The straightforward, but tedious, proof of this is left to the reader. ///

We now prove the above mentioned statement. Let $M = (K,\Sigma,\Gamma,R,k_o,Z)$ be a dpda such that $L(M)$ is a syntdet language. By the above lemma, we can find a dpda $N = (K,\Sigma,\overline{\Gamma},\overline{R},k_o,\overline{Z})$ such that $L(N) = L(M)$ and such that conditions (1) - (3) in that lemma hold (in what follows we shall adopt the terminology used in the lemma). We now construct a special dpda N_1 such that $L(N_1) = L(N)$. N_1 is obtained from N by deleting a number of superfluous rules from $\overline{R}$ as follows.

Consider an arbitrary k in K and $\overline{S}$ in $\overline{\Gamma}$, such that $\overline{R}(k,\overline{S}) \neq \emptyset$. †
We now indicate which rules have to be deleted from $\overline{R}(k,\overline{S})$. Let $\overline{S} = (S,f,g)$ for some f and g in C. If $\overline{R}(k,\overline{S})$ is a singleton, then no rules should be deleted from $\overline{R}(k,\overline{S})$. Now suppose that $\overline{R}(k,\overline{S}) = \{(k,\sigma_1,\overline{S}) \to (k_1,\bar{\alpha}_1),\ldots,(k,\sigma_n,\overline{S}) \to (k_n,\bar{\alpha}_n)\}$ for certain $n \geq 2$, $\sigma_1,\ldots,\sigma_n$ in Σ, $k_1,\ldots,k_n$ in K and $\bar{\alpha}_1,\ldots,\bar{\alpha}_n$ in $\overline{\Gamma}^*$. If there are i and j in $\{1,\ldots,n\}$ with $i \neq j$, such that, for all p in P, $\{\sigma_i,\sigma_j\} \neq \{p,\bar{p}\}$, and $f(k,\sigma_i) = f(k,\sigma_j) = 1$, then all rules should be deleted from $\overline{R}(k,\overline{S})$. If there are no such i and j, then all rules $(k,\sigma_m,\overline{S}) \to (k_m,\bar{\alpha}_m)$ such that $f(k,\sigma_m) = 0$ $(1 \leq m \leq n)$ should be deleted from $\overline{R}(k,\overline{S})$.

It obviously follows from the above construction that N_1 is a special dpda. We now show that all deleted rules are useless for N in the sense that no such rule is ever applied in any computation of the form $(k_o,\phi,\overline{Z}) \overset{*}{\underset{N}{\vdash}} (k',\varepsilon,\varepsilon)$ (with ϕ in Σ^* and k' in K). This implies that $L(N_1) = L(N)$, and the statement is proved. Let k, $\overline{S}$ and $\overline{R}(k,\overline{S})$ be as above, so $\overline{S} = (S,f,g)$ and $\overline{R}(k,\overline{S}) = \{(k,\sigma_1,\overline{S}) \to (k_1,\bar{\alpha}_1),\ldots,(k,\sigma_n,\overline{S}) \to (k_n,\bar{\alpha}_n)\}$.

Suppose that there are i and j in $\{1,\ldots,n\}$ with $i \neq j$, such that, for all p in P, $\{\sigma_i,\sigma_j\} \neq \{p,\bar{p}\}$, and $f(k,\sigma_i) = f(k,\sigma_j) = 1$. Assume that there is a computation of the form $(k_o,\phi,\overline{Z}) \overset{*}{\underset{N}{\vdash}} (k,\sigma\psi,\overline{S\alpha})$ for some ϕ, ψ in Σ^*, σ in $\{\sigma_1,\ldots,\sigma_n\}$ and $\bar{\alpha}$ in $\overline{\Gamma}^*$. In other words, assume that there is a computation in which the rule with left hand side $(k,\sigma,\overline{S})$ is applicable. We shall show that this contradicts the syntactic determinism of L(N). Obviously, there exists ϕ_1 in Σ^* such that $\phi = \phi_1\sigma\psi$ and $(k_o,\phi_1,\overline{Z}) \overset{*}{\underset{N}{\vdash}} (k,\varepsilon,\overline{S\alpha})$. Hence, by condition (2) of the lemma, $(k_o,\phi_1,Z) \overset{*}{\underset{M}{\vdash}} (k,\varepsilon,S\alpha)$, where α is defined in that condition. Now, since $f(k,\sigma_i) = 1$, there is a word ψ_i in Σ^* such that $(k,\sigma_i\psi_i,S\alpha) \overset{*}{\underset{M}{\vdash}} (k',\varepsilon,\varepsilon)$ for some k' in K. And so $(k_o,\phi_1\sigma_i\psi_i,Z) \overset{*}{\underset{M}{\vdash}} (k,\sigma_i\psi_i,S\alpha) \overset{*}{\underset{M}{\vdash}} (k',\varepsilon,\varepsilon)$. Hence $\phi_1\sigma_i\psi_i \in L(M)$. Similarly, there is a word ψ_j in Σ^* such that $\phi_1\sigma_j\psi_j \in L(M)$. But, since, for all p in P, $\{\sigma_i,\sigma_j\} \neq \{p,\bar{p}\}$, this contradicts the syntactic determinism of L(M). Hence all rules of $\overline{R}(k,\overline{S})$ are useless.

---

† For the notation $\overline{R}(k,\overline{S})$, see Notation 21.1.

Now suppose that there are no such i and j. Let m be in $\{1,2,\ldots,n\}$ such that $f(k,\sigma_m) = 0$. Assume that there is a computation of N in which the mth rule is applied. In other words, assume that there is a computation of the form $(k_o,\phi,\bar{Z}) \vdash_{N}^{*} (k,\sigma_m\psi,\overline{S\alpha}) \vdash_{N}^{*} (k',\varepsilon,\varepsilon)$ for some ϕ,ψ in Σ^*, k,k' in K and $\bar{\alpha}$ in $\bar{\Gamma}^*$. Then, by condition (2) of the lemma, $(k,\sigma_m\psi,S\alpha) \vdash_{M}^{*} (k',\varepsilon,\varepsilon)$. And so, by condition (3.1) of the lemma, $f(k,\sigma_m) = 1$. This is a contradiction, and so the mth rule is useless.

This proves our statement.

Remark. On the other hand, if all deleted rules are useless, then L(N) is syntdet. (Proof: if the deleted rules are useless, then $L(N_1) = L(N)$, and, since N_1 is a special dpda, $L(N_1)$ is syntdet). Consequently, starting from an arbitrary dpda M, we have that L(M) is syntdet if and only if the deleted rules in N are useless. Now it can easily be seen that we can effectively determine which rules of N are useless. These considerations imply that it is decidable for an arbitrary dpda M whether L(M) is syntdet. Together with the fact that prefix-freedom is decidable for dpda languages †, this easily implies that it is decidable for an arbitrary dpda M whether $L_f(M)$ is syntdet. In other words, the pss SyntdetDPDA is a decidable subset of the class of all dpda's. ///

---

† Geller and Harrison [1973, Theorem 3.2].

CONCLUSION, INDEXES

AND REFERENCES

Conclusion

It may have already occurred to the reader that, while viewing program schemes from a language theoretic point of view, a kind of basic research methodology for solving problems concerning program schemes appears to be natural. It is the easiest to describe it as the following procedure.

(1) Decide on a class of program schemes that is of interest to you.

(2) Characterize the set of histories of computation of these program schemes as a class of languages.

(3) Translate problems concerning program schemes of the given class into problems concerning languages from the class obtained in (2).

(4) Solve the problems obtained in (3) for your class of languages.

(5) Retranslate the solutions into program scheme terminology.

Using basically this approach we have succeeded in solving a number of problems concerning program schemes of various types. One could try to use this approach and to extend our theory of L-schemes so as to incorporate more classes of program schemes, as for example the following.

- Program schemes with counters, pushdown stores and other additional memory mechanisms.
- Program schemes with features like constants, equality, boolean procedures, etc.
- Program schemes with variables. In this case, the languages involved obviously have to be languages of terms (tree languages). For example, in the case of a flowchart one can easily think of a macro grammar which generates an equivalent term language (where the variables of the flowchart are used as variables of the macro grammar)†.

---

† We are grateful to P.R.J. Asveld for pointing this out to us (personal communication).

Index of terms

The digits following a term refer to the definition (example etc.) in which (or close to which) the term occurs for the first time. (Most of the terms defined in section 1 are not included in this index).

Index of symbols and notation

For the symbols listed below we indicate their most frequent use. (Most of the notation introduced in section 1 is not included in this index).

$P_K, \overline{P}_K$	20.3
R	set of rules of a grammar or machine
R(S)	1.4.1.2
R(k,S)	21.1
S	standard mapping 10.17
	procedure symbol, nonterminal, pushdown symbol
T	set of tests page 97
	procedure symbol, nonterminal, pushdown symbol
T_S	set of standard tests 10.1
U,V,W	program schemes
W_S	set of standard words 10.3
Z	main procedure symbol, start symbol
a	predicate symbol
a_k	20.3
b	predicate symbol, arc
bound(t)	set of bound function variables of t 6.1
b(S)	body of S 4.1, 5.3
d	element of D
e	3.1
$e_k, \overline{e}_k$	20.3
f,g	function symbols
free(t)	set of free function variables of t 6.1
h	2.1
h_I	2.1
i	natural number
j	element of J, natural number
k	element of K, natural number
k_o	initial marker, initial state
ℓ	3.1, 8.8
m	natural number, node
n	natural number, node
n^o	start node

p	positive predicate symbol	
	"partial functions"	2.3
q	positive predicate symbol	
s	substitution	
s_K	20.14	
t	test, term	
	"total functions"	2.3
v	substitution	19.7
	variable	
x,y,z	elements of D, variables	
Γ	alphabet of pushdown symbols	
Δ	alphabet	
Σ	alphabet of instruction symbols	page 32
Σ_K	20.3	
α,β,γ	elements of $(\Sigma \cup N)^*$ and Γ^*	
ε	empty word	
∈	element of	
θ	set of program schemes of a pss	
μ	section 6	
π	"partial predicates"	2.3, section 12
σ	element of Σ	
τ	"total predicates"	2.3, 9.2
φ,ψ,ω	elements of Σ^*	
≡, ≤	for program schemes:	9.1, 9.2
	for pss's:	19.3
$\equiv_\ell$, $\subset_\ell$	8.8	
$\equiv_{\ell(eff)}$, $\subset_{\ell(eff)}$	8.11	

References

Aho [1968]: A.V. Aho, "Indexed grammars - an extension of context-free grammars", Journal of the Association for Computing Machinery 15(1968), pp. 647-671.

Ashcroft and Manna [1971]: E. Ashcroft and Z. Manna, "The translation of "go to" programs to "while" programs", Proc. IFIP Congress 71.

Ashcroft, Manna and Pnueli [1973]: E. Ashcroft, Z. Manna and A. Pnueli, "Decidable properties of monadic functional schemas", Journal of the Association for Computing Machinery 20 (1973), pp. 489-499.

de Bakker [1969]: J.W. de Bakker, "Semantics of programming languages", Advances in Information Systems Science, Vol.2, Plenum Press, 1969, pp. 173-227.

de Bakker [1971]: J.W. de Bakker, "Recursive procedures", Mathematical Centre Tracts 24, Mathematisch Centrum, Amsterdam, 1971.

de Bakker and Meertens [1973]: J.W. de Bakker and L.G.L. Th. Meertens, "On the completeness of the inductive assertion method", Report IW 12/73 (prepublication), Mathematisch Centrum, Amsterdam, 1973.

de Bakker and de Roever [1973]: J.W. de Bakker and W.P. de Roever, "A calculus for recursive program schemes", Automata, Languages and Programming (M. Nivat ed.), North Holland Publ. Co. and American Elsevier Publ. Co., 1973, pp. 167-196.

de Bakker and Scott [1969]: J.W. de Bakker and D. Scott, "A theory of programs", Unpublished notes, Vienna, 1969.

Birkhoff [1967]: G. Birkhoff, "Lattice theory", AMS Colloquium Publications Vol. XXV, AMS, 1967, Third Edition.

Blikle [1971]: A. Blikle, "Nets; complete lattices with a composition", Bulletin de l'Academie Polonaise des Sciences, Série des sciences math., astr. et phys. 19 (1971), pp. 1123-1127.

Blikle [1973]: A. Blikle, "Equations in nets - computer oriented lattices", CCPAS Reports 99, Warsaw, 1973.

Böhm and Jacopini [1966]: C. Böhm and G. Jacopini, "Flow diagrams, Turing machines and languages with only two formation rules", Communications of the Association for Computing Machinery 9 (1966), pp. 366-371.

Book [1973]: R.V. Book, "Topics in formal language theory", Currents in the Theory of Computing (A.V.Aho ed.), Prentice-Hall, 1973, pp. 1-34.

Brown, Gries and Szymanski [1972]: S. Brown, D. Gries and T. Szymanski, "Program schemes with pushdown stores", SIAM Journal on Computing 1 (1972), pp. 242-268.

Bruno and Steiglitz [1972]: J. Bruno and K. Steiglitz, "The expression of algorithms by charts", Journal of the Association for Computing Machinery 19 (1972), pp. 517-525.

Burstall and Landin [1969]: R.M. Burstall and P.J. Landin, "Programs and their proofs: an algebraic approach", Machine Intelligence 4 (B. Meltzer and D. Michie eds.), Edinburgh at the University Press, 1969, pp. 17-43.

Burstall and Thatcher [1974]: R.M. Burstall and J.W. Thatcher, "The algebraic theory of recursive program schemes", Proc. of the First International Symposium on Category Theory applied to Computation and Control, University of Mass., 1974, pp. 154-160.

Chandra [1973]: A.K. Chandra, "On the properties and applications of program schemas", Ph.D. Thesis, Report CS-336, AIM-188, Stanford University, 1973.

Chandra [1974]: A.K. Chandra, "Degrees of translatability and canonical forms in program schemas: Part I", Sixth Annual ACM Symposium on Theory of Computing, 1974, pp. 1-12.

Chandra and Manna [1972]: A.K. Chandra and Z. Manna, "Program schemas with equality", Fourth Annual ACM Symposium on Theory of Computing,1972, pp. 52-64.

Chandra and Manna [1973]: A.K. Chandra and Z. Manna, "On the power of programming features", Report CS-333, AIM-185, Stanford University,1973.

Cherniavsky and Constable [1972]: J.C. Cherniavsky and R.L. Constable, "Representing program schemes in logic", IEEE 13th Annual Symposium on Switching and Automata Theory, 1972, pp. 27-39.

Constable and Gries [1972]: R.L. Constable and D. Gries, "On classes of program schemata", SIAM Journal on Computing 1 (1972), pp. 66-118.

Cooper [1967]: D.C. Cooper, "Böhm and Jacopini's reduction of flow charts", Communications of the Association for Computing Machinery 10 (1967), pp. 463,473.

Cooper [1971]: D.C. Cooper, "Program schemes, programs and logic", Symposium on Semantics of Algorithmic Languages (E. Engeler ed.), Lecture Notes in Mathematics 188, Springer-Verlag, 1971, pp. 62-70.

Dubinsky [1973]: A. Dubinsky, "The functions computed by a monadic program schema with one location", Automata, Languages and Programming (M. Nivat ed.), North-Holland Publishing Co. and American Elsevier Publishing Co., 1973, pp. 521-535.

Elgot [1970]: C.C. Elgot, "The common algebraic structure of exit-automata and machines", Computing 6 (1970), pp. 349-370.

Elgot [1971]: C.C. Elgot, "Algebraic theories and program schemes", Symposium on Semantics of Algorithmic Languages (E. Engeler ed.), Lecture Notes in Mathematics 188, Springer-Verlag, 1971, pp. 71-88.

Elgot [1972]: C.C. Elgot, "Remarks on one-argument program schemes", Formal Semantics of Programming Languages (R. Rustin ed.), Prentice-Hall, 1972, pp. 59-64.

Engeler [1967]: E. Engeler, "Algorithmic properties of structures", Mathematical Systems Theory 1 (1967), pp. 183-195.

Engelfriet [1971 a]: J. Engelfriet, "Generalisierte Ianovschemata", Mitteilungen der Gesellschaft für Mathematik und Datenverarbeitung Nr. 17, 1971, Bonn, pp. 15-18.

Engelfriet [1971 b]: J. Engelfriet, "Ianov schemes and formal languages", Seminar on Some syntactical and semantical problems in theoretical computer science, Abstract No. 2, Utrecht, 1971.

Engelfriet [1972 a]: J. Engelfriet, "Program schemes and formal languages", Séminaires IRIA, Théorie des algorithmes, des langages et de la programmation, Rocquencourt, 1972, pp. 25-31.

Engelfriet [1972 b]: J. Engelfriet, "A note on infinite trees", Information Processing Letters 1 (1972), pp. 229-232.

Engelfriet [1972 c]: J. Engelfriet, "Programmschemata mit Hilfsvariablen", Mathematisches Forschungsinstitut Oberwolfach, Tagungsbericht 43, 1972, pp. 7-8.

Engelfriet [1973]: J. Engelfriet, "Translation of simple program schemes", Automata, Languages and Programming (M. Nivat ed.), North-Holland Publishing Co. and American Elsevier Publishing Co., 1973, pp. 215-223.

Ershov [1971]: A.P. Ershov, "Theory of program schemata", Proc. IFIP Congress 71.

Fischer [1968]: M.J. Fischer, "Grammars with macro-like productions", IEEE 9th Annual Symposium on Switching and Automata Theory, 1968, pp. 131-142.

Floyd [1967]: R.W. Floyd, "Nondeterministic algorithms", Journal of the Association for Computing Machinery 14 (1967), pp. 636-644.

Garland and Luckham [1973]: S.J. Garland and D.C. Luckham, "Program schemes, recursion schemes and formal languages", Journal of Computer and System Sciences 7 (1973), pp. 119-160.

Geller and Harrison [1973]: M.M. Geller and M.A. Harrison, "Characterizations of LR(0) languages", IEEE 14th Annual Symposium on Switching and Automata Theory, 1973.

Ginsburg [1966]: S. Ginsburg, "The Mathematical Theory of Context-free Languages", McGraw-Hill Book Company, 1966.

Ginsburg and Greibach [1966]: S. Ginsburg and S. Greibach, "Deterministic context free languages", Information and Control 9 (1966), pp. 620-648.

Ginsburg, Greibach and Hopcroft [1969]: S. Ginsburg, S. Greibach and J.E. Hopcroft, "Studies in abstract families of languages", Memoirs of the American Mathematical Society, Number 87, AMS, 1969.

Goguen [1972]: J.A. Goguen, Jr., "On homomorphisms, simulations, correctness and subroutines for programs and program schemes", IEEE 13th Annual Symposium on Switching and Automata Theory, 1972, pp. 52-60.

Goguen [1973]: J.A. Goguen Jr., "Axioms, extensions and applications for fuzzy sets: languages and the representation of concepts", IBM Research Report RC 4547, 1973.

Gruska [1971]: J. Gruska, "A characterization of context-free languages", Journal of Computer and System Sciences 5 (1971), pp. 353-364.

Harrison and Havel [1973]: M.A. Harrison and I.M. Havel, "Strict deterministic grammars", Journal of Computer and System Sciences 7 (1973), pp. 237-277.

Hermes [1965]: H. Hermes, "Enumerability, decidability and computability; an introduction to the theory of recursive functions", Springer-Verlag, 1965.

Hopcroft and Ullman [1969]: J.E. Hopcroft and J.D. Ullman, "Formal languages and their Relation to Automata", Addison-Wesley Publishing Co., 1969.

Ianov [1960]: Iu. I. Ianov, "On the logical schemes of algorithms", Problems of Cybernetics 1 (1960), pp. 82-140.

Indermark [1973]: K. Indermark, "On Ianov schemes with one memory location", GI 1.Fachtagung über Automatentheorie und Formale Sprachen, Lecture Notes in Computer Science 2, Springer-Verlag, 1973, pp. 284-293.

Igarashi [1963]: S. Igarashi, "On the logical schemes of algorithms", Information Processing in Japan 3 (1963), pp. 12-18.

Ito [1968]: T. Ito, "Some formal properties of a class of non-deterministic program schemata", IEEE 9th Annual Symposium on Switching and Automata Theory, 1968, pp. 85-98.

Kaluzhnin [1961]: L.A. Kaluzhnin, "Algorithmization of mathematical problems", Problems of Cybernetics 2 (1961), pp. 371-391.

Kaplan [1969]: D.M. Kaplan, "Regular expressions and the equivalence of programs", Journal of Computer and System Sciences 3 (1969), pp. 361-386.

Karp [1960]: R.M. Karp, "A note on the application of graph theory to digital computer programming", Information and Control 3 (1960), pp. 179-190.

Kfoury [1973]: D. Kfoury, "Comparing algebraic structures up to algorithmic equivalence", Automata, Languages and Programming (M. Nivat ed.), North-Holland Publishing Co. and American Elsevier Publishing Co., 1973, pp. 253-263.

Knuth and Floyd [1971]: D.E. Knuth and R.W. Floyd, "Notes on avoiding "go to" statements", Information Processing Letters 1 (1971), pp. 23-31.

Korenjak and Hopcroft [1966]: A.J. Korenjak and J.E. Hopcroft, "Simple deterministic languages", IEEE 7th Annual Symposium on Switching and Automata Theory, 1966, pp. 36-46.

Langmaack [1973]: H. Langmaack, "On procedures as open subroutines", Report A 73/04, Universität des Saarlandes, Saarbrücken, 1973.

Luckham, Park and Paterson [1970]: D.C. Luckham, D.M.R. Park and M.S. Paterson, "On formalised computer programs", Journal of Computer and System Sciences 4 (1970), pp. 220-249.

Manna [1969]: Z Manna, "Properties of programs and the first-order predicate calculus", Journal of the Association for Computing Machinery 16 (1969), pp. 244-255.

Manna [1973]: Z. Manna, "Program Schemas", Currents in the Theory of Computing (A.V. Aho ed.), Prentice-Hall, 1973, pp. 90-142.

Mazurkiewicz [1972 a]: A. Mazurkiewicz, "Iteratively computable relations", Bulletin de l'Academie Polonaise des Sciences, Série des sciences math., astr. et phys. 20 (1972), pp. 793-798.

Mazurkiewicz [1972 b]: A. Mazurkiewicz, "Recursive algorithms and formal languages", Bulletin de l'Academie Polonaise des Sciences, Série des sciences math., astr. et phys. 20 (1972), pp. 799-803.

McCarthy [1962]: J. McCarthy, "Towards a mathematical science of computation", Proc. IFIP Congress 1962, pp. 21-28.

McCarthy [1963]: J. McCarthy, "A basis for a mathematical theory of computation", Computer Programming and Formal Systems (P. Braffort and D. Hirschberg eds.), North-Holland Publishing Co., 1963, pp. 33-70.

Mezei and Wright [1967]: J. Mezei and J.B. Wright, "Algebraic automata and context-free sets", Information and Control 11 (1967), pp. 3-29.

Milner [1970]: R. Milner, "Equivalences on program schemes", Journal of Computer and System Sciences 4 (1970), pp. 205-219.

Morris [1971]: J.H. Morris Jr., "Another recursion induction principle", Communications of the Association for Computing Machinery 14 (1971), pp. 351-354.

Nivat [1973]: M. Nivat, "Langages algébriques sur le magma libre et sémantique des schémas de programme", Automata, Languages and Programming (M. Nivat ed.),North-Holland Publishing Co. and American Elsevier Publishing Co., 1973, pp. 293-307.

Paterson [1967]: M.S. Paterson, "Equivalence problems in a model of computation", Ph.D. Thesis, University of Cambridge, 1967.

Paterson [1972]: M.S. Paterson, "Decision problems in computational models", Proc. of an ACM Conference on Proving Assertions about Programs, SIGACT News 14, 1972, pp. 74-82.

Paterson and Hewitt [1970]: M.S. Paterson and C.E. Hewitt, "Comparitive schematology", Record of the Project MAC Conference on Concurrent Systems and Parallel Computation, 1970, pp. 119-127.

Rogers [1967]: H. Rogers, Jr., "Theory of recursive functions and effective computability", McGraw-Hill Book Company, 1967.

Rosen [1972]: B.K. Rosen, "Program equivalence and context-free grammars", IEEE 13th Annual Symposium on Switching and Automate Theory, 1972, pp. 7-18.

Rounds [1970]: W.C. Rounds, "Tree-oriented proofs of some theorems on context-free and indexed languages", Second Annual ACM Symposium on Theory of Computing, 1970, pp. 109-116.

Rutledge [1964]: J.D. Rutledge, "On Ianov's program schemata", Journal of the Association for Computing Machinery 11 (1964), pp. 1-9.

Salomaa [1973]: A. Salomaa, "Formal Languages", Academic Press, 1973.

Scott [1970]: D. Scott, "An outline of a mathematical theory of computation", Proc. of the Fourth Annual Princeton Conference on Information Sciences and Systems, 1970, pp. 169-176.

Scott [1971]: D. Scott, "The lattice of flow diagrams", Symposium on Semantics of Algorithmic Languages (E. Engeler ed.), Lecture Notes in Mathematics 188, Springer-Verlag, 1971, pp. 311-366.

Stearns [1967]: R.E. Stearns, "A regularity test for pushdown machines", Information and Control 11 (1967), pp. 323-340.

Strong [1971 a]: H.R. Strong Jr.,"High level languages of maximum power", IEEE 12th Annual Symposium on Switching and Automata Theory, 1971, pp. 1-4.

Strong [1971 b]: H.R. Strong Jr., "Translating recursion equations into flow charts", Journal of Computer and System Sciences 5 (1971), pp. 254-285.

Zeiger [1969]: H.P. Zeiger, "Formal models for some features of programming languages", First Annual ACM Symposium on Theory of Computing, 1969, pp. 211-215.